When Mandates Work

When Mandates Work

RAISING LABOR STANDARDS
AT THE LOCAL LEVEL

Edited by
Michael Reich
Ken Jacobs
Miranda Dietz

UNIVERSITY OF CALIFORNIA PRESS
Berkeley   Los Angeles   London

University of California Press, one of the most distinguished university presses in the United States, enriches lives around the world by advancing scholarship in the humanities, social sciences, and natural sciences. Its activities are supported by the UC Press Foundation and by philanthropic contributions from individuals and institutions. For more information, visit www.ucpress.edu.

University of California Press
Berkeley and Los Angeles, California

University of California Press, Ltd.
London, England

Library of Congress Cataloging-in-Publication Data

When mandates work : raising labor standards at the local level / edited by Michael Reich, Ken Jacobs, Miranda Dietz.
    pages cm
  ISBN 978-0-520-27813-4 (cloth : alk. paper) —
  ISBN 978-0-520-27814-1 (pbk. : alk. paper) —
  ISBN 978-0-520-95746-6 (e-book)
  1. Labor policy—California—San Francisco. 2. Labor laws and legislation—California—San Francisco. 3. Wages—Government policy—California—San Francisco. 4. Employee rights—California—San Francisco. I. Reich, Michael. II. Jacobs, Ken, 1962– III. Dietz, Miranda, 1983–
  HD8085.S36W44 2014
  331.12′042—dc23   2013030868

Manufactured in the United States of America

23 22 21 20 19 18 17 16 14
10 9 8 7 6 5 4 3 2 1

In keeping with a commitment to support environmentally responsible and sustainable printing practices, UC Press has printed this book on Natures Natural, a fiber that contains 30% post-consumer waste and meets the minimum requirements of ANSI/NISO Z39.48–1992 (R 1997) (*Permanence of Paper*).

Contents

Figures

Tables

Acknowledgments

The idea for this book originated in a session of the Labor and Employment Research Association's 2009 annual meetings. The session, "San Francisco and the New Social Compact," was organized by David Weinberg and Michael Theriault. Their encouragement resulted in the conference paper and presentation that ultimately provided the outline for this volume. One of us, Michael Reich, had testified before the San Francisco Board of Supervisors several times a decade ago, reporting on his prospective impact studies on behalf of a number of alternative versions of the policies that we analyze here. During that same time, Ken Jacobs cochaired the San Francisco Living Wage Coalition. This policy engagement spurred both of us to subsequently conduct a series of state-of-the-art research studies evaluating those policies.

The authors of each of the chapters in this volume not only contributed quality research. When we met as a group in summer 2012, their questions and suggestions sharpened the volume as a whole. Indeed, this book would not have been possible without the numerous studies of

San Francisco's policies that we and others conducted over the past fifteen years. Citations to those studies appear in each chapter. During this time we benefited frequently from the many discussions of the issues raised in this book and the insights of our past and current Berkeley colleagues, especially those at the Institute for Research on Labor and Employment and the Center for Labor Research and Education: Sylvia Allegretto, David Card, Arindrajit Dube, Netsy Firestein, Peter Hall, Ethan Kaplan, William Lester, Enrico Moretti, Suresh Naidu, Steven Pitts, Katie Quan, Steven Raphael, and Carol Zabin.

Rob McKay and Barry Hermanson provided small grants for our initial work on labor standards policies in San Francisco more than a decade ago. UC Berkeley's support for research at the Institute for Research on Labor and Employment provided the funding for our subsequent studies and for the preparation of this book.

Vince Chhabria, Margot Feinberg, Julian Gross, Andy Katz, Jen Kern, Scott Kronland, Stacey Layton, David Rosenfeld, and Paul Sonn are among the many people working in the field who contributed to our understanding of the legal and institutional issues surrounding local labor standards policies. Too many individuals have been engaged in passing and implementing the policies to mention here. But we want to especially acknowledge some of those who graciously answered our many questions in the course of the research for this book: Donna Levitt, Ellen Love, and Donna Mandel at the Office of Labor Standards Enforcement, Tim Paulson, Shelley Kessler, Connie Ford, Ian Lewis, Sara Flocks, and Tangerine Brigham. Special thanks to then-supervisor, now Assembly member Tom Ammiano for his leadership and vision.

We also wish to thank Eileen Appelbaum, Stephanie Luce, and Robert Pollin for their helpful comments on the manuscript. We are grateful to Zachary Goldman, Jared Park, and Luke Reidenbach for their excellent research assistance and to Jenifer MacGillvary for her help with preparing the manuscript. Peter Richardson at UC Press took an immediate interest in the topic and helped shepherd the book through the review process. He has been a terrific editor.

Abbreviations and Glossary

AFL-CIO:	American Federation of Labor and Congress of Industrial Organizations, the umbrella organization of unions in the United States
CBA:	Community benefits agreement
ERISA:	Employee Retirement Income Security Act
HCAO:	Health Care Accountability Ordinance
HCSO:	Health Care Security Ordinance
HRA:	Health Reimbursement Account
IHSS:	In-Home Support Services
MCO:	Minimum Compensation Ordinance
NLRA:	National Labor Relations Act
NLRB:	National Labor Relations Board
OLSE:	Office of Labor Standards Enforcement
PSL(O):	Paid Sick Leave (Ordinance)

PTO:	Paid Time Off
QCEW:	Quarterly Census of Employment and Wages
QSP:	Quality Standards Program
QWI:	Quarterly Workforce Indicators
SEIU:	Service Employees International Union
SFO:	San Francisco International Airport
UFCW:	United Food and Commercial Workers International Union
UNITE HERE:	Union of Hotel and Restaurant Employees
YWU:	Young Workers United

GLOSSARY

Card check agreement: A simplified form of union recognition in which an employer agrees to recognize the union if a majority of workers sign authorization cards. Also referred to as a "majority sign-up."

Community benefits agreement (CBA):   A legal contract between developers and coalitions of community-based organizations in which the developer agrees to conditions aiding the local community in exchange for their public support for the development.

Employee Signature Authorization Ordinance (ESAO):   San Francisco law requiring that in projects for which the City was a landlord, lender, or loan guarantor, employers have to agree to card check and a labor peace policy.

Employee Retirement Income Security Act (ERISA):   Federal law governing pension and health benefits provided by private employers.

Healthy San Francisco: A program to provide comprehensive health services to uninsured San Francisco residents.

Labor peace agreement: A union agreement not to strike, often made in exchange for the employer agreeing not to interfere with employees' decision on whether to unionize.

Living wage: Policies that set wage standards for government contractors or lessees above the state or federal minimum wage. They may include provisions for paid time off and other benefits.

National Labor Relations Act (NLRA):   Federal law regulating workplace organizing and unions in the private sector and creating the National Labor Relations Board (NLRB).

Prevailing wage: Policies that require employers to pay no less than the common area wage for a specific occupation, which is often the union wage rate.

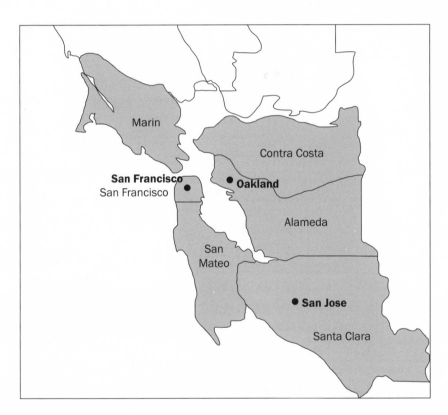

Figure 1.1   San Francisco Bay Area counties and major cities.

ONE When Do Mandates Work?

Ken Jacobs and Michael Reich

Beginning in the late 1990s, the City of San Francisco enacted a notable series of laws designed to improve pay and benefits, expand health care access, and extend paid sick leave for low-wage San Francisco residents and workers. Remarkably, and despite many warnings about dire negative effects, these new policies raised living standards significantly for tens of thousands of people, and without creating any negative effects on employment. While modest by most European and Canadian standards, San Francisco's policies represent a bold experiment in American labor market policies that provides important lessons for the rest of the United States.

*Portions of this chapter are based on or appeared in Ken Jacobs, "San Francisco Values: The New Social Compact," Labor and Employment Relations Association Series, *61st Annual Proceedings,* edited by Adrienne E. Eaton, 180–87 (n.p.).

In contrast, over the past three decades living standards have stag-
nated—at best—for a majority of Americans, decreased for large swaths
of America, and increased dramatically for a very select few. The causes
of stagnating living standards and rising inequality are much debated.
One side focuses on technological change and the effects of globalization,
each of which is said to reduce the demand for less educated workers.
Another side focuses on changes in business and public policy, particularly on changes that loosened standards that put floors on worker pay
and benefits while allowing incomes at the very top to rise dramatically.

Our volume addresses this debate through a novel perspective: an
examination of the scope and effects of the innovative but relatively
unknown set of public policy experiments in San Francisco. Although other
cities and states have adopted somewhat similar policies, the number,
scope, and reach of the San Francisco standards are unequaled anywhere
else in the United States. It is not an exaggeration to state that they represent
a new social compact among businesses, workers, and government.[1]

The first set of policies mandated wage and benefit standards for firms
doing business with the city, beginning with equal benefit laws and continuing with a set of living wage standards. While these living wage
standards resembled policies that have been adopted by more than 130
local governmental entities in the United States, the scope and share of
workers affected exceeded those of any other city. These early initiatives
were followed by pioneering new laws that applied higher standards to
all firms operating within San Francisco's geographic boundaries. These
citywide programs established a minimum wage that applied to all
employers, a universal health access program for all San Francisco residents with a mandated employer health spending requirement, and a
minimum level of paid sick days for all San Francisco workers.

San Francisco's innovative labor standards policies have gone further
than those in other U.S. cities or states. As this chapter and the chapters
that follow show, their implementation did not hurt jobs or the local

---

[1] San Francisco is also unusual in the range of its regulations governing affordable housing, neighborhood preservation, and environmental standards. While we touch on these
below when considering the city's political evolution, a sustained discussion is beyond the
scope of this volume.

economy. Indeed, in recent decades San Francisco has enjoyed more prosperity than most U.S. cities. What lessons can we draw from this experience? Are the circumstances that led to the adoption and benevolent effects of these policies unique to San Francisco, or are they generalizable to other areas?

As it turns out, the local economic setting—a city in recovery from the hollowing out of industry and a loss of middle-paying jobs, with growth alongside increasing economic inequality—is representative of trends in the majority of metropolitan areas and the United States as a whole. The San Francisco experience thus does carry important lessons for city, state, and national policy.

The evidence collected in this book demonstrates how the specific crafting of San Francisco's mandates contributed to their success. In particular, San Francisco has been attentive to the issue of compliance, wage increases were indexed so the benefits persist over time, and an inclusive political process accounted for local economic conditions and community needs. With similarly careful consideration of local conditions, San Francisco–type standards would work in many other places. Indeed, many of San Francisco's innovative policies have been adopted in other localities, and more are seriously considering doing so.

· · · · ·

San Francisco's pay and benefit standards were not only more far-reaching than those in other cities; they also have been studied intensively. A wealth of careful new research, mostly conducted by scholars at the University of California, Berkeley, has documented the effects of the policies on employee compensation, productivity, job creation, and health coverage. Although opponents of the laws predicted significant negative impacts on jobs and the local economy, the research evidence indicates more positive results. Our volume brings this evidence together for the first time, reviews it as a whole, and makes it accessible to a broader audience.

To introduce the volume, this chapter provides first a brief historical account of each of the policies and how it came into being. Section 2 presents the economic and political context in San Francisco that led to the adoption of the pay and benefit mandates. In section 3, we discuss the economic theory of pay and benefit mandates. Our goal is to provide a unified explanatory framework that accounts for the impacts of the policies. Section 4 assesses how the San Francisco economy has performed, relative to its immediate neighbors, as a result of the aggregate effects of all these policies. In section 5, we discuss the lessons that the San Francisco experience holds for local, state, and national policy. Finally, section 6 provides an overview of the volume and summarizes the findings in each of the chapters, which individually examine the impacts on pay, employment, and other outcomes.

1. A NEXUS OF MANDATES

The series of pay and benefit standards enacted by San Francisco began in 1996. The first set of mandates applied primarily to contractors doing business with the City. These contractor-only policies began with a legally contentious battle to extend benefits to domestic partners (1996), continued with a labor peace and majority sign-up agreement with simplified union recognition procedures (1997), an overhaul of prevailing wage law in 1999, and the creation of a labor standards enforcement office in 2000. From 1998 to 2001 the set of contractor-only policies was extended in a series of laws that included not only city contractors, but, in some cases, companies doing business on City-owned land, such as at the airport, the port, and the major league baseball park. In 2006 the city passed a sweat-free contracting ordinance, and in 2008 it entered into an expansive community benefits agreement that covers all employers in a new large-scale economic development project.

By 2003, San Francisco's policy initiatives began to focus on programs that would affect all employers in the city, not just city contractors. This shift represented a major expansion in coverage. The citywide policies included a minimum wage (enacted in 2003 and implemented in 2004), a local earned income tax credit (2005), a health access program (passed in 2006 and implemented in 2008), and paid sick leave for all workers (enacted in 2006 and implemented in 2007).

Table 1.1   Timeline of San Francisco Mandates

Contractor-Only Policies	Date Passed	Citywide Policies
Equal Benefits for Domestic Partners	November 1996	
Employee Signature Authorization (majority sign-up)	December 1997	
Prevailing Wage Revisions	November 1999	
Airport Quality Standards Program	January 2000	
Minimum Compensation Ordinance (living wage)	August 2000	Office of Labor Standards Enforcement created
Health Care Accountability Ordinance	July 2001	
	November 2003	Minimum Wage
	July 2006	Health Care Security Ordinance
	November 2006	Paid Sick Leave
Hunters Point Shipyard Community Benefits Agreement	June 2008	

While the greatest impact of these policies is on low-wage workers, the health and sick leave policies also reach into the middle-income workforce. For low-wage workers, these standards do not operate independently of each other. They form a nexus of mandates that affect workers and firms in an interdependent manner. Table 1.1 summarizes their evolution as a timeline. The rest of this section elaborates the evolution in more detail.

Contractor-Only Policies

EQUAL BENEFITS FOR DOMESTIC PARTNERS

In November 1996, the San Francisco Board of Supervisors enacted the Equal Benefits Ordinance, requiring firms that did business with the City of San Francisco to provide the same benefits to employees' domestic partners that they provide to married spouses. The law applied to all firms entering into contracts or leases of more than $5,000 with the City. Benefits were defined broadly as including health insurance, retirement plans, leaves of absence, use of company facilities, and employee discounts.

United Airlines, Federal Express, and the Air Transport Association sued the City, arguing preemption under federal law, including the Employee Retirement Income Security Act (ERISA), and violation of the commerce clause of the U.S. Constitution. The federal district court upheld the ordinance, with several important restrictions. Outside of the city or land owned by the city, the ordinance could apply only where work related to a city contract is being performed. Employees of United Airlines not working in San Francisco or at San Francisco International Airport (SFO) would not be covered by the law, but employees working on service agreements for the City of San Francisco would be, even if they are located outside of the city.

The court further determined that when the city is acting as a regulator, rather than in its proprietary interest as a consumer, the ordinance could apply only to benefits not covered under ERISA, such as bereavement leave, paid family leave, and company discounts. In the case of the airlines, the court found that the city's monopoly power over the airport meant that it wielded greater power than an ordinary consumer so was not shielded from preemption as a market participant (*Air Transport Ass'n v. City and County of San Francisco*, 1998). The distinction between the city acting as a market participant or as a regulator would prove important for other San Francisco laws.

While the Equal Benefits law was fundamentally a human rights ordinance, it did broaden health coverage. Many contractors chose to extend the same rules to their entire workforce, not only to those covered by the law. A 2002 report by the San Francisco Human Rights Commission estimated that more than fifty thousand people in 39 states and 500 cities had taken advantage of health insurance offered to domestic partners by firms contracting with the city (Goldstein 2002). By 2013, 62 percent of Fortune 500 companies provided health benefits to domestic partners (Human Rights Campaign Foundation 2013).

With the Equal Benefits Ordinance, San Francisco directly established labor standards conditions on a wide range of firms, and it did so in a manner that survived legal challenge. The law then served as a blueprint for many of the labor standards policies passed in San Francisco in the succeeding years. It has also served as a model for laws passed in nineteen other cities around the country as well as the state of California.

MAJORITY SIGN-UP (CARD CHECK)

The next major piece of labor standards legislation came in December 1997, when the San Francisco Board of Supervisors passed the Employee Signature Authorization Ordinance, sometimes referred to as the labor peace ordinance. The first of its kind in the United States, the ordinance requires that employers in hotel or restaurant developments in which the city has a proprietary interest as a landlord, lender, or loan guarantor enter into a card check agreement with a labor organization requesting such an agreement.[2] The agreement must provide for a card check procedure with a neutral third party, binding arbitration over disputes, a prohibition on economic action by the union against the employer at work sites covered by the agreement as long as the employer is in compliance, and a prohibition on coercion or intimidation of workers by the labor organization or employer during the process.

The stated purpose of the ordinance is to protect the city's economic interest from the threat of labor-management conflict where it is acting as a market participant, with the same risks and liabilities as others participating in similar ventures. It is expressly not intended to affect the outcome of the determination of preference regarding unionization.

PREVAILING WAGE REVISIONS AND CREATION OF THE OFFICE OF LABOR STANDARDS ENFORCEMENT

A 1998 ordinance mandated that local prevailing wages, including the cost of benefits, be paid to janitors working on city contracts.[3] This mandate was later extended to include window cleaners, parking lot

---

[2] In a card check agreement an employer agrees to recognize a union if a majority of workers sign authorization cards indicating they want the union to represent them.

[3] Prevailing wage laws require employers to pay no less than the common area wage for a specific occupation, which is often the union wage rate.

attendants, theatrical workers, solid waste haulers, and movers contracting with the city. In addition, the 1998 Displaced Worker Protection Act required new city janitorial and security contractors and subcontractors to retain the same workers for a transitional employment period of ninety days.

The following year, the Board of Supervisors overhauled and strengthened the city's prevailing wage policy for public construction projects. But labor organizations soon became concerned about whether the law would be enforced. In 2000 they successfully advocated that the city create the Office of Labor Standards Enforcement to promote compliance.

LIVING WAGE LAWS (COMPENSATION CONDITIONS ON PUBLIC CONTRACTS AND LEASES)

San Francisco was a relative latecomer in passing a living wage law. Labor and community organizations and policy makers drew from the experiences of other cities in crafting the San Francisco laws. At the same time, they introduced their own innovations and used San Francisco's power as both a city and a county to reach greater numbers of workers. Between 1999 and 2001 a series of policies placing conditions on firms doing business with the city were passed by the San Francisco Airport Commission, the Board of Supervisors, and the Redevelopment Commission.

Living Wages for Screeners and Baggage Handlers at SFO (Quality Standards Program). In January 2000, the San Francisco Airport Commission passed the Quality Standards Program, which was designed to improve safety and security at the San Francisco International Airport. At the time, the turnover rate for airport security screeners at SFO was nearly 100 percent a year (Reich, Hall, and Jacobs 2005). Officials at SFO expressed concerns over the impact of the high turnover rates on worker performance and airport security. Airport director John Martin reported seeing workers sleeping in the stairways between two shifts.

With many security and airline service jobs carried out by airline contractors, the airport had no direct relationship with—or oversight of—many of the firms operating there. SFO crafted an innovative policy designed to give it greater oversight of airline contractors and to address the high turnover rates. The Quality Standards Program established a permitting process for airline contractors operating in secure areas of the airport or carrying out security functions; and minimum training and compensation standards were required as a condition for receiving a permit. This policy went into effect in April 2000. Nearly one-third of the airport's thirty thousand workers received pay increases in the year following the implementation of the ordinance (Reich, Hall, and Jacobs 2005). As of January 1, 2013, the minimum compensation rate under the program at SFO was $12.93 an hour, fifty cents above the rate for other airport workers as established by the minimum compensation ordinance.

Living Wages on City Contracts and Leaseholders at SFO (Minimum Compensation Ordinance). In August 2000 the San Francisco Board of Supervisors passed an ordinance establishing living wage standards for firms contracting with the city or holding leases at San Francisco International Airport. At the time of implementation, the policy affected an estimated 4,200 lower-wage workers on city contracts and 3,000 workers at SFO working in restaurant and retail concessions and parking and rental car facilities and not covered by the Quality Standards Program (Reich, Hall, and Hsu 1999; Reich and Hall 1999). It also applies to San Francisco's 18,000 In-Home Supportive Service (IHSS) workers. The San Francisco Redevelopment Agency adopted the living wage requirements the following year. The wage is indexed to the Bay Area Consumer Price Index. As of January 1, 2013, the required rate was $12.43 an hour, $11.03 for nonprofit organizations (including IHSS).

HEALTH BENEFITS FOR EMPLOYEES WORKING ON CITY
CONTRACTS OR ON CITY LEASED LANDS (HEALTH CARE
ACCOUNTABILITY ORDINANCE)

In 2001 the Board of Supervisors passed companion legislation to the living wage ordinance. This legislation required firms with city contracts or leases to provide health insurance or pay $1.50 an hour per worker to the San Francisco Department of Public Health to cover the costs of the uninsured in the city. The payment rate is adjusted periodically for medical cost inflation on the recommendation of the health director. As of July 1, 2013, the rate was $4.00 an hour, not to exceed $150.00 per workweek.

While limited to firms doing business with the city, the Health Care Accountability Ordinance could be considered the first pay or play health care policy to go into effect in the United States.

San Francisco's living wage policies were largely variations on policies being carried out in other cities. They differed mainly in the number of workers covered. San Francisco was able to reach more workers through these policies in part as a result of its joint powers as a city and a county. San Francisco policy could reach the airport, the thousands of home care and human service workers (a county function), and city service contractors.

HUNTERS POINT SHIPYARD COMMUNITY BENEFITS AGREEMENT

In 2008, a coalition of unions and community organizations negotiated a community benefits agreement with the Lennar Corporation covering a massive redevelopment project at the site of the former Hunters Point Shipyard.[4] The project is expected to generate up to ten thousand permanent jobs. It will include 635,000 square feet of retail space, 2.65 million square feet of office and research and development space, and a hotel. More than 30 percent of the housing built on the site will be below market rate, double what is required by California law. Lennar further committed to contribute $27.4 million to a fund to assist community residents in purchasing market-rate units in the district.

The agreement applies living wage conditions to the broadest scope of employers in a private commercial development anywhere in the United States. All firms with twenty workers or more operating in the redevelopment area will be required to meet the living wage standard of $12.43 an hour and provide twelve days of paid time off a year (or a cash equivalent). The agreement also requires majority sign-up for union recognition for hotels, restaurants, grocery stores, and security and custodial workers. Housing production commenced in July 2013, though full funding for the development was not yet secured (Dineen 2013).

---

[4] Community Benefits Agreements are binding legal contracts between developers and coalitions of community-based organizations in which the developer agrees to set-asides for the community and labor standards in the project area in exchange for their public support for the development.

Citywide Policies

As we have noted, San Francisco's greatest innovation is the set of policies that apply to all employers in the city. We turn to these next.

MINIMUM WAGE

Building on the success of the living wage campaign, a coalition of labor and community organizations placed on the ballot in November 2003 an initiative to create a citywide minimum wage. The initiative passed with 60 percent of the popular vote. It was the first minimum wage law implemented in a major city, not including a much more limited ordinance in Washington DC. In a prospective study, Reich and Laitinen (2003) estimated that the minimum wage would affect 54,000 workers, 11 percent of the city's workforce. This estimate included workers who were earning under the minimum wage rate and would receive a mandated increase and those earning slightly above the new minimum wage; employers were expected to raise wages to retain these employees. The San Francisco minimum, which applies to all employers and workers covered under state minimum wage law, was set at $8.50 an hour and indexed annually to the Bay Area Consumer Price Index. The minimum wage rate in 2013 was $10.55 an hour, the highest in the nation.

WORKING FAMILIES CREDIT

Established as a pilot program in 2005, the Working Families Credit was designed to encourage take-up of the Earned Income Tax Credit (EITC), promote savings, and help working families stay in San Francisco. Initially funded with public and private sources, the program provided a 10 percent supplement to the EITC.[5] In 2005 approximately ten thousand families received an average credit of $220. When private funding ran out at the end of the pilot program, the city switched to a flat per-family credit, currently set at $125 and available only to first-time applicants. When families apply for the credit, they are also connected to other programs for low-income working families (Flacke and Wortheim 2006).

---

[5] The largest contributor, H&R Block, donated $1 million to the program.

HEALTH CARE SECURITY ORDINANCE

The San Francisco Health Care Security Ordinance was approved in July 2006 and launched in July 2007. The ordinance has two central elements: It establishes a new health program, Healthy San Francisco, to provide comprehensive health services to uninsured San Francisco residents, with a focus on prevention, and it sets a minimum health spending requirement for firms with twenty or more workers.

Healthy San Francisco is open to uninsured San Francisco residents regardless of health, employment, or immigration status on a sliding scale based on income. Enrollees are assigned a medical home and a primary care physician through one of the city's public or nonprofit clinics. Acute care and specialty care are provided by San Francisco General and a network of the city's nonprofit hospitals. Healthy San Francisco is a health access program, not insurance. Health services are not available through the program outside of the local network. The program is funded by the public, individuals, and employers. It also receives in-kind contributions from nonprofit hospitals.

The minimum health spending requirement originally mandated that businesses with twenty to ninety-nine workers spend a minimum of $1.17 an hour per employee on health services. Businesses with one hundred or more workers are required to spend a minimum of $1.76 an hour per employee on health services. The minimum spending amounts are indexed to health premium costs. In 2013 the amounts are $1.55 and $2.33 an hour, respectively. Employers may meet the requirement through contributions to health benefits, health savings accounts, direct reimbursement of health care costs, or payment into the city program. The requirement was designed to level the playing field for firms that already provide coverage, to discourage firms from dropping coverage and placing a greater burden on the new public program, and to help reduce the taxpayer cost of caring for uninsured workers.

The employer spending requirement went into effect in April 2008 for employers with 50 or more workers and April 2009 for employers with 20 to 49 workers. By June 2010 nearly a thousand employers had chosen to pay into the city plan, contributing a total of nearly $80 million on behalf of over 55,000 workers (Department of Public Health and Office of Labor Standards 2010). Healthy San Francisco is available only to San Francisco residents. If an employer pays its obligation to the city, funds are set aside in Medical Reimbursement Accounts (MRAs) for workers who are not eligible for the program. Close to 50,000 individuals were enrolled in Healthy San Francisco in March 2013, and another 10,000 transitioned from Healthy San Francisco to new insurance offerings made available through a State Medicaid waiver to bridge coverage to the new programs created by the Affordable Care Act (Healthy San Francisco 2013).

PAID SICK LEAVE

In November 2006 San Francisco became the first U.S. city to require employers to provide paid sick leave. A ballot initiative establishing the policy passed with 61 percent of the vote. In order to give employers time to come into compliance, implementation of the ordinance began in June 2007. The law requires employers to provide one hour of paid sick time for every thirty hours worked. Workers for businesses with fewer than ten employees may accrue at least a minimum of forty hours of paid sick time; for all other businesses the minimum required accrual is seventy-two hours. Employees may use the time for their own health care or to care for a family member who is sick.

2. THE ECONOMIC AND POLITICAL CONTEXT

As we have seen, San Francisco has gone much further than other cities in instituting innovative mandates. We argue in this section that the economic context in which these mandates were instituted was similar to those in many other cities. In particular, the structure of San Francisco's economy is not wildly different from that of many other U.S. cities. The move to enact local labor standards emerged in the context of eroding federal protections, the revival of the central city, and rising economic inequality. Compared to many other cities, San

Francisco was a bit ahead on these trends; but it has not traveled on an exceptional trajectory.

We also argue that political coalitions among business, labor, and neighborhood organizations emerged in San Francisco that did distinguish it from other cities. In particular, the emergence in San Francisco of coalitions among labor and community-based organizations shifted policy making in new directions. These coalitions supported mandates that also encouraged economic development.

Eroding Federal Protections of Labor Standards

Over the course of the 1980s the real value of the federal minimum wage declined by 30 percent (Reich and Laitinen 2003). In 2000, 14.9 percent of workers nationally were covered by a union contract, a drop of 42 percent over two decades (Hirsch and McPherson 2012). Unionization in California was slightly above the national average, with 17.7 percent of workers covered.[6] These erosions of protections led to a countertrend that began in 1994, when Baltimore enacted the first modern local living wage law. This law required service companies contracting with the city to meet wage standards well above the federal minimum wage.

Ten years later, more than 130 local jurisdictions had passed living wage laws (Fairris and Reich 2005). Over the course of the decade, these laws became more complex, applying to wider categories of workers and containing a broader mix of protections, including minimum paid time off, requirements that workers be retained if the city contract changes hands, and protections against employer retaliation against workers who file complaints.

In this same period, over thirty states passed state minimum wage laws that exceed the federal floor and ten states indexed their minimum wage standards to inflation. As we discuss below, a number of cities and states also passed laws providing paid family and medical leave, paid sick leave, and other policies that protect living standards.

---

[6] Union density remained remarkably stable in California over the next decade, even as the share of workers covered by union contracts continued to fall nationally.

While many cities and states have passed such laws, other states have also been active, but to reduce worker protections further. A number of states moved to preempt local jurisdictions from establishing such policies. In the Great Lakes region, many states reduced protections for state and local government workers. Thus the greater activism of states and localities has had mixed effects on worker protections.

Economic Context: The Revival of Many Central Cities but with More Inequality

In the half century from 1940 to 1990, economic activity and population in urban areas shifted from central cities to the suburban rings of metropolitan areas. This shift began with the emergence in the 1920s and subsequent spread of decentralized truck- and car-based transport modes that replaced centrally located rail and harbor facilities. In the immediate postwar period, the greater availability of land in the suburbs, postwar federal subsidies for suburban housing developments, and the creation of the interstate highway system also contributed to the decentralization of economic activity. As a result, although most central cities in the United States nonetheless continued to grow in absolute terms, they did so at a declining rate. In the 1980s, rapid deindustrialization of the U.S. economy multiplied the economic problems of most central cities, and declining growth gave way to absolute population and economic shrinkage (Boustan and Shertzer 2010).

San Francisco experienced these same trends, except that they emerged earlier than in the nation as a whole (Glaeser and Gottlieb 2008; Birch 2009, table 1). Indeed, in the early postwar years San Francisco declined more than most cities, as it lost most of its industrial base, first to the suburbs and then to overseas competition. By 1999 less than 5 percent of San Francisco's workers were employed in manufacturing, one of the lowest proportions among U.S. cities. In this dimension, San Francisco has not been an exception but rather ahead of other cities, whose industrial bases also declined in the same period.

Beginning in the late 1980s and continuing in the 1990s, many, but not all, central cities were experiencing positive growth (Boustan and

Shertzer 2010, fig. 1a). The decline of San Francisco relative to its surrounding counties ended in the early 1990s. Although the city's concentration in high technology led to substantial declines again after the dot-com bust of 2000, the city recovered again in the subsequent years.

San Francisco's previous decline and more recent revival are especially apparent in data on the median income of San Francisco households, both in real terms and relative to California households and to all U.S. households. These patterns are presented in the left columns of table 1.1 for the period 1969–2010. After stagnating in the 1980s, median household income in San Francisco rose in real terms in the 1980s and 1990s. In the 2000s, although not shown in table 1.2, median income increased until the Great Recession and then fell less than in California or the United States. In 2010 San Francisco's median household income ranked third among major U.S. cities, behind San Jose, California, and Austin, Texas.[7]

Median income among San Francisco households, expressed relative to that of California and U.S. households, followed a similar pattern. In the 1970s, the median income of San Francisco households was lower than in California as a whole. Beginning in the 1980s, the relative median income of San Francisco households rose sharply and continued to do so into the 2000s. The same pattern appears when San Francisco is compared to the United States as a whole.

San Francisco's economic resilience continued even after the onset of the Great Recession. Although not shown in table 1.2, from 2006 to 2010 median income continued to rise in the city while declining by 6 percent in California and 4.4 percent nationwide. Of course, the wealth of the average home-owning household fell substantially with the sharp

---

[7] The increase in real median household income is notable because it indicates some gains for San Francisco's beleaguered middle class. Relatedly, it is not the case that the percentage of San Francisco households with children declined disproportionately to comparable areas. From the 1970s to 2000 the proportion of children in San Francisco's population did decline but at the same rate as in surrounding counties. Since 2000 the proportion has leveled off in San Francisco while continuing to decline elsewhere (RAND California 2012).

Table 1.2   Median Household Income and Income Inequality
San Francisco, California, and the U.S., 1969–2010

Year	Median Household Income San Francisco	San Francisco Relative to California	San Francisco Relative to U.S.	Mean to Median Ratio San Francisco	Mean to Median Ratio California	Mean to Median Ratio U.S.
1969	$49,271	0.86	0.94	—	—	—
1979	$50,327	0.87	0.94	1.30	1.23	1.21
1989	$59,539	0.93	1.11	1.37	1.29	1.28
1999	$73,156	1.16	1.31	1.45	1.38	1.35
2010	$71,745	1.17	1.37	1.43	1.37	1.37

SOURCE: Social Explorer 2013; United States Census 2013.

decline in home prices that began in 2006, erasing many of the steep gains in property values of the previous decade. This decline did not affect the highest-income households to the same extent, since more of their wealth was held in securities that had recovered their prerecession values by 2012.

San Francisco's prosperity has also produced increasing inequality, a pattern that has been repeated in other growing cities, in individual states, and in the United States as a whole.[8] This increase has occurred in both the upper and lower halves of the income distribution. We focus here on the upper half of the distribution and discuss in section 4 developments in the lower half. The three columns on the right side of table 1.2 display the ratio of mean to median income over time in San Francisco and the United States for the period 1979–2010. A rising ratio of mean to median income indicates the growth of inequality among the more affluent half of households. This ratio increases during these decades in all three columns. By this measure, San Francisco exhibits more inequality than California or the United States as a whole.

[8] Glaeser and Gottlieb (2008) show that economic inequality increased in most metropolitan areas between 1980 and 2000.

San Francisco's prosperity, like that of other recent "superstar" cities, such as San Jose and Austin, has been based more on innovation than mass production. Figure 1.2 displays the changes between 1990 and 2010 in the economic structure of San Francisco and of the twenty largest central U.S. cities. To keep the figure readable, we have included only eight sectors. The selected sectors include three that are high paying: financial services; information and communications; and professional, scientific, and management services. Two of the sectors in figure 1.2 pay middle-level wages—manufacturing and health, education, and social services—and three are relatively low paying—administrative support services, retail, and accommodation and food services. We have analyzed the data for the remaining sectors and found that they do not change the patterns that we observe among these eight.

Two major patterns can be seen in figure 1.2. The first pattern is shown by the relative importance of each of these sectors in 1990. Relative to the twenty other largest central cities, San Francisco's industrial mix in 1990 was already overrepresented in the high- and low-paying sectors and underrepresented in the middle-paying sectors. Surprisingly, however, the importance of the accommodation and food services sector, which includes the tourism industry, is only 2 percent higher in San Francisco than in the comparison central cities.

The second pattern in figure 1.2 is shown by changes in the relative importance of these sectors over the 1990–2010 period. Two of the three high-paying sectors—financial services and information and communications—did not increase in economic importance. The proportion of the San Francisco economy in one of the three high-paying sectors—professional, scientific, and management services—increased in San Francisco and in the twenty comparison cities, but the increase was greater in San Francisco. Changes over time in the importance of the two middle-paying sectors—manufacturing and health, education, and social services—offset each other in both San Francisco and the twenty comparison cities. Changes in the importance of each of the three low-paying sectors were remarkably similar in San Francisco and the twenty comparison central cities.

These comparisons suggest that San Francisco's relative prosperity is reproducible in other cities. Indeed, Moretti (2011, 2012) argues that the cit-

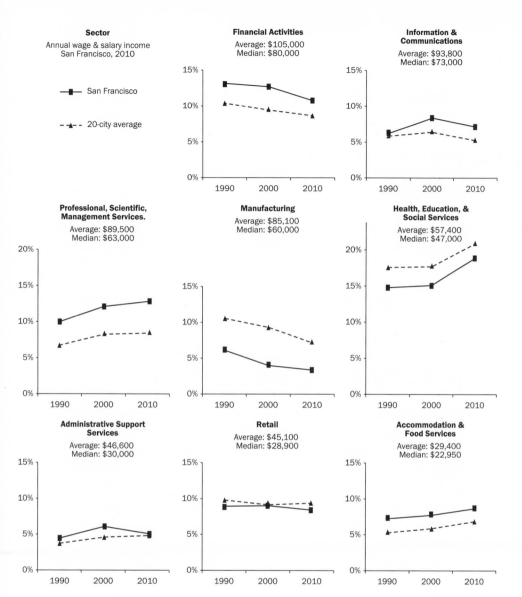

Figure 1.2 Employment shares by industry, San Francisco and average of 20 other largest central cities, 1990, 2000, and 2010.

NOTES: About 25–30 percent of workers are in other sectors not shown. Sectors correspond as closely as possible to NAICS. To adjust for changes in classification across time, these sectors were compiled of the following industries.

Information & Communications: newspaper publishing, other publishing, radio and television, telephone, miscellaneous communications, computer and data processing services, theaters and motion pictures, and libraries.

Professional, Scientific, Management Services: advertising, legal, engineering and architecture, accounting, research and development, veterinary services, management and public relations, and miscellaneous professional services.

Administrative Support Services: landscape, building, personnel, protective services, and miscellaneous business services. The comparison group is composed of place of work public use microdata areas (pw-puma) that best approximate the central cities of the twenty largest metropolitan statistical areas in the U.S., absent Miami and Denver. Geographic areas covered by pw-puma vary in how closely they align with actual city boundaries.

SOURCE: American Community Survey and Decennial Census from Ruggies et al., 2010.

ies that have seen the biggest revivals had greater concentrations of highly educated, highly productive, and innovative workers. This workforce created agglomeration economies and knowledge spillovers that made all workers—including those with only high school degrees—more productive and better paid. These agglomeration economies in turn attracted more highly skilled workers to the area, in a virtuous circle. In contrast, economic recovery was much weaker in cities that were weaker in these dimensions.

San Francisco and nearby San Jose had the two highest proportions of college graduates in 1970 and in every succeeding decade.[9] As Moretti shows, the relative abundance of skilled workers in 1970 or 1980 predicts the relative success of these cities by 2000, as measured, for example, by median earnings or median household income. This success is evident in the left-hand columns of table 1.2. In 1969 and 1979 median household income in San Francisco stood at 86 or 87 percent of the state median. Twenty years later—in 1999—the comparable figure had risen to a substantially higher level, 116 percent.

San Francisco's boom was based in particular on such high-paying industries as finance, high-tech, and biotech, as well as on tourism, which generates low- and middle-paid jobs. According to Moretti's calculations, every additional job in innovative industries generates five additional jobs, three of which are filled by workers who have not attended college. Highly paid workers in the innovative industries spend a large part of their income on local services—many of which employ large numbers of low-paid workers.

These highly paid workers also spend large shares of their growing incomes on housing, driving up house prices relative to less prosperous areas. Rising housing costs put increased pressure on working families. Median home prices in San Francisco rose from $270,000 in 1996 to $590,000 in 2002 to $760,000 in 2008 (California Association of Realtors 2013). In 2010 the California Budget Project estimated that a full-time single worker would need to earn $15.37 an hour to meet basic needs in San Francisco. For a single-parent family, the comparable figure was $36.64 (California Budget Project 2010).

[9] Excluding Washington DC, where the main industry is government (Tavernise 2012).

The presence of middle-income families had already diminished because of the decline of middle-paying jobs in industry in the central city. The growth of house prices, which was greater in San Francisco than in its neighboring counties as well as in other regions of the United States, further fueled the exodus of middle-income families.[10] The result of these economic forces: prosperity for some hand in hand with economic stagnation for many. In other words, growth occurred together with increasing inequality.

To summarize, while San Francisco's economy was doing relatively well by the 1990s, income inequality was increasing. A growing number of San Francisco's workers were earning very low pay in an increasingly high-income economy. Indeed, many of these low-paid workers were employed in industries that provided services directly to ever more affluent San Franciscans.

These conditions led to calls for greater economic justice as well as to the recognition that the affluent could easily afford to pay a bit more for these services. In the language of economics, the price elasticity of these services is relatively low, indicating that modestly higher labor costs could be passed on to affluent consumers in higher prices without substantially reducing demand for the services. Mandates, therefore, might lead to greater shared prosperity without substantially reducing the number employed.

Political Trends: The Rise of a Progressive Economic Development Coalition

San Francisco has long been a Democratic Party stronghold, as well as a strong labor city with a rich tradition of community organizing. It shares these features with many other central cities in the United States. As in most cities, a pro-growth coalition of business allied with unions and middle-class professions had responded to the postwar decline of central

---

[10] An important question concerns whether the growth of house prices resulted from San Francisco's relative prosperity, from the limited land available in the city, or from the regulatory constraints that neighborhood-oriented activists placed on the growth of housing supply. A large literature has examined this question, with evidence supporting each mechanism, but these issues are beyond the scope of this volume.

city manufacturing and transportation by promoting urban redevelopment. The growth model was based upon real estate, finance, and tourism and on building a transportation infrastructure that would better serve suburban white-collar commuters (Mollenkopf 1983).

Beginning in the 1950s, Democrats in most major cities built electoral bases around urban renewal policies that fostered economic growth, with benefits not just for downtown businesses but also for some unions and racial minorities. In the 1980s, when federal funds for urban redevelopment dried up, growth strategies in San Francisco and other cities increasingly involved public-private partnerships. During this period, San Francisco was distinctive from other cities in the degree to which its redevelopment policies became more inclusive of the interests of neighborhood groups. A further shift took place in the late 1990s, with the emergence of new labor-community coalitions focused on job quality.

As in many other cities, San Francisco's postwar urban redevelopment growth strategy provoked protests from affected local neighborhoods. A variety of San Francisco political histories (DeLeon 1992; Hartman 2002; Beitel 2003) describe the city's long tradition of active neighborhood-based organizing that sought to limit the city's economic growth. One strain of neighborhood activists wanted to stop development so as to preserve their neighborhoods' traditional character; a second sought to keep development from displacing low-income residents and gentrifying their community; and a third group, concerned with environmental issues, fought economic development in order to keep their communities from becoming swallowed up by high-rise buildings that would expand the size of the downtown area ("the Manhattanization of San Francisco"). By the mid-1980s, these organizations were able to wrest some concessions from the pro-growth coalition, such as increasing the supply of affordable housing through inclusionary zoning requirements for low-income housing as a condition of new development.[11]

---

[11] Inclusionary zoning policies require or encourage developers to meet minimum standards for the share of new housing units affordable to low- and moderate-income households. See chapter 10 for a more detailed discussion of inclusionary zoning.

In this same period, the city's private sector labor organizations generally favored economic development projects proposed by city agencies and downtown interests. These unions, particularly those in construction and in the hospitality and tourism industry, sought to maintain collective bargaining rights and to increase the number of jobs for their members. Unions had the power to secure their interests without the support of community-based organizations, and their political support for development projects was not contingent on conditions that were advanced by those organizations. Indeed, the pro-growth business-labor coalition was repeatedly in conflict with neighborhood groups.

By the 1990s, the relationships among these groups began to shift substantially. As the economy changed, service and public sector unions became the dominant players in the San Francisco Labor Council. Internal changes in a number of major San Francisco unions brought a more inclusive set of leaders into power (Wells 2002). Another key change occurred in 1996, when labor succeeded in getting the city to enact a law that placed labor-oriented conditions on economic development projects. This law required employer neutrality during unionization drives and labor peace on economic development projects that involved city subsidies or city land. Their success with using essentially the same strategy that neighborhood organizations had already successfully adopted provided a new development model to labor organizations. Further, such conditions could be written into other contractor and development agreements.

Both community activists and labor then began to join together to use this strategy of placing a variety of conditions on development. Moreover, since they were not trying to stop development altogether, the community activists and labor organizations could then begin to work together with some parts of the business community on policies that were of interest to all three parties.[12] This pattern was especially evident in a number

[12] This shift in policy to more inclusionary economic development was not unique to San Francisco, nor was it universal. Alongside the successful coalitions, conflicts continued around many development projects. In some other cities, notably Los Angeles and San Jose, labor and community activists were able to unite more consistently around including community-based conditions in economic redevelopment projects.

of explicit public-private bargains among developers, organized labor, and neighborhood groups, including legally binding community benefit agreements (Wolf-Powers 2010).

Changes in electoral law in this period also increased the strength of the neighborhood organizations. Since 2000, the San Francisco Board of Supervisors has been elected through district rather than citywide elections. With this shift a much more progressive electoral coalition began to dominate City Hall. Moreover, public financing of election campaigns began in 2002 for supervisors and for the mayor in 2006.[13] Together, these reforms reduced the power of downtown real estate interests and increased the influence of labor, community organizations, and the city's many Democratic Party neighborhood clubs.

Finally, as a city and a county, San Francisco shares the legal powers of the two levels of government. This characteristic both broadens the reach of specific laws and allows for the passage of laws with a single act, whereas coordination among multiple jurisdictions would be required elsewhere.[14]

3. THE POSSIBLE ECONOMIC EFFECTS OF PAY AND BENEFIT MANDATES

While some mandates create requirements for *individuals*, the mandates in San Francisco apply to *employers*. These employer mandates are of two types: one sets a floor on pay, and the other sets a floor on benefits.[15]

---

[13] Fourteen localities across the United States provide public financing of local campaigns (Levinson and Long 2009). Banks et al. (2006) evaluate the effectiveness of San Francisco's law.

[14] Other major consolidated cities and counties include Denver, Honolulu, Lexington, KY, New Orleans, Philadelphia, and Washington DC. New York City is made up of five boroughs, which serve some of the functions of counties.

[15] Federal and state laws set numerous other work-related mandates, such as paying overtime rates, meeting OSHA safety standards, contributions to social insurance and worker compensation funds, family and medical leaves, and plant-closing notification requirements. Summers (1989) and Krueger (1994) provide general theoretical discussions of the efficiency and distributional effects of mandates. Empirical studies of a variety of

Economists have long considered that the two types of employer mandates may have differing labor market effects.

In the case of mandates concerning pay, the simplest labor market model of supply and demand suggests that an increase in the cost of labor will lead to less demand for labor. This model underlies the familiar "job killer" description applied to minimum wage policies. In the case of mandates concerning benefits, the same basic model suggests that employers and workers will adjust primarily by reducing pay rather than employment. In this model, a mandate on benefits leaves total compensation (pay plus benefits) unchanged and employment will not be reduced. For workers who are already paid at or near the minimum wage, pay cannot be reduced by the full amount of the cost of the mandates. As a result, the simple supply-and-demand theory predicts that benefits mandates for such low-wage workers will fall partly on their pay and partly upon their employment levels.

Economists have revised the simple supply-and-demand model by adding important features that better account for the specific characteristics of labor markets. The most important of these features in low wage settings concern the costs of higher labor turnover, the positive effects of higher pay on worker productivity, and the possibility of passing on higher labor costs to consumers through higher prices. Each of these effects can mitigate or even eliminate the negative employment effects of a pay mandate and the negative pay effects of a benefit mandate. To discover whether there are negative effects then rests not on theoretical arguments but on careful empirical analysis.

In 1994 David Card and Alan Krueger published a groundbreaking study that changed how many economists view the minimum wage. Card and Krueger looked at employment in fast-food restaurants across the New Jersey and Pennsylvania border after New Jersey increased its state minimum wage. They found no measurable negative impact on employment. Dube, Lester, and Reich (2010, 2013) expanded the approach

---

benefit mandates support their analyses. See, for example, Gruber (1994) on mandated maternity benefits and Kolstad and Kolakowsi (2012) on the effects of health insurance reform in Massachusetts.

of Card and Krueger, comparing counties across every state border in the United States that had differences in the minimum wage over a sixteen-year period and reached the same conclusions.

Labor economists' expanded models offer important insights that help to explain what happened in San Francisco. First, workers are not widgets. If you pay more for a hammer, the quality of the hammer does not change. In contrast, paying workers more can change their work performance. It can change their attitude about their job, how hard they work, and their ability to make it to the job on time. Second, low-wage labor markets have high levels of frictional unemployment. Turnover levels are high as workers leave jobs for wage gains or may be unable to stay in their jobs due to poverty-related problems, such as difficulties with transportation, child care, or health. This effect suggests that rather than kill jobs, increases in minimum wages kill job vacancies, leaving employment unchanged.[16]

Firms can absorb higher labor costs through other means as well. They can pass on some of the increased costs to consumers through higher prices, earn lower profits, or reduce managerial salaries. There could be a combination of all these effects (Schmitt 2013). Indexing the minimum wage, as is done in San Francisco, allows workers' wages to keep up with the cost of living and avoids the larger wage shocks to employers that come from more intermittent adjustments.

4. THE AGGREGATE EFFECTS OF SAN FRANCISCO'S NEXUS OF MANDATES

San Francisco's new labor standards policies have brought substantial improvements in compensation and access to health care to thousands of low-wage workers and their families. Mandated minimum compensation costs for a large employer in 2013 were $13.31; $10.55 in minimum wage; $2.33 in mandated health allocation; and one hour of paid sick

---

[16] Studies of California's paid family leave law, the first in the nation and enacted in 2002, arrive at similar findings. See Rossin-Slater, Ruhm, and Waldfogel 2012; Milkman and Appelbaum 2013.

leave for every thirty hours worked, or an extra 43 cents per hour. However, employers in San Francisco in effect face a somewhat lower minimum compensation cost on average, both because not all the health care security ordinance money is claimed and because not all paid sick leave hours are used.[17, 18] Taking into account these two adjustments, the average actual minimum compensation cost that an employer faced in 2013 was $12.83 for firms with one hundred or more employees, $12.13 for midsized firms, and $10.65 for firms with few than twenty employees not subject to the Health Care Security Ordinance.[19]

Given these average actual minimum compensation costs, in 2013 minimum wage workers in San Francisco received wages and benefits worth 33 to 60 percent more, on average, than minimum wage workers in the rest of California and 47 to 77 percent more than minimum wage workers under the federal minimum wage. Figure 1.3 shows minimum compensation standards across jurisdictions, including the range of minimum compensation in San Francisco, from minimum wage only to minimum wage with the full monetary value of paid sick leave and mandated health allocation.

Effects of the Mandates on Low-Paid Workers

In section 2 we discussed evidence indicating that economic prosperity in San Francisco also generated increased upper-half inequality—as shown by the growing gap between mean and median household incomes. A similar increase in inequality occurred in the bottom half of the income distribution. We use a common measure of lower-half inequality: the 50:10 wage ratio, which is the median hourly wage divided by the hourly

[17] Some employers use Health Reimbursement Accounts (HRAs) to comply with the law, but in 2010 and 2011 only 20 to 26 percent of the money allocated to HRAs was actually paid out in reimbursements. Averaged across all employers we estimate that employers retain 5 to 7 percent of their mandated health allocation (San Francisco OLSE 2012).

[18] For paid sick leave, only 62 percent of workers actually took any paid sick leave; if they did, they tended to take a total of four days, only 44 percent of the nine days a full-time worker would accrue in a year. In effect employees use only an average of a quarter of an hour (27 percent) of paid sick leave for every 30 hours that they work (Lovell, chapter 7 this volume).

[19] These numbers should be understood in the context of living costs in San Francisco. In 2010, the nonprofit California Budget Project estimated the minimum hourly amount needed for a full-time working single adult to meet basic expenses in San Francisco at $15.37 an hour.

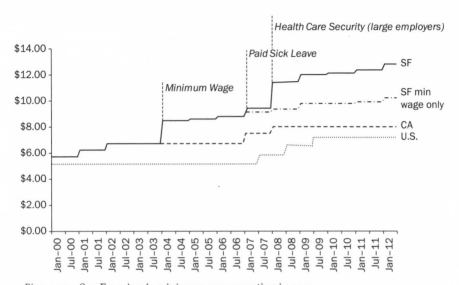

Figure 1.3   San Francisco's minimum compensation in 2012.

SOURCE: Authors' calculations based on San Francisco Office of Labor Standards Enforcement.

wage at the 10th percentile. While the median wage was increasing dramatically in the 1980s and 1990s, the real minimum wage in California fell substantially until it regained some of its lost ground with state and federal minimum wage increases in 1996–98. As the minimum wage is highly correlated with wages at the 10th percentile, it follows that the 50–10 ratio was increasing during this period.

While the median wage is not affected by San Francisco's mandates, the 10th percentile wage definitely is. As figure 1.4 shows, the 10th percentile wage jumped in 2004, when the city's minimum wage was increased from $6.75 to $8.50, and then has remained constant in real dollars, reflecting how indexing of the city's minimum wage protects workers from real wage cuts because of inflation.

In contrast, as figure 1.4 shows, the 10th percentile wage did not increase in San Francisco's surrounding counties but instead declined after the onset of the Great Recession. This difference in wage patterns suggests that the mandate had positive and persisting effects on low-

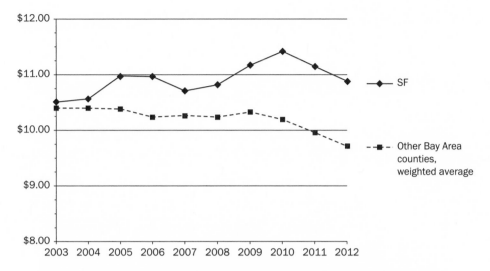

Figure 1.4 San Francisco and other Bay Area counties, 10th percentile hourly wage, 2003–2012.

NOTE: This figure shows the 10th percentile wage in San Francisco growing relative to other Bay Area counties. Other Bay Area counties include San Mateo, Alameda, and Santa Clara and San Benito counties, weighted by county civilian labor force. Data are adjusted using the CPI-W for San Francisco, Oakland, and San Jose.

SOURCE: California Employment Development Department, Labor market Information Division analysis of OES data, all industries and all occupations.

paid San Francisco workers. However, this impact was not sufficient to prevent a further widening of the 50–10 gap.

What about the effects of the mandate on employment? Contrary to arguments that minimum wage increases kill jobs, these policies do not appear to have reduced private employment in the city (fig. 1.5). Employment trends in San Francisco during this period of policy change were similar to those in the rest of the Bay Area, with the recessions in 2001 and 2008–9 playing a much more obvious role both in San Francisco and throughout the region. From the first quarter of 2004, when the minimum wage ordinance went into effect, to the first quarter of 2011, overall private employment grew by 5.6 percent in San Francisco and 3.0 percent in Santa Clara County and fell by 4.4 percent overall in other counties of the Bay Area.

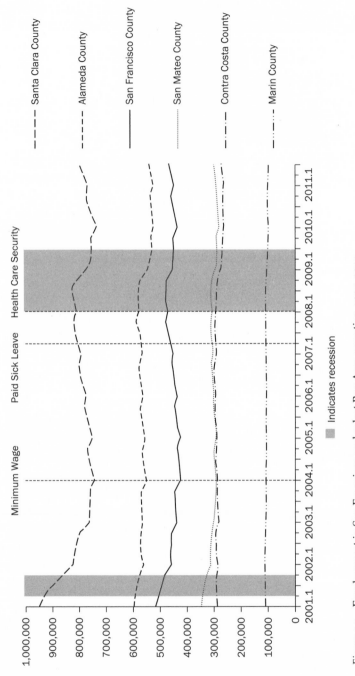

Figure 1.5 Employment in San Francisco and select Bay Area counties, 2001–2011.

NOTE: This figure shows San Francisco employment trends mirroring trends in neighboring counties.

SOURCE: Quarterly Census of Employment and Wages, average quarterly employment, private sector workers.

These general trends are robust when analyzing employment trends for food service workers, who are more likely to be directly affected by minimum wage laws. Within the relatively low-wage bar and restaurant industry there are no obvious employment effects (fig. 1.6). From the first quarter of 2004 to the first quarter of 2011, employment in food services and drinking places grew by 17.7 percent in San Francisco, faster than either the other counties of the Bay Area (13.2 percent growth) or Santa Clara County (13.1 percent growth). San Francisco's patterns again mimic those of surrounding counties.

5. LESSONS FOR URBAN AND NATIONAL POLICY

San Francisco's policies offer important lessons for the rest of the country. With the exception of the Health Care Security Ordinance, none of the policies are unique to San Francisco. Some were implemented first in San Francisco; many were not. What is unique is the broad mix of policies and the extent of their reach. San Francisco's experience suggests that cities, states, and the federal government could do much more to protect labor standards without negatively affecting employment.

San Francisco's Equal Benefits Ordinance has been widely replicated; nineteen other cities have passed similar laws, as did the state of California (table 1.3). More than 130 cities, counties, and university campuses have living wage policies, as does the state of Maryland. The Federal Service Contract Act serves a similar function on a federal level, requiring contractors to pay prevailing wage for contracted service. Community Benefits Agreements are becoming a part of the development landscape in many major urban areas.

In 2013 eighteen states had minimum wage policies above the federal wage minimum wage. Citywide minimum wage policies are also in effect in Albuquerque and Santa Fe, New Mexico, San Jose, California, and Washington DC. Connecticut, Washington DC, Milwaukee, Portland, Oregon, New York City, and Seattle all have passed paid sick leave laws (although Milwaukee's was overturned by the state). While San

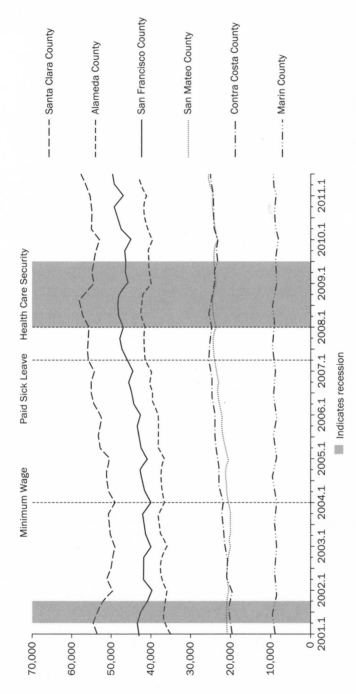

Figure 1.6 Employment in restaurants in San Francisco and select Bay Area counties, 2001–2011.

NOTE: This figure shows that restaurant employment in San Francisco grew at the same rate as in surrounding counties even after employer mandates were put in place.

SOURCE: Quarterly Census of Employment and Wages, average quarterly employment, food service and drinking places (NAICS 722)

Table 1.3 Presence of San Francisco–Type Laws in Other Jurisdictions

Law	Other Cities and Localities	States
Equal Benefits for Domestic Partners	19 other localities including Los Angeles, Minneapolis, Philadelphia, and Seattle	California
Union majority sign-up / card check / labor peace	A handful of localities including airports, school districts, and cities	
Living wage at airports	Los Angeles, Miami, Oakland, San Jose, St. Louis	
Living wage	First enacted in Baltimore, living wage laws now exist in over 130 cities, counties, and university campuses.	Maryland
Contractor pay-or-play health policy	Houston	New Mexico
Minimum wage	Albuquerque ($8.50), San Jose ($10.00), Santa Fe ($10.29), Washington DC ($8.25)	18 states with minimum wage laws above federal minimum wage and/or indexed to cost of living. Above federal: AK, CA, CT, IL, NM, MA, ME, MI, RI Above federal and indexed: AZ, CO, FL, MT, NV, OH, OR, VT, WA
Paid Sick Leave	New York City, Portland, OR, Seattle, Washington DC	Connecticut
Health spending mandates		Similar elements in HI and in national Affordable Care Act
Community benefits agreements	Atlanta, Denver, Los Angeles, Milwaukee, New Haven, New York, Oakland, Philadelphia, Pittsburgh, San Jose, San Diego, Seattle, Syracuse, Washington DC, among others	

Francisco's Health Care Security Ordinance takes a unique approach to setting health spending standards, Hawaii and Massachusetts also have employer requirements as part of their health reform laws, as does the Affordable Care Act nationally. Research on the employment effects of these laws echoes the results found in the research on San Francisco.

An argument can be made that labor standards policies work best at the state or federal level because they create a common set of rules for businesses and a level playing field between jurisdictions. This logic already underlies federal preemption policy in the National Labor Relations Act and the Employee Retirement Insurance Security Act. At the same time, the Fair Labor Standards Act permits states to go beyond its standards. While federal policy may establish the floor, it does not establish a ceiling. While state and local governments must adhere to federal standards, they may go beyond those standards to reflect local conditions.

The ability of local jurisdictions to set wage standards depends on state law. California specifically permits cities and counties to establish minimum wage standards.[20] Local wage policies can provide a useful adjustment for the cost of living in a specific geographic area or can be tailored to address conditions in specific industries, as with living wage laws. The failure of Congress to pass majority verification for union recognition at the federal level, the low level and lack of indexing for the federal minimum wage, and the ongoing political stalemate in Washington on economic policy are likely to place greater attention again on state and local governments as places for action to address poverty and economic inequality. The San Francisco experience thus provides an important case study on what is possible at the local level.

To be sure, we would not argue that mandates will work well everywhere. Addressing inequality-producing growth through mandates to make prosperity broader based may be less salient when a city is not growing and is not prosperous.

---

[20] Localities have the power to enact higher minimum wages in Arizona, California, New Mexico, Washington, Maryland, and Illinois. The legality of local standards has not been tested in many other states (Paul Sonn, pers. com., Apr. 1, 2013).

Moreover, provisions in some laws could encourage distortions that hurt economic efficiency. For example, in the Affordable Care Act an employer with fifty full-time employees who does not pay the mandated cost of health benefits is penalized for *every* worker working over thirty hours per week. This creates a "cliff" that may encourage employers to adjust work hours to keep greater numbers of workers employed under thirty hours. In San Francisco, the "pay" penalty in the play or pay design is scaled to the number of hours a person works, for those working eight hours or more per week, so there is no cliff on work hours. It does, however, include cliffs for numbers of employees—at twenty and one hundred.

The reach of San Francisco's mandates is high when it is measured in absolute terms against other areas and against wage levels in restaurants, retail, and other low-wage industries. But its reach is not high compared to the median wage in San Francisco. Indeed, the ratio of the minimum wage to the median wage is .39 in San Francisco, identical to the comparable ratio for the United States as a whole. San Francisco thus could be said to have been quite conservative in its mandates, adjusting for local conditions and cautious not to risk negative employment effects.[21]

6. OVERVIEW OF THE BOOK

The book is divided into three parts. Part 1 takes up the pay mandates, part 2 takes up the benefit mandates, and part 3 examines the conditions that make the mandates work. Each of the chapters in the first two parts examines the impacts of San Francisco's policies with a focus on workers and firms. In doing so, they address how San Francisco was able to improve labor standards without creating any measurable negative effects on employment levels.

---

[21] Interestingly, the same pattern appears when comparing minimum wage levels across states to the state's median wage. State minimum wage levels that are higher than the federal minimum are generally in line with the relative level of median wages in those states.

Many of the chapters are based on research papers that use state-of-the-art statistical methods and that have appeared in refereed scholarly journals. The authors have revised their studies to make the findings accessible to a broader audience, to bring them up to date, and to include a discussion of the extent to which the policies they discuss were subsequently adopted elsewhere.

Part 1: The Pay Mandates

In chapter 2, "Labor Market Impacts of San Francisco's Minimum Wage," Arindrajit Dube, Suresh Naidu, and Michael Reich discuss their study of San Francisco's minimum wage policy. Their data come from their survey of restaurants in San Francisco and surrounding areas before and nine months after implementation of the citywide minimum wage ordinance. The authors found a small but not statistically significant increase in employment in affected restaurants compared to their control group. The length of employee tenure increased in limited service restaurants by an average of 3.5 months, as did the share of employees working full time. Restaurants in San Francisco raised prices 2.8 percent more than the control group during the same time period.

In chapter 3, "Liftoff: Raising Wages at San Francisco Airport," Peter Hall, Ken Jacobs, and Michael Reich examine the impact of living wage policies at San Francisco International Airport. They find that the program had a sharp and immediate impact on employee turnover and job performance. Fifteen months after the policy went into effect, turnover had fallen by one-third among all firms and by 60 percent among the firms with the greatest share of affected workers. Annual turnover of security screeners fell 80 percent. Sizable numbers of employers reported higher morale, fewer grievances, fewer absences, and better customer service. Employees reported that they were working harder, that more skills were required of them on the job, and that the pace of work had increased.

In chapter 4, "Living Wage and Home Care Workers," Candace Howes argues that San Francisco set the standard for job quality in consumer-directed home care services, one of the fastest growing occupations in the country. She provides an overview of the long-term care industry and examines how San Francisco's mandates affected home care workers in the city. She finds that the policy led to a sharp and persisting drop in turnover among home care workers. Howes also examines how the San Francisco model has diffused in the rest of California and in other states.

Part 2: The Benefit Mandates

Chapter 5, "Health Spending Requirements in San Francisco," by Carrie Colla, William Dow, and Arindrajit Dube, discusses the impacts of San Francisco's 2006 health care reform law. From the evidence thus far, employers have largely opted to leave their current benefit programs intact, and there is substantial demand for the city program for workers who do not have health coverage. A number of restaurants have adapted to the ordinance by adding surcharges to the cost of dining, ranging from one dollar an entrée to 5 percent of the bill. The authors find little measurable impact on employment or earnings in the sectors most affected by the law.

Christy Mallory and Brad Sears discuss the Equal Benefits Ordinance in chapter 6, "Requiring Equal Benefits for Domestic Partners." They evaluate the implementation and enforcement of the law in San Francisco and twenty other jurisdictions that have replicated the policy and consider the potential for a presidential executive order requiring federal contractors to offer domestic partner benefits. They find widespread compliance and few complaints by contractors. They also find that the policies have not been disruptive to the contracting process, either for contractors or for governments, while providing benefits to both parties.

Employer fears concerning paid sick leave focus on the costs: whether workers will treat it as additional paid vacation time that can be disruptive to firm performance because employees are not required to provide advance notice when they will be using it. However, as Vicky Lovell reports in chapter 7, "Universal Paid Sick Leave," most workers treat paid sick leave as insurance—something they want to use only when they really need it; workers report using only a quarter of their available sick days. Lovell finds that two of five San Francisco workers benefited directly from the ordinance and employers have been surprisingly positive about the law.

Part 3: Making the Mandates Work

In chapter 8, "Enforcement of Labor Standards," Miranda Dietz, Donna Levitt, and Ellen Love discuss the best practices that have emerged in San Francisco to enforce the mandates analyzed in the previous chapters. In 2000 San Francisco established the Office of Labor Standards Enforcement (OLSE) to oversee enforcement of the city's prevailing wage laws for construction and living wage law. The office has since been expanded and given enforcement responsibilities over many of the laws discussed in this volume. OLSE proposes regulations, sends out notifications to employers about changes in the laws, investigates worker complaints, and conducts audits of city contractors. The city also contracts with a group of local community-based organizations to educate workers about their rights under the laws. This group includes organizations working in the Chinese and Latino communities, where language can be a barrier to enforcement.

In chapter 9, "Labor Policy and Local Economic Development," Miriam Wells provides a detailed history of the Employee Signature Authorization Ordinance and its impacts, placing it in the context of weakening federal labor laws and the prior history of neighborhood activism in the city. While many scholars rightly focus on how globalization reduces federal protections for labor rights, Wells demonstrates how local actors have turned successfully to municipal-level activism to gain more effective worker protections.

In chapter 10, "Community Benefit Agreements and Economic Development at Hunters Point Shipyard," Ken Jacobs discusses the emergence of new proactive coalitions around a comprehensive approach to urban economic development that includes affordable housing, workforce development, and strong labor standards. Community Benefit Agreements provide an important tool to local actors to engage in the economic development process. In contrast to the highly contentious political battle over the original living wage law in San Francisco, the labor standards provisions in the Hunters Point Shipyard Community Benefits Agreements were agreed to quietly and with little fanfare. This contrast suggests how much such policies have become normalized by businesses in San Francisco.

Finally, in Chapter 11, we discuss the lessons learned from these policies and the prospects for their future beyond San Francisco.

ACKNOWLEDGMENTS

We are grateful to Miranda Dietz and Jared Park for their assistance in preparing this chapter.

REFERENCES

Air Transport Ass'n v. City and County of San Francisco, 992 F.Supp. 1149 (1998).

Banks, Gina, Sasha Horwitz, Adam Lang, and Ernie Tedeschi. 2006. "Evaluating San Francisco's Partial Public Campaign Financing Program after Two Elections." Report to the San Francisco Ethics Commission. UC Berkeley, Goldman School of Public Policy.

Beitel, Karl. 2003. "Transforming San Francisco: Community, Capital, and the Local State in the Era of Globalization, 1956–2001." PhD diss., University of California, Davis, 2003.

Birch, Eugenie. 2009. "Downtown in the 'New American City.'" *Annals of the American Academy of Political and Social Science* 626: 134–53.

Boustan, Leah, and Allison Shertzer. 2010. "Demography and Population Loss from Central Cities, 1950–2000." Working Paper 16435. National Bureau of Economic Research.

California Association of Realtors. 2013. "Historical Housing Data: Median Prices of Existing Detached Homes." www.car.org/marketdata/data /housingdata/.

California Budget Project. 2010. "Making Ends Meet: How Much Does It Cost to Raise a Family in California?" www.lafla.org/pdf/MakingEndsMeet.pdf.

California Employment Development Department, Labor Market Information Division. 2012. "Quarterly Census of Employment and Wages (QCEW) Data Search Tool." www.labormarketinfo.edd.ca.gov/cgi/dataanalysis /areaselection.asp?tablename = industry.

————. 2013. "Occupational Employment Survey (OES), 10th Percentile Wage, All Industries, Total All Occupations." www.labormarketinfo.edd.ca.gov /cgi/dataanalysis/areaselection.asp?tablename=oeswage.

Card, David, and Alan Krueger. 1994. "Minimum Wages and Employment: A Case Study of the Fast Food Industry in New Jersey and Pennsylvania." *American Economic Review* 84, 4: 772–98.

DeLeon, Richard. 1992. *Left Coast City: Progressive Politics in San Francisco, 1975– 1001*. Lawrence: University Press of Kansas.

Department of Public Health and Office of Labor Standards Enforcement. 2010. "Status Report on the Implementation of the San Francisco Health Care Security Ordinance." www.healthysanfrancisco.org/files/PDF/June_2010_ BoS_Report.pdf.

Dineen, J.K. 2013. "Lennar Kicks off Construction at Hunters Point Shipyard." *San Francisco Business Times*. Updated June 27. www.bizjournals.com /sanfrancisco/blog/2013/06/lennar-kicks-off-construction-at.html.

Dube, Arindrajit, William Lester, and Michael Reich. 2010. "Minimum Wage Effects across State Borders: Estimates Using Contiguous Counties." *Review of Economics and Statistics* 92, 4: 945–64.

————. 2013. "Minimum Wage Shocks, Employment Flows and Labor Market Frictions." Working Paper 149–13. Institute for Research on Labor and Employment, University of California, Berkeley.

Dube, Arindrajit, Suresh Naidu, and Michael Reich. 2007. "The Economic Effects of a Citywide Minimum Wage." *Industrial and Labor Relations Review* 60, 4: 522–43.

Ettlinger, Michael. 2006. "Securing the Wage Floor: Indexing Would Maintain the Minimum Wage's Value and Provide Predictability to Employers." *Briefing Paper No. 177*. Washington DC: Economic Policy Institute.

Fairris, David, and Michael Reich. 2005. "The Impacts of Living Wage Policies: Introduction to the Special Issue." *Industrial Relations* 44, 1: 1–13.

Flacke, Tim, and Tina Wortheim. 2006. "Delivering a Local EITC, Lessons from the San Francisco Working Families Credit." *Survey Series.*Washington DC: Brookings Institution.

Glaeser, Edward, and Joshua Gottlieb. 2008. "The Economics of Place-Making Policies." *Brookings Papers on Economic Activity* (Spring): 155–253.

Goldstein, Cynthia. 2002. *Five Year Report on The San Francisco Equal Benefits Ordinance*. San Francisco Human Rights Commission. www.sfgov.org/site /sfhumanrights_page.asp?id=6295.

Gruber, Jonathan. 1994. "The Incidence of Mandated Maternity Benefits." *American Economic Review* 84, 3: 622–41.

Hartman, Chester. 2002. *City for Sale: The Transformation of San Francisco*. Berkeley: University of California Press.

Healthy San Francisco. 2013. "Program Stats as of March 8, 2013." www.
healthysanfrancisco.org/about_us/Stats.aspx#.

Hirsch, Barry, and David McPherson. 2012. "U.S. Historical Tables: Union
Membership, Coverage, Density and Employment, 1973–2007." www
.unionstats.com.

Human Rights Campaign Foundation 2013. "Corporate Equality Index 2013."
www.hrc.org/files/assets/resources/CorporateEqualityIndex_2013.pdf.

Kolstad, Jonathan, and Amanda Kowalski. 2012. "Mandate-Based Health
Reform and the Labor Market: Evidence from the Massachusetts Reform."
Working Paper 17933. National Bureau of Economic Research.

Krueger, Alan. 1994. "Observations on Employment-Based Government
Mandates, With Particular Reference to Health Insurance." Working Paper
323. Industrial Relations Section, Princeton University.

Levinson, Jessica, and Smith Long. 2009. "Mapping Public Financing in
American Elections." Los Angeles, CA: Center for Governmental Studies.

Milkman, Ruth, and Eileen Appelbaum 2013. *Unfinished Business: Paid Family
Leave in California and the Future of U.S. Work-Family Policy*. Ithaca, NY:
Cornell University Press.

Mollenkopf, John. 1983. *The Contested City*. Princeton, NJ: Princeton University
Press.

Moretti, Enrico. 2011. "Local Labor Markets." In *Handbook of Labor Economics*, ed.
Orley Ashenfelter and David Card, vol. 4, 1237–1313. Amsterdam: Elsevier.

———. 2012. *The New Geography of Jobs*. New York: Houghton Mifflin.

RAND California. 2012. "Bridged-Race Postcensal Population Estimates by
Race/Ethnicity and Age Group." Last modified Nov. 9. http://ca.rand.org
/stats/popdemo/popraceage.html.

Reich, Michael, Arindrajit Dube, and Gina Vickery. 2005. "Minimum Wages and
the California Economy: The Economic Impact of AB 48." Policy Brief.
Institute for Research on Labor and Employment, University of California,
Berkeley. September.

Reich, Michael, and Peter Hall. 1999. "Living Wages at the Airport and Port of
San Francisco: The Benefits and the Costs." Briefing Paper. Institute of
Industrial Relations, University of California, Berkeley.

Reich, Michael, Peter Hall, and Fiona Hsu. 1999. "Living Wages and the San
Francisco Economy: The Benefits and the Costs." Briefing Paper. Institute of
Industrial Relations, UC Berkeley.

Reich, Michael, Peter Hall, and Ken Jacobs. 2005. "Living Wage Policies at the
San Francisco Airport: Impacts on Workers and Businesses." *Industrial
Relations* 44, 1: 106–38.

Reich, Michael, and Amy Laitinen. 2003. "Raising Low Pay in a High Income
Economy: The Economics of a San Francisco Minimum Wage." Report for

San Francisco Board of Supervisors. Institute of Industrial Relations, UC Berkeley. www.irle.berkeley.edu/research/minimumwage/minwage_may03.pdf.

Rossin-Slater, Mayra, Christopher J. Ruhm, and Jane Waldfogel. 2012. "The Effects of California's Paid Family Leave Program on Mothers' Leave-Taking and Subsequent Labor Market Outcomes." Working Paper 17715. NBER, Cambridge, MA.

Ruggles, Stephen J., Trent Alexander, Katie Genadek, Ronald Goeken, Matthew B. Schroeder, and Matthew Sobek. 2010. *Integrated Public Use Microdata Series: Version 5.0* [Machine-readable database]. Minneapolis: University of Minnesota.

San Francisco Health Commission. 2008. "Healthy San Francisco Program Update." www.healthysanfrancisco.org/files/PDF/August_2008_Program_Update.pdf.

San Francisco International Airport. 2009. *Quality Standards Program.* www.flysfo.com/web/export/sites/default/download/about/rules/pdf/QSP.pdf.

San Francisco Administrative Code, Chapter 23, Article VI. "Labor Representation Procedures in Hotel and Restaurant Developments in Which the City Has an Ongoing Proprietary Interest, Findings and Declarations." www.amlegal.com/nxt/gateway.dll?f=templates&fn=default.htm&vid/amlegal:sanfrancisco_ca.

San Francisco Office of Labor Standards Enforcement. "Health Care Accountability Ordinance." www.sfgov.org/olse/hcao.

———. "Health Care Security Ordinance." www.sfgov.org/olse/hcso.

———. "Minimum Compensation Ordinance." www. sfgov.org/olse/mco.

———. "Minimum Wage Ordinance." www.sfgov.org/olse/mwo.

———. "Paid Sick Leave Ordinance." www.sfgov.org/olse/psl.

Schmitt, John. 2013. "Why Does the Minimum Wage Have No Discernible Effect on Employment?" Research report. Center for Economic Policy and Research, Washington DC.

Social Explorer. 2013. "Demographic Reports: Census and American Communities Survey." Accessed May 2013. www.socialexplorer.com/pub/reportdata/home.aspx.

Summers, Lawrence. 1989. "Some Simple Economics of Mandated Benefits." *American Economic Association Papers and Proceedings* 79, 2: 177–83.

Tavernise, Sabrina. 2012. "A Gap in College Graduates Leaves Some Cities Behind." *New York Times,* May 12.

United States Census. 2013. "Historical Income Data: Decennial Census Tables." Rev. Mar. 28. www.census.gov/hhes/www/income/data/historical/index.html.

Universal Health Care Council. 2006. "San Francisco Health Access Program: Serving Uninsured Adults." Final Report to Mayor Gavin Newsom. www.sfhp.org/files/PDF/about_us/UHC_Report_to_Mayor_06–23–06.pdf.

Wells, Miriam. 2002. "When Urban Policy Becomes Labor Policy: State Structures, Local Initiatives, and Union Representation at the Turn of the Century." *Theory and Society* 31, 1: 115–46.

Wolf-Powers, Laura. 2010. "Community Benefits Agreements and Local Government: A Review of Recent Evidence." *Journal of the American Planning Association* 76, 2: 141–59.

PART ONE   The Pay Mandates

TWO Labor Market Impacts of San Francisco's Minimum Wage

Arindrajit Dube, Suresh Naidu, and Michael Reich

1. INTRODUCTION

In November 2003 San Francisco voters passed a ballot proposition to enact a minimum wage covering all employers in the city. The new standard set a minimum wage at $8.50 per hour—over 26 percent above the then-current California minimum wage of $6.75—and an annual adjustment for cost of living increases (reaching $10.55 in 2013). This standard, which first became effective in late February 2004, constituted the

---

*Portions of this chapter are based on or appeared in Arindrajit Dube, Suresh Naidu, and Michael Reich, "The Economic Effects of a Citywide Minimum Wage," *Industrial and Labor Relations Review* 60, 4 (2007): 522–43. http://digitalcommons.ilr.cornell.edu/cgi/viewcontent.cgi?article=1293&context=ilrreview.

highest minimum wage in the United States and the first implemented universal municipal minimum wage in a major city. In a prospective study of this policy, Reich and Laitinen (2003) estimated that about 54,000 workers, amounting to 10.6 percent of the city's workforce, would receive wage increases, either directly or indirectly, if such a policy were adopted and that the increased wage costs on average would amount to about 1 percent of business operating costs.

Simple trends from county-level administrative data comparing San Francisco with nearby Alameda County suggest that the policy did increase pay and moreover did so without affecting employment. Figures 2.1 and 2.2, below, present these comparisons for restaurants, the industry with the greatest proportion and absolute number of minimum wage workers. In the years prior to the enactment of the San Francisco policy, restaurant pay and employment in these two geographic areas exhibited quite similar trends. After the policy was implemented, restaurant pay increased in San Francisco relative to Alameda County while relative employment trends did not change. Of course, these simple comparisons are only suggestive, as they could be affected by other changes, such as changes in the size or type of restaurant in the two areas.

In this chapter, we estimate the effects of the San Francisco minimum wage ordinance, drawing on data from a commissioned panel survey of restaurants. The survey's first wave was fielded just prior to the implementation of the new policy, with reinterviews of the same restaurants nine to ten months later. The sample includes small restaurants that were exempt from the policy in its first year, restaurants that did not have any workers paid below $8.50, and restaurants from the neighboring East Bay region that were not covered by the policy. We compare changes in restaurant-level outcomes between those restaurants that were affected by the minimum wage and those that were not, controlling for a variety of potential confounding factors.

The principal outcomes we examine are average pay, the distribution of pay, total employment, and part-time and full-time employment. Other outcomes we examine are menu prices, employee tenure, health insurance coverage, proportion of workers who receive tips, and employer compliance with the law.

In addition to presenting the findings, this chapter builds on the existing understanding of minimum wage effects. First, by providing the first study of how a citywide minimum wage policy operates, we can shed light on whether employment effects of city policies differ from those of state minimum wage laws. Second, some features of the policy—notably its delayed application to very small employers—and the geography of the San Francisco Bay Area allow us to have better controls for identifying minimum wage effects than are typical in the literature. Third, we collected data on a greater range of outcomes than previous studies have examined, permitting us to investigate the impacts of the policy on work hours, wage compression, employee tenure, and health insurance coverage. Fourth, we are able to examine whether the experiences of fast-food restaurants differed from those of table-service restaurants. Fifth, we examine other factors that may affect employment response, such as differing patterns of demand (restaurants that are located in tourist areas) and noncompliance with the law (restaurants that hire large numbers of immigrants). Sixth and finally, we relate these findings to subsequent research that has generalized the case study approach utilized in this chapter.

Existing Research on Minimum Wages and Theoretical Predictions

An extensive literature has surveyed the effects of minimum wages at both the national and state levels (Brown 1999; Lee 1999; Neumark and Wascher 2008; Belman and Wolfson forthcoming). Methodologically, our study is most closely related to that of Card and Krueger (1994), which surveyed fast-food restaurants in New Jersey and Pennsylvania to evaluate the employment effects of a minimum wage law passed in New Jersey. The controversy surrounding their findings of negligible or mildly positive employment effects and the subsequent set of studies it spawned are well known (Neumark and Wascher 2000; Card and Krueger 2000). As we discuss further below, our more recent studies have generalized the Card-Krueger approach by examining all contiguous border-county pairs that have a minimum wage policy discontinuity and by using up to twenty years of data (Dube, Lester, and Reich 2010; Allegretto et al. 2013).

The recent minimum wage literature draws on two models of the labor market. The standard competitive model predicts that a minimum wage will have measurable negative employment effects, to the extent that (a) the policy is binding, (b) there are opportunities to substitute higher- and lower-skilled workers for each other, and/or (c) product demand is price sensitive. In the absence of (b) and (c), a minimum wage could still increase prices but not reduce employment substantially. A minimum wage increase can also be offset by compensating reduction in benefits, such as reductions in health insurance coverage, or by changing the component of income that takes the form of tips relative to employer-paid compensation. These compensating offsets may mitigate any negative employment effects.

Noncompetitive labor market models have received increased attention in the minimum wage literature, in part because of the positive employment effects reported in Card and Krueger (1994) and their dynamic monopsony explanation (Card and Krueger 1995). In a dynamic monopsony model, the presence of labor market frictions makes job search and employer-worker matching costly. As a result, recruitment and quits are not infinitely elastic to wage changes and employers have some wage-setting power (Manning 2003). In such models, an increase in the minimum wage can increase employment, as workers' increased willingness to take and stay in higher-paying jobs reduces vacancies and separations. More generally, labor economists increasingly recognize that the presence of search frictions makes the magnitude and the direction of minimum wage effects ambiguous (Manning 2003; Flinn 2010; Dube, Lester, and Reich 2013).

We collected data on a number of the outcomes relevant for both the competitive model and a model with search frictions. To determine wages, we asked each firm to report the number of workers paid an hourly wage in five bins, under $6.75, $6.75–$8.49, $8.50–$9.49, $9.50–$10.99, and $11 or higher. We asked about the hours of the average full-time and part-time worker and the number of workers in each category, as well as the separation rate and typical employee tenure. We also collected data on employee health coverage and tips and the price of the most popular menu item.

2.   SAMPLING AND RESEARCH DESIGNS

The presence in the San Francisco Bay metropolitan area of several major central urban areas besides San Francisco itself (such as the cluster of older cities—Berkeley, Hayward, Oakland, and San Leandro—in the East Bay) provides a quasi-experimental context for testing predictions about the economic effects of a policy that is specific to San Francisco.[1] Since our treatment and control samples are all part of the same San Francisco-Oakland-Fremont Metropolitan Statistical Area, they are likely to provide closer comparisons than cross-state studies.

Sampling Strategy

Our establishment sample draws from fast-food and table-service restaurants in San Francisco and the East Bay. We included both fast-food and table-service restaurants in order to test for differences in responses by types of restaurant.

Focusing only on restaurants provides two advantages. First, by comparing trends in the same industry, we eliminate industry-based growth differentials that are unrelated to the minimum wage increase. Second, restaurants are the most intensive users of minimum wage labor and they account for a substantial portion of all low-wage workers.[2] A large part of the minimum wage impact literature has focused on this industry (or subsets, such as fast-food establishments) partly for this reason.

To summarize, the sampling frame included small San Francisco restaurants (4–8 workers), midsize San Francisco restaurants (14–35 workers), and midsize East Bay restaurants. The treatment group consists of those midsize San Francisco restaurants that had to raise the pay of at least one employee. Since small East Bay restaurants would not be

---

[1] For further details about our methods, including the econometric specifications, see Dube, Naidu, and Reich 2007.

[2] Prior to the enactment of the minimum wage ordinance, 15.5 percent of the low-wage (under $7.75 per hour) San Francisco workforce was employed in restaurants. The comparable figure among the largest 50 cities in the United States was 15.7 percent. (Computed by the authors from the 2000 Census, PUMS dataset.)

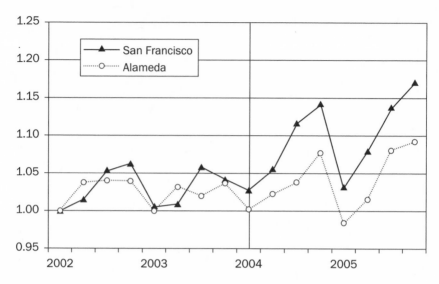

Figure 2.1   Average earnings for restaurant workers indexed to 2002 Q1 level.

NOTE: This figure shows that average restaurant worker earnings in San Francisco rose relative to those in Alameda county beginning in 2004.

SOURCE: Quarterly Census of Wages and Employment.

directly comparable to the treatment group and since the time available to conduct the survey was limited, we chose to leave out this group. One implication of this sampling frame, which will be discussed further in the next section, is that controlling for both size and region effectively draws from the midsize San Francisco restaurants, comparing those that had to raise wages to those that did not.

The first wave of our study was conducted during January and most of February 2004, ending just before the new minimum wage went into effect but after the November 2003 vote that made the policy law. Although firms might have adjusted employment in anticipation of the law, in a high-turn-over market, such as the one for restaurant labor, there is little incentive to reduce the labor force through attrition before the policy is implemented. Also, evidence from aggregate payroll data in figures 2.1 and 2.2 suggests that anticipation effects were minimal. The second wave of the survey was conducted in November and December 2004. The second wave included completed surveys for 301 of the original 354 restaurants in wave 1.

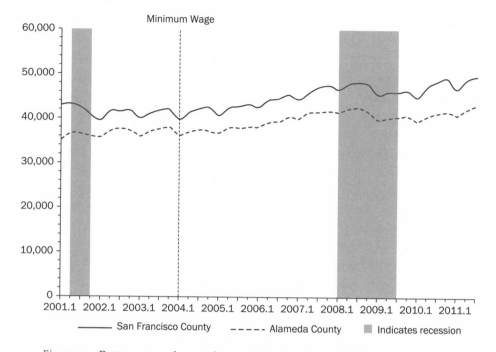

Figure 2.2 Restaurant worker employment, San Francisco and Alameda Counties.

NOTE: This figure shows restaurant employment in San Francisco growing at least as quickly as in Alameda County.

SOURCE: Quarterly Census of Employment and Wages, average quarterly employment, food service and drinking places (NAICS 722)

Research Design

Our research design uses the policy as a "quasi-natural experiment," with covered firms that are economically affected as the "treatment group." Specifically, a restaurant is considered to be in the "treatment group" if (1) it employed at least one worker whose hourly wage was below $8.50 in wave 1 and (2) it was covered by the law—that is, it was located in San Francisco and employed at least ten workers in wave 1.

In this chapter, we compare the average changes in the outcomes for this treatment group relative to those in three distinct control groups: small San Francisco restaurants, the unaffected midsize San Francisco restaurants that were already paying above minimum wages, and midsize East

Bay restaurants. Using three different control groups allows our research design to account for differential trends by restaurant size and region.

Typically, in the minimum wage literature, the subpopulation consists of teens, fast-food workers, or some other high-impact group. When comparing minimum wage effects, it is critical to ensure that the minimum wage coverage rates are similar in the different populations. Since they are in the same basic industry, our estimates of the effects are comparable to those from the fast-food industry studies. The teen population is also comparable to our population in this sense, as 25 percent of all teenage workers are directly affected by a typical minimum wage increase (Brown 1999), nearly identical to the percentage of San Francisco midsize restaurant workers who received a pay raise in our sample (23 percent).

We focus here on group mean comparisons between the treatment group and alternative control groups. Since we examine the differences between the treatment and control groups both before and after the implementation of the minimum wage, our key statistic is what is called the difference-in-difference measure.[3]

3. EFFECTS ON THE LEVEL AND THE DISTRIBUTION OF PAY

In this section, we report our estimates of the impact of the wage policy on the level and distribution of restaurant workers' pay. Table 2.1 provides the changes in average wage and the proportion of workers earning under $8.50 per hour for the treatment group and the various control groups.[4] As shown in the table, the average wage rose from $10.22 to $11.01 at restaurants in the treatment group; in other restaurants, it increased from $9.78 to $10.09. Comparing the three control groups, we find that wages also grew in small San Francisco restaurants, though substantially less than in the treatment group.

---

[3] Our regression-adjusted estimates are provided in Dube, Naidu, and Reich 2007, which explains the regression methodology in detail.

[4] Compared to the treatment group, initial wages are lower in the East Bay control group but not in the San Francisco control groups. Wages overall are lower in the East Bay.

Table 2.1   Average Wage and Proportion Paid under $8.50

Sample	Average Wage				Percent under $8.50			
	WAVE 1	WAVE 2	PERCENT CHANGE	DIF-IN-DIF	WAVE 1	WAVE 2	PERCENT CHANGE	DIF-IN-DIF
Treatment group	10.22	11.01	7.74*		49.72	5.00	-89.94*	
	(0.25)	(0.19)	(2.67)		(2.98)	(2.21)	(4.48)	
All controls	9.78	10.09	3.17*	4.57+	43.34	38.11	-12.07*	-77.88*
	(0.12)	(0.12)	(1.24)	(2.60)	(2.26)	(2.03)	(5.01)	(6.72)
Alternative control samples								
Small SF	10.44	10.91	4.50	3.24	33.44	18.90	-43.48*	-46.46*
	(0.26)	(0.24)	(2.37)	(2.58)	(0.15)	(0.34)	(9.11)	(10.16)
Unaffected								
Midsize SF	11.06	11.01	-0.45	8.19*	0.00	2.83	n/a	n/a
	(0.21)	(0.20)	(2.08)	(3.40)	(0.00)	(2.02)		
Midsize East Bay	9.13	9.40	2.96+	4.79+	58.84	59.68	1.43	-91.37*
	(0.14)	(0.17)	(1.72)	(2.88)	(3.02)	(2.98)	(5.20)	(6.88)

+ significant at 10%; * significant at 5%.

Table 2.2   Wage Distributions in Waves 1 and 2 (%)

Wage	Treatment Group		All Control Groups	
	WAVE 1	WAVE 2	WAVE 1	WAVE 2
$11/hr or more	22.63	25.00	14.30	16.26
$9.50–$10.99	15.39	21.18	15.36	15.30
$8.50–$9.49	10.22	49.46	24.12	26.00
$6.75–$8.50	51.68	4.35	46.18	42.37
Under $6.75	0.08	0.00	0.05	0.07

The fraction of workers in the treatment group receiving a wage below $8.50 declined from over 50 percent to under 5 percent between waves 1 and 2 (table 2.2). In contrast, among firms in the control group overall, that fraction remained relatively stable, declining from 43 percent to 38 percent. The difference-in-difference estimate for the proportion of workers earning below $8.50 per hour shows that the pay raise at the bottom in the treatment group was statistically significant and large vis-à-vis all the control groups. This result demonstrates clearly that the minimum wage policy in San Francisco had a strong impact in raising pay at the bottom, as compared to restaurants not affected by the policy. The average wage increase was higher among treated fast-food restaurants than among treated table-service restaurants.[5]

4. EFFECTS ON EMPLOYMENT AND FULL-TIME EQUIVALENT EMPLOYMENT

In this section we report our findings using two different employment measures—head count and full-time equivalent employment. We use the term *employment* specifically to refer to the head count number of workers. Our survey asked firms to report the number of full-time and part-

---

[5] Besides raising average wages, the policy substantially reduced the dispersion of wages among restaurant workers.

time workers, as well as the average number of hours per week worked by each. Using this information, we constructed a measure of employment hours, a finer measure of employment than has been used in previous studies, most of which have relied on head count or have imputed full-time equivalent employment based on partial information. We compute full-time equivalent employment as the total number of hours worked per week divided by 40.

Table 2.3 provides the differences in means between the treated group and the various control groups, for both employment and full-time equivalent employment. The upper panel reports these results for the balanced panel—all the restaurants that responded to both waves of the survey. The lower panel takes into account the businesses that closed or relocated and thus did not respond to the second wave of the survey.

Considering first the balanced panel, the treatment group exhibits an increase in employment (2.79 percent); this growth exceeds that in the control group overall (1.10 percent), although it is below the employment growth in other midsize San Francisco controls only (5.91 percent). For full-time equivalent employment, the treatment group registered a 4.81 percent growth, while the growth for other control groups ranged between 0.06 and 3.81 percent. Overall, total hours of work grew more in the treated sample than any of the other control groups, though the differences were not statistically significant, as shown by the standard errors of the difference-in-difference estimate.

The lower panel of table 2.3 again estimates the change in employment and full-time equivalent employment, but it now also includes the fifteen restaurants that were closed between waves 1 and 2. We continue to find that the growth in employment and full-time equivalent employment was larger in the treatment group; all the control samples registered negative growth. Even when factoring in the closed restaurants, we find that overall growth remained positive for the treatment sample.

Fast-Food versus Table-Service Restaurants

Since fast-food restaurants employ a higher proportion of minimum wage workers than do table-service restaurants, we might expect to find

Table 2.3   Employment and Full-Time Equivalent Employment

	Employment				Full-Time Equivalent Employment			
	WAVE 1	WAVE 2	% CHANGE	DIF-IN-DIF	WAVE 1	WAVE 2	% CHANGE	DIF-IN-DIF
Excluding business closures								
Treatment group	20.42	20.99	2.79		16.23	17.01	4.81	
	(0.68)	(1.46)	(5.79)		(0.74)	(1.29)	(6.34)	
All controls	15.5	15.67	1.10	1.69	11.18	11.41	2.06	2.75
	(0.27)	(0.43)	(2.24)	(6.21)	(0.29)	(0.35)	(2.62)	(6.95)
Alternative control samples								
Small SF	6.14	6.3	2.61	0.19	4.73	4.91	3.81	1.00
	(0.15)	(0.31)	(4.04)	(7.09)	(0.18)	(0.26)	(4.52)	(7.89)
Unaffected								
Midsize SF	20.63	21.85	5.91	−3.12	15.97	15.98	0.06	4.74
	(0.61)	(1.59)	(7.54)	(9.53)	(0.67)	(1.00)	(6.16)	(8.93)
Midsize East Bay	20.43	20.34	−0.44	3.23	14.02	14.34	2.28	2.52
	(0.48)	(0.70)	(2.49)	(6.33)	(0.49)	(0.58)	(3.41)	(7.31)
Including business closures								
Treatment group	20.24	20.28	0.20		16.12	16.43	1.92	
	(0.67)	(1.49)	(5.94)		(0.72)	(1.31)	(6.56)	
All controls	15.4	14.88	−3.38	3.57	11.11	10.82	−2.61	4.53
	(0.27)	(0.47)	(2.62)	(6.49)	(0.28)	(0.37)	(2.99)	(7.20)
Alternative control samples								
Small SF	6.15	5.84	−5.04	5.24	4.69	4.53	−3.41	5.33
	(0.15)	(0.34)	(4.95)	(7.75)	(0.18)	(0.26)	(5.09)	(8.32)
Unaffected								
Midsize SF	20.64	20.54	−0.48	0.68	15.83	15.01	−5.18	7.10
	(0.60)	(1.62)	(7.78)	(9.80)	(0.67)	(1.00)	(6.39)	(9.18)
Midsize East Bay	20.45	19.66	−3.86	4.06	14.1	13.87	−1.63	3.55
	(0.48)	(0.78)	(3.13)	(6.74)	(0.49)	(0.58)	(4.00)	(7.70)

a greater minimum wage impact in the fast food segment. In order to determine if the response was different, we estimated employment in the two restaurant types separately. We found that employment effects for both types of restaurants were small and statistically indistinguishable from zero (Dube, Naidu, and Reich 2007, 534).

Employment Response in Tourist Areas

The demand for restaurant meals may be less responsive to price increases in tourist areas than elsewhere, leading to a smaller disemployment effect in restaurants serving tourists than among restaurants in other areas. To see if this is the case, we test for differences in the impact of the policy on restaurants that are likely to attract many tourists. Since we do not directly observe the actual composition of customers for each restaurant, we use location in the city to predict if a restaurant's clientele is more or less made up of tourists relative to the city's average. To do so, we calculate the ratio of hotel workers to the overall workforce in each San Francisco zip code, using Zip Code Business Patterns data. We then consider the subsample in which this ratio is greater than the median ratio, under the assumption that these areas are likely to have heavier tourist traffic than other areas (Dube, Naidu and Reich 2007, 356). The employment effect was not statistically significant in the tourist subsample or in the remaining areas.

Employer Compliance with Minimum Wage Laws

It is possible that noncompliance with the new wage standard is responsible for the lack of employment effects found above. On the other hand, we already have found that the law had a noticeable effect on wages. Even if many restaurants were not complying, the policy did raise the wages they paid and was, in that sense, successful. To examine this issue further, we identified restaurants that were likely to have higher concentrations of immigrant workers, since noncompliance is usually more of a concern in these establishments than in others. In San Francisco, these restaurants are located in the Chinatown and Mission district neighbor-hoods.[6]

Our wage data indicate that the fraction of workers paid under $8.50 fell at the same rate in the Chinatown/Mission sample of treated firms (from 49 percent to 5 percent) as in the rest of the treatment group (from 55 percent to 6 percent). If reported truthfully, wages increased substan-tially in these neighborhoods. However, the wage reports may not be truthful. To assess that possibility, we devised an indirect test. In the competitive model, if restaurants in Chinatown/Mission are less compli-ant with the new standard than are restaurants elsewhere in the city, they should exhibit less negative or more positive employment effects than the rest of the treatment group. To conduct this test, we split the San Francisco sample accordingly and estimated the treatment effect.

The results indicate that the effect on full-time equivalent employ-ment for Chinatown/Mission is negative while the estimate for the rest of the city is positive (Dube, Naidu, and Reich 2007, 534). However, nei-ther effect is statistically significantly different from zero. The combina-tion of a negative effect for the Chinatown/Mission sample and a posi-tive effect for the others is inconsistent with the hypothesis that firms hiring immigrant workers do not raise wages or reduce employment. We conclude that lack of compliance is unlikely to explain the lack of nega-tive employment response predicted by the competitive model.

In summary, and consistent with some of the recent literature on state-level changes in the minimum wage, our employment estimates are small, positive, and not statistically significant.

Subsequent Studies

In follow-up work since the San Francisco survey, we have included all thestate border contiguous county comparisons in minimum wage

---

[6] According to the 2000 Census, 23 percent of the residents in the four zip codes corre-sponding to Chinatown and the Mission district were noncitizens, as compared to 14 percent in the rest of San Francisco. Chinatown and the Mission district together comprise about 17 percent of residents in the city and 22 percent of the San Francisco restaurants in our sample.

changes and over a much longer period. We used this expanded approach to study the effect of minimum wages on employment in restaurants (Dube, Lester, and Reich 2010), as well as on teens (Dube, Lester, and Reich 2013). These expanded studies use administrative payroll data submitted by employers for Unemployment Insurance purposes; the two datasets we use are the Quarterly Census of Employment and Wages (QCEW) and the Quarterly Workforce Indicators (QWI). We find minimum wage elasticities for employment that are small (at most a 1 percent reduction in employment for a 10 percent increase in the minimum wage in all cases) and statistically indistinguishable from zero. This finding holds even after allowing for longer lagged effects, covering up to sixteen quarters after a minimum wage increase. Overall, the research since our San Francisco study suggests that our results are not specific to San Francisco, nor are they particular to the 2004 minimum wage ordinance.

5.   FINDINGS FOR OTHER OUTCOMES

We present in table 2.4 the results for our other outcome variables for treated and control restaurants in each wave. These outcome variables are price, tenure, turnover, incidence of full-time work, health insurance coverage, and proportion of workers receiving tips. Below we report the results for the treatment effect on these outcome measures.

Effect on Prices

The survey instrument asked respondents in the first wave to list the name and price of the most popular entrée. "Price" refers to dinner price if the restaurant served dinner, lunch price if it served lunch only, or a general price if there was no distinction. In the second wave, respondents were asked about the price of this same entrée. If this entrée was no longer served, respondents were asked for (a) the current price and (b) the price in January 2004 (the interview period for the first wave) of the currently most popular dish.

Table 2.4   Other Outcomes

| | Treatment | | Small SF | | Unaffected Midsize | | | |
| | | | | | SF | | Midsize East Bay | |
	WAVE 1	WAVE 2	WAVE 1	WAVE 2	WAVE 1	WAVE 2	WAVE 1	WAVE 2
Price	13.65	13.75	8.72	8.94	12.56	12.68	10.17	10.17
	(0.88)	(0.92)	(0.59)	(0.61)	(1.35)	(1.37)	(0.69)	(0.72)
Separation	0.28	0.29	0.28	0.24	0.27	0.32	0.31	0.29
rate (annual)	(0.05)	(0.04)	(0.05)	(0.04)	(0.03)	(0.05)	(0.03)	(0.02)
Tenure (months)	14.83	18.5	17.21	21.39	16.00	16.08	13.69	13.55
	(1.84)	(2.26)	(1.74)	(2.94)	(1.57)	(1.52)	(1.19)	(1.18)
Average hours—	20.86	21.45	22.26	21.26	21.05	20.83	20.91	21.17
part-time	(0.65)	(0.67)	(0.71)	(0.63)	(0.61)	(0.71)	(0.62)	(0.58)
Average hours—	40.43	39.68	37.80	39.34	39.45	38.74	39.74	39.07
full-time	(0.78)	(0.58)	(1.16)	(0.3)	(0.47)	(0.33)	(0.78)	(0.4)
Percent full-time	0.58	0.58	0.56	0.57	0.56	0.50	0.38	0.41
	(0.03)	(0.04)	(0.03)	(0.04)	(0.03)	(0. 03)	(0.03)	(0.03)
Health insurance	0.13	0.22	0.16	0.16	0.25	0.20	0.12	0.16
coverage rate	(0.03)	(0.08)	(0.04)	(0.04)	(0.04)	(0.03)	(0.02)	(0.04)
Percent tipped	0.40	0.67	0.30	0.49	0.46	0.58	0.23	0.37
workers	(0.06)	(0.06)	(0.05)	(0.05)	(0.05)	(0.05)	(0.04)	(0.04)

Unlike employment, which the firm chooses, the price may be determined at the level of the product market. For this reason, we began by comparing relative price changes in San Francisco and the East Bay. Table 2.4 shows that San Francisco restaurants in the sample increased their prices relative to their counterparts in the East Bay. However, this difference was not statistically significant. Considering fast-food restaurants only, we do find a statistically significant 6.2 percent rise in prices in San Francisco as compared to the East Bay (Dube, Naidu, and Reich 2007, 536). To put these findings in perspective, consider that just under 50 percent of workers in these restaurants were initially paid less than

$8.50, that the minimum wage increase was 26 percent, and that labor costs in fast-food restaurants account for 35 percent of operating costs. Multiplying these three numbers implies a cost pressure on prices of 4.4 percent.

We next investigated whether the price change was proportional to the cost pressures implied by the extent of treatment in an individual restaurant, that is, proportional to the fraction of workers earning under $8.50 initially in the covered restaurants. We find no evidence of such a relationship (Dube, Naidu, and Reich 2007, 541). Moreover, the treatment variable is not correlated with price growth among either fast-food or table-service restaurants. The effects are small and not statistically significant.

Taken together, these results suggest that the price adjustment occurred primarily at the geographic market level (as opposed to the individual restaurant level), and primarily among fast-food restaurants. This pattern would be expected if product markets are competitive and if the elasticity of substitution between restaurants within broad categories (such as all fast-food restaurants) is high. In other words, prices at fast-food restaurants increased more in locations affected by the minimum wage than in unaffected locations, but no similar difference is apparent across affected and unaffected restaurants within the treatment location. Moreover, the price increase (6.2 percent; see table 2.4) is comparable to the cost pressures on prices among San Francisco fast-food restaurants.

Tenure and Turnover

The positive association among lower wages, voluntary quits, and shorter tenure more generally is well documented in labor economics (Brown 1999). More recently, Reich, Hall, and Jacobs (2005) found that turnover among San Francisco airport security screeners fell by 80 percent when their pay rose from the minimum wage of $5.75 to $10.00 per hour (the data for this study were gathered before the 9/11 attacks). Card and Krueger (1995) suggested that a dynamic monopsony model applies to fast-food restaurant chains, which exhibit short employee tenure and high rates of voluntary quits.

To study the effect on churning in the labor market, we included in the survey instrument a question that asked the respondent how long the firm's "typical worker" had been working at the restaurant. The results, controlling again for firm size and region, indicate a substantial positive treatment effect of 5.01 months on the tenure of the "typical worker," with statistical significance at the 10 percent level. Interestingly, this effect was concentrated in fast-food restaurants.

Surprisingly, we do not detect a reduction in the overall separation rate, defined as the number of workers who stopped working over the past year as a proportion of the current workforce. This result held even among fast-food restaurants, which reported a rise in the tenure of their "typical worker." It appears, therefore, that the change in the separation rate may have been duration-dependent, leading to increased differences in tenure. In other words, the combination of a fall in the separation rate among workers with initially higher tenure with an increase in the separation rate among the rest is consistent with a rise in the tenure of the "typical worker." This may reflect an increased segmentation of the workforce: a core workforce that experiences increased stabilization and a peripheral workforce that perhaps is composed of more temporary workers. This San Francisco finding, however, is not consistent with results from elsewhere in the country. When Dube, Lester, and Reich (2013) considered a large number of adjacent counties with minimum wage changes they found that on average the separation rate does fall in response to minimum wage increases.

Full-Time Work

The proportion of full-time jobs rose at fast-food restaurants (Dube, Naidu, and Reich 2007, 541). This increase was statistically significant at the 10 percent level. In contrast, we do not detect a significant change in the proportion of full-time workers in table-service restaurants. Approximately 50 percent of the workers in the treated fast-food restaurants earned below $8.50 in wave 1. Consequently, the coefficient of 0.118 in the fast-food regression equation implies roughly a 6 percentage point increase in the incidence of full-time work in these restaurants due to the policy. Increased full-time work could reflect a move toward workers with more commitment to the job, which is consistent with the finding of increases in job tenure.

Health Insurance

We do not detect any compensating differential for the increased wages through reduced health insurance. The treatment effect on health insurance coverage is typically positive and not statistically significant. This absence of a negative benefit effect is inconsistent with the competitive labor market model.

Proportion of Workers Receiving Tips

The San Francisco policy applies to tipped and nontipped workers equally. California does not allow a tip credit. In many other states, employers can count tips as wages in complying with minimum wage standards. In the survey instrument, we asked respondents to report the proportion of their "near minimum wage workers"—those earning below $9.50—who receive tips and the proportion who do not receive tips. We can therefore discern whether the wage mandate generated any change in the tip status of workers in this pay range.

We find a substantial and statistically significant rise in the proportion of tipped workers in table-service restaurants. We estimate that the wage mandate increased the tipped proportion of the "near minimum wage" workforce in the treated table-service restaurants by 15.55 percentage points. Since the initial proportion of tipped workers was 37 percent, the wage mandate increased the proportion tipped by 42 percent (15.55/.37) over its initial level. This increase in the tipped proportion of the work-force may result from a compensating differential. In the absence of a "tip credit," wages went up for serving staff in many restaurants. Restaurants likely increased the pool of workers who received some tip income (cooks, dishwashers, and others) as a way to partly offset the increased income of the wait staff. Providing some tip income to cooks, for example, would mean they would require a lower base wage. The muted increase in the average income in table-service restaurants is also consistent with this finding, which would be predicted by a competitive model.

6. SUMMARY AND CONCLUSIONS

We find that the San Francisco wage floor policy increased pay significantly at affected restaurants and compressed the wage distribution among restaurant workers. The policy increased average pay by twice as much among fast-food restaurants as among table-service restaurants. We do not detect any increased rate of business closure or employment loss among treated restaurants; this finding holds across a variety of alternative specifications and control subsamples. Our employment findings are precise enough to rule out some of the larger negative and positive effects in the literature, including Card and Krueger (1994, 2000) and Neumark and Wascher (2000).

Changes in menu prices, proportion of full-time work, and employee tenure differed significantly between fast-food and table-service restaurants. At fast-food restaurants, but not at table-service restaurants, prices, employment of full-time workers, and employee job tenure all increased significantly. These findings, taken together with the greater wage effects among fast-food restaurants, suggest that the policy improved job quality and worker attachment in this restaurant segment and reduced the gaps in job quality between the two types of restaurants. We did find that table-service restaurants increased their use of tipped workers. Regarding other potential avenues for employment effects, we also found that restaurants in tourist areas did not experience different outcomes from those not in tourist areas. Moreover, with respect to policy compliance and employment effects, restaurants in immigrant-intensive areas were no different from restaurants elsewhere in San Francisco.

What do our results suggest about the competitiveness of the low-wage labor market? The combination of no negative employment effect and the presence of a small positive price effect is consistent with a competitive model, in which small price increases do not significantly reduce product demand. The absence of any reductions in health insurance coverage among affected restaurants is not consistent with the compensating differences predictions of a competitive model. At the same time, the increase in the proportion of tipped workers in table-service restaurants suggests a compensating difference that spreads tips among more workers. The increases in job tenure among fast-food restaurants are consistent with a model with search frictions, in which wages improve worker retention and recruitment in affected restaurants. However, the lack of a reduction in separations poses somewhat of a puzzle for that perspective.

Can San Francisco's experience be generalized to other cities? As the introduction to this book documents, the composition of San Francisco's industries is similar to that in other major U.S. cities, suggesting that the policy effects are not likely to be artifacts of any peculiarities of the city's industrial structure. At the same time, it is also true that San Francisco is a high-income city, and this factor may affect the nature of the demand for goods and services produced by low-wage workers.

The generalizability of our study of San Francisco should be interpreted in the context of our subsequent minimum wage studies (Dube, Lester, and Reich 2010, 2013). These studies draw on evidence from over twenty years of minimum wage changes, and they compare many dozens of neighboring areas with minimum wage gaps comparable to those between San Francisco and its surrounding counties. That evidence suggests that the key patterns we found in San Francisco—sizable wage gains and no visible changes in employment—are in fact the norm and not an aberration in the U.S. labor market.

The United States has been moving toward a more decentralized system of minimum wage determination, with greater variation in wage floors among both states and cities. Indeed, more cities have implemented citywide mandates, including Washhington DC, Santa Fe, New Mexico, and, more recently, San Jose, California, and Albuquerque, New Mexico. San Francisco's experience shows that wage standards that are more generous than those that are often discussed can indeed be adopted without affecting employment.

REFERENCES

Allegretto, Sylvia, Arindrajit Dube, Michael Reich, and Ben Zipperer. 2013. "Credible Research Designs for Minimum Wage Studies." Working Paper 149–13. Institute for Research on Labor and Employment, University of California, Berkeley.

Belman, Dale and Paul Wolfson. Forthcoming. *What Does the Minimum Wage Do?* Kalamazoo, MI: Upjohn Institute.

Brown, Charles. 1999. "Minimum Wages, Employment, and the Distribution of Income." In *Handbook of Labor Economics,* ed. Orley Ashenfelter and David Card, 2101–63. New York: Elsevier.

Card, David, and Alan B. Krueger. 1994. "Minimum Wage and Employment: A Case Study of the Fast-Food Industry in New Jersey and Pennsylvania." *American Economic Review* 84, 4: 772–93.

———. 1995. *Myth and Measurement: The New Economics of the Minimum Wage.* Princeton: Princeton University Press.

———. 2000. "Minimum Wage and Employment: A Case Study of the Fast-Food Industry in New Jersey and Pennsylvania: Reply." *American Economic Review* 90, 5: 1397–1420.

Dube, Arindrajit, T. William Lester, and Michael Reich. 2010. "Minimum Wages across State Borders: Evidence from Contiguous Counties." *Review of Economics and Statistics* 92, 4: 945–64.

———. 2013. "Minimum Wage Shocks, Employment Flows and Labor Market Frictions." Working Paper 148–13. Institute for Research on Labor and Employment, University of California, Berkeley.

Dube, Arindrajit, Suresh Naidu, and Michael Reich. 2007. "The Economic Effects of a Citywide Minimum Wage." *Industrial and Labor Relations Review* 60, 4: 522–43.

Fairris, David, and Michael Reich. 2005. "The Impacts of Living Wage Policies." *Industrial Relations* 44, 1: 1–13.

Flinn, Christopher. 2010. *The Minimum Wage and Labor Market Outcomes.* Cambridge, MA: MIT Press.

Lee, David S. 1999. "Wage Inequality in the U.S. during the 1980s: Rising Dispersion or Falling Minimum Wage?" *Quarterly Journal of Economics* 114, 3: 941–1023.

Manning, Alan 2003. *Monopsony in Motion: Imperfect Competition in Labor Markets.* Princeton: Princeton University Press.

Neumark, David, and William Wascher. 1994. "Employment Effects of Minimum and Subminimum Wages: Reply to Card, Katz, and Krueger." *Industrial and Labor Relations Review* 47, 3: 497–512.

————. 2000. "Minimum Wages and Employment: A Case Study of the Fast-Food Industry in New Jersey and Pennsylvania: Comment." *American Economic Review* 90, 5: 1362–96.

————. 2008. *Minimum Wages.* Cambridge, MA: MIT Press.

Reich, Michael, Peter Hall, and Ken Jacobs. 2005. "Living Wage Policies at the San Francisco Airport: Impacts on Workers and Businesses." *Industrial Relations* 44, 1: 106–38.

Reich, Michael, and Amy Laitinen. 2003. "Raising Low Pay in a High Income City: The Economics of a San Francisco Minimum Wage." Working Paper 99. Institute of Industrial Relations, University of California, Berkeley.

THREE Liftoff

RAISING WAGES AT SAN FRANCISCO AIRPORT

Peter V. Hall, Ken Jacobs, and Michael Reich

1. INTRODUCTION

Most of the first wave of living wage ordinances that were enacted in the mid-1990s involved minimum pay scales that were substantially above federal and state minimum wages. Typically they set a standard of $8.00 or more per hour when the minimum wage was $5.15. Policy makers generally assumed that a living wage policy could not work in trade-based

*Large portions of this chapter appeared in earlier form in Michael Reich, Peter V. Hall, and Ken Jacobs, *Living Wages and Economic Performance: The San Francisco Airport Model*, IRLE Monograph, 2003, www.irle.berkeley.edu/research/livingwage/sfo_mar03.pdf; and Michael Reich, Peter V. Hall, and Ken Jacobs, "Living Wages Policies at the San Francisco Airport: Impacts on Workers and Businesses," *Industrial Relations* 44, 1 (2005): 106–38. Both publications provide further details on the QSP and on our methods, data, and findings.

goods- or service-producing sectors that were subject to the forces of technological change and global competition. Consequently, living wage ordinances typically covered only workers on municipal service contracts, or only about 3 percent to 5 percent of the low-wage workers in a city. The implementation of these ordinances often involved granting numerous waivers and exemptions, further reducing their impact. Consequently, the first ordinances were thought to have small spillover impacts on the local low-wage labor market (Freeman 2005).

This chapter examines the impact of the living wage policies at San Francisco International Airport (SFO) with these issues in mind. The living wage policy at SFO, known as the Quality Standards Program (QSP), was adopted in January 2000. It covered virtually all the low-wage workers—about one-third of the thirty thousand employees—at SFO. This SFO policy represented one of the largest living wage experiments in the nation at the time. It was unusual also in including higher educational standards for new hires and training mandates intended to improve airport security and customer service. Given the very high density of workers affected and the broader scope of the living wage policy, SFO provides a laboratory for observing the impact of grander labor market interventions. As we shall show, the successful adoption of the QSP and its demonstrated benefits and low costs contained valuable policy implications for other mandates that were subsequently implemented in San Francisco as well as for living wage policies at other airports in the United States.

The QSP initially established a minimum pay standard of $9.00 plus full health benefits, or $10.25 without health benefits, and it mandated twelve days per year of paid time off. It also established a high school completion hiring requirement and a training standard of forty hours for new employees. The basic wage was increased to $10.00 in January 2001 and inflation-indexed thereafter. The QSP covers ground-based workers who are employed in positions related to safety and security, generally those who are nonmanagerial employees of airlines and of airline services firms.

The QSP constituted only one of a related set of policies that substantially restructured the institutions regulating pay, benefits, and labor relations policies at SFO between 1999 and 2001. At the time of our original study, the Minimum Compensation Ordinance (MCO) and Health Care Accountability Ordinance (HCAO) had only affected approximately 100 workers at SFO. While these policies would eventually cover most of the approximately 2,700 ground-based nonmanagerial workers, including passenger service workers and employees of concession holders, not covered by the QSP, they went into effect only when leases were renegotiated.

A labor peace/card check policy also went into effect in February 2000; it had a substantial impact on labor relations at SFO. Approximately 2,000 workers were organized into unions during the period of study. However, since the QSP set the general wage rate in collective bargaining agreements reached for workers covered by the program during the study period, it will be regarded as the main policy that set wage and benefit standards at the airport. Of course, this focus on the QSP was not always apparent to all the actors. They experienced all the policies, along with increased unionization and worker expectations that were altered by the union and living wage organizing campaigns, as a totality that changed the economic and labor relations environment at the airport.

In 2009, the QSP was effectively merged with other citywide policies: the hourly wage rate is now set at 50 cents above the citywide MCO (SFO 2009). It reached $12.93 in January 1, 2013. The health benefit provisions were replaced by the HCAO mandate as of April 1, 2010.

The QSP experience also provides a case study of service sector work that is intimately tied up in the trading activities of a postindustrial economy. Transportation labor markets since the deregulation of the early 1980s are notorious for their uneven and broadly deteriorating effects on working conditions (Peoples 1998; Hall 2009). Rubery et al. (2003) have also noted the challenges posed by multiemployer environments, such as airports, that are characterized by a high degree of subcontracting. In contrast, the policies enacted at SFO, a major transportation node, contain large components of what some commentators have labeled the "high road" path of economic development. The high road program promises to raise low pay while also improving workers' skills and productivity and to reduce economic inequality while also enhancing economic performance. Airport living wage laws are also in effect Los Angeles, Oakland, and San Jose, and other airports are considering similar policies.

Several studies have examined the economic effects of living wage ordinances. Brenner (2005) and Fairris (2005) studied policies in Boston and Los Angeles, respectively, finding substantial positive wage and turnover effects for covered workers. Fairris (2005), however, did not include data from "any establishment at the Los Angeles airport and any establishment in the airline services industry for fear that 'before/after' comparisons would be tainted by the devastating impact of the events of 9/11 on this sector" (94). Lester (2012) uses a panel regression model to analyze the impact of business assistance living wage laws on employment and establishment growth and finds no evidence that those living wage ordinances affect economic development outcomes. This chapter uses evidence from surveys before and after the implementation of the policy at SFO to examine the impact of the policy on workers, firms, and airline activity.

In the following section, we describe the state of the local labor market at SFO prior to the implementation of the living wage policy. In section 3 we discuss our research strategy to identify the effects of the policy and the data sources we collected to conduct a before and after examination of the policy's effects. Section 4 examines the effects on employee pay as well as on health insurance benefits, paid time off, and quality of life indicators. In section 5 we consider the effects on airport activity, on overall airport employment, and on low-wage employment. Section 6 examines the costs of the policy. In section 7 we examine dynamic effects on employee turnover, worker effort, and productivity. We present our conclusions in section 8.

2. THE SFO LABOR MARKET PRIOR TO ADOPTION OF THE LIVING WAGE POLICIES

Prior to 1999, the employment and pay structure among SFO's 30,000 workers was typical of most large U.S. airports. As table 3.1 shows, passenger and cargo airlines accounted for approximately two-thirds of private sector employment, with the remainder concentrated among airline

Table 3.1   Private Sector Employers and Workers at SFO, Pre-QSP

Sector	Workers	Employers
Airlines[a]		
Passenger airlines	21,800	45
Cargo airlines	240	15
Airline Services		
Airline catering	1,340	3
Security/Skycaps[b]	1,000	4
Aviation services	1,070	33
Passenger Services		
Retail concessions[c]	800	19
Food concessions[c]	870	10
Airport parking	150	1
Rental cars	1,040	10
Total	28,310	140

SOURCES: Authors' own analysis and adjustments of *The Economic Impact of San Francisco International Airport*, March 1998; CLRE Airport Study, 1999. Employment data are for 1998. All figures have been rounded.

[a] This figure includes airlines with active permits to land at SFO but not currently operating. There were 39 active passenger airlines and 10 active cargo airlines at the time of the SFO Employer Survey.

[b] Most skycaps are subcontracted by the airlines.

[c] Retail and food concessions figures together conform to those in the Economic Impact Report; classification of firms into these categories may differ in other sources.

service companies and passenger service companies. Average pay growth in air transportation had lagged behind other sectors, including even retail, since airline deregulation began in 1978. Table 3.2 shows that the low-wage workforce at SFO was concentrated among the 11,000 ground-based, nonmanagerial workers, including customer service and ramp workers, baggage handlers, screeners, cabin cleaners, and restaurant and retail workers. By 1999, over half of the ground-based nonmanagerial workers were paid less than $10 per hour.

Subcontracting accounted for a disproportionate share of the low-wage workforce. Airlines experimented with new approaches to labor

Table 3.2   Pay before and after QSP, Selected Job Titles

Job Titles	Number of Workers	Minimum Entry Wage ($)		Average Wage ($)	
		BEFORE QSP	AFTER	BEFORE QSP	AFTER
Customer service agents	3,700	5.75	10.00	10.15 (0.70)	11.85 (0.48)
Administration/ clerical	200	7.40	9.00	10.90 (1.07)	13.45 (1.73)
Baggage/ramp agents	2,500	6.95	10.00	10.50 (0.78)	12.35 (0.31)
Cabin cleaners	700	6.00	10.00	9.95 (1.38)	11.45 (0.49)
Screeners	1,000	5.75	10.00	6.50 (0.33)	10.05 (0.0)
Skycaps	200	5.75	10.00	6.35 (0.38)	10.00 (0.0)
All ground-based nonmanagerial employees	11,000	5.75	6.25	9.60 (0.35)	11.70 (0.33)

SOURCE: UCB-SFO Employer Survey, 2001, conducted by authors.

NOTE: Standard errors shown in parentheses. All amounts have been rounded to nearest 100 employees/$0.05. Low-wage job titles not listed here include wheelchair agents, fuelers, car rental service agents, restaurant workers, and retail cashiers. Sample size before QSP = 5,497 employees and after QSP = 5,827 employees.

relations following airline deregulation in 1978 (Cappelli 1985), including deunionization and increasing use of contracted-out ground-based services (Peoples 1998). Employees of the airline service firms at SFO received lower wages and benefits and less training and had fewer opportunities for advancement than direct airline employees in the same occupational categories.

3.   METHODS AND DATA

Our research uses comparisons of surveyed firms and workers before and after QSP implementation. These comparisons were made easier because all but one of the firms operated at the airport at both points in time and because they all faced the same changes in the airport's business environment. We obtained data from representative samples of the airport firms both before and after the policy went into effect. A series of adjustments are also made to control for effects that are not directly related to the QSP in the period 1998–2001, such as any changes in passenger volume at SFO and other Bay Area airports, the opening of the new international terminal, improvements in management-labor relations, and the overall strength (weakness) of the national and regional economy.

Because the QSP and the living wage ordinance covered all employers and low wage workers at SFO, we could not compare covered firms and workers with a control group of noncovered firms and workers. As an alternative differencing technique, we estimate the impacts of the QSP by comparing the firms in which the policy change had a small impact on wage costs to those in which it had a large impact. This technique is similar to comparisons in minimum wage impact studies that examine differences between low-wage and high-wage industries.

We collected the post-QSP data for this study soon after the ordinances went into effect and just prior to September 11, 2001. Consequently, while they reflect the implementation of the ordinances, they were not affected by the subsequent and more turbulent conditions of the airline industry. The primary pre- and post-QSP data comparison dates are June 1999 and June 2001. Both dates occur during summer peak period employment, ruling out seasonality effects. As we discuss below, we also control for the downturn in the economy that began in early March 2000 and for the airport's international terminal expansion that occurred simultaneously with the implementation of the QSP.

Data

The QSP was phased in during the period April 1, 2000, to October 1, 2000. The majority of covered employees began to receive increases from June 1, 2000. We collected data from several sources to compensate for small sample sizes and to allow us to confirm our findings through triangulation.

The pre-QSP employment and wage data are based on an employer survey that we conducted in June 1999 (Reich, Hall, and Hsu 1999). The Airport Commission's 1998 Economic Impact Report (SFO 1998) provided an initial employment baseline. A telephone survey was then conducted of airport employers for wage and benefit coverage information as of June 1999.

The principal post-QSP data for this study come from an employer survey that we conducted in 2001. The survey instrument included questions on employment and wages by occupation, as well as evaluation questions that allowed employers to reflect on the implementation effects of the QSP. Mailing of the questionnaire was followed by telephone and in-person interviews and resulted in a response rate of 35 percent. The responding firms employ approximately half of the ground-based non-managerial airport workers (5,626 of an estimated 11,000). Responses from each firm were weighted to derive an estimate for all SFO employers. Although the sample size is small, the employer survey provides a representative profile of employment and wages at the airport. The employer responses to the qualitative questions on the survey indicated that the respondents covered the full spectrum of favorable and unfavorable views of the policies.

We also drew on several supplementary sources that combine information from direct surveys of employers and employees with administrative data. These multiple sources of data add confidence to the findings. They include:

1. SFO Badge Office: This database derives from administrative data on security badges issued to employees at the time of hire; it includes detailed firm and occupational employment counts, as well as data on demographics and employment tenure, for about 17,500 workers as of June 1, 2001. Although these badge data tend to overestimate the aggregate number of employees at SFO, because of the delay in returning badges when employment is terminated, we were able to correct for this bias and to confirm the validity of our survey data on a firm- and occupation-specific basis.

2. SFO Employment Office: Working conditions, wages and benefits, and job descriptions for various occupations from an archive of employment advertisements.

3. Airline passenger numbers: The SFO website and Bureau of Transportation Statistics provide data for the period 1997–2011.

4. Structured interviews with eleven union organizers from six union locals and the AFL-CIO.

5. A short self-administered questionnaire that was completed by a sample of 99 workers.

4. OBSERVED EFFECTS ON PAY AND BENEFITS

Between the inception of the QSP in April 2000 and the data collection ending date of June 2001, almost 90 percent of the 11,000 ground-based nonmanagement workers at SFO—or approximately 9,700 workers— obtained a wage increase. These workers' pay increased by approximately 22 percent, which amounts to a total increase of $56.6 million in annual earnings. Some 1,300 workers received no increase at all; most of these were United Airlines employees who were awaiting a new contract during the study period.

The largest pay increases were recorded among entry-level workers in QSP covered positions. The average entry wage increased 33 percent for QSP-covered positions, compared to 10 percent for non-QSP-covered positions. Table 3.2 shows entry-level and average pay for selected job titles, before and after the implementation of the QSP. The largest average wage increases went to screeners, baggage handlers, fuel agents, customer service agents, ramp workers, cabin cleaners, and skycaps. For example, security screeners, who averaged $13,400 a year with no benefits prior to the QSP, earned $20,800 plus full benefits by January 2001, a 55 percent increase in wages and a 75 percent increase in total compensation.

Prior to the new city and airport policies, 55 percent of the ground-based nonmanagerial jobs paid an average of less than $10 an hour (table 3.3). By June 2001, only 5 percent of these jobs were paying an average of less than $10 per hour. The proportion of entry-level positions receiving $10 per hour or more increased from less than 3 percent to over 80 percent. Not surprisingly, these differences are highly significant statistically, as the note to table 3.3 reports.

Table 3.3   Wage Distribution for SFO Workers, before and after QSP

Average Hourly Wage in Nominal Dollars	Before QSP (mid-1999)	After QSP (mid-2001)
Less than $8.00	23.1	0.2
$8.00–$9.99	32.0	4.7
$10.00–$11.99	26.9	61.5
$12.00–$13.99	16.0	28.2
$14.00 or more	2.0	5.5
All ground-based nonmanagerial employees	100.0	100.0

SOURCE: UCB-SFO Employer Survey, 2001, conducted by the authors.

NOTE: Chi-squared test indicates that the before and after QSP wage distributions are significantly different (p = 0.000). Sample size before QSP = 5,497 employees and after QSP = 5,827 employees.

The pay increases mandated by the QSP significantly reduced the pay differences between in-house (airlines) and contracted-out (airline services) ground based jobs. Prior to the QSP, lower wages in the airport labor market were concentrated among employees of airline service contractors. The differences in entry-level pay rates have been eliminated entirely. Indeed, in-house employees in entry-level positions now earn slightly less than contracted-out employees in the same positions, as the airlines tend to offer full benefits while some airline service firms offer the $1.25 premium in lieu of benefits.

Attributing the Wage Increases: Direct, Indirect, and General Labor Market Effects

To what extent can these wage increases be related to the policy change? In order to attribute which part of the $56.6 million increase in annual earnings for ground-based nonmanagerial employees resulted from the policies, we distinguished among three types of wage increases:

1. *Direct wage increases* are the $34.6 million received by the 5,400 workers who were covered by the QSP policy and who earned less than the mandated wage level, net of any wage increases these workers would have received without the QSP. To calculate this estimate, we assumed that these workers would not have received any significant increases without the QSP. Records of job advertisements obtained from the SFO Employment Office showed that pay in many of these jobs tracked the state minimum wage, which did not increase during the study period (i.e., June 1999–June 2001). Also, United Airlines, which accounted for half of all employment and activity in 2001, did not award any increases during the study period because of ongoing contract negotiations.

2. *General labor market-based wage increases* result from labor market tightening or general wage inflation and would have occurred without the QSP policy. Without the policy change, we expected that wage rates at the airport would rise at no more than the same rate as wage rates in comparable occupations in the San Francisco metropolitan area during the same period. Available data from California's Employment Development Department indicates that the average wage for a comparable group of service sector occupations in the area rose about 10 percent from 1999 to 2001. Some 1,750 workers received general labor market increases only, representing $10 million of the total increase.

3. *Indirect wage increases* are the remaining $12 million received by 2,550 workers not covered by the policy but still affected by it. In other words, they are increases in excess of what would have been expected from general labor market–based wage increases. Indirect increases can result from either vertical or horizontal wage pushes. Vertical wage increases occur in firms covered by the QSP when workers earning at or above the mandated wage receive increases in order to maintain some or all of the customary wage differentials within the firm. Horizontal wage increases occur when employees working in firms and/or jobs not directly covered by the QSP receive increases because of competitive pressure to pay workers more and/or to hire more skilled workers.

Our evidence suggests that vertical indirect wage increases were relatively small and that most of the indirect wage increases were across, rather than within, firms. In the airport services sector, the only reported wage increases were those mandated by the QSP, and among airline employees, vertical indirect wage increases above the mandated minimum were limited by the fact that wage rates at United Airlines were effectively fixed during the study period. Conversely, the percentage wage increases in the non-QSP retail concessions sector were only slightly smaller than the increases received by those directly covered by the QSP and were substantially above the rate of wage increase in the general economy. This pattern suggests that horizontal indirect wage increases within this localized labor market were significant. In other words, employers not covered by the QSP raised pay at a faster rate than they otherwise would have, in order to keep employees from leaving for higher-paying jobs covered by the QSP and to match the new wage norms.

Additional Benefits of the QSP for Employees

As a result of the QSP, all covered workers now receive twelve days of paid time off per year. These can be used for national holidays, vacation leave, and sick leave. Data on leave prior to the QSP are incomplete, but worker interviews, and the review of union contracts and job advertisements, suggested that many airport workers did receive paid leave prior to the QSP.

Of greater impact, the QSP required employers to provide health benefits or pay workers an extra $1.25 per hour. Approximately 24 percent of the employees covered by the QSP—2,000 workers—who were not previously offered employer-paid health benefits received the full QSP-mandated benefit package or the wage premium. In addition, other QSP-covered workers that had previously been offered health benefits received an improved benefit package as a result of the policy. Anecdotal evidence suggests that firms eased initial eligibility period requirements and improved their share of out-of-pocket expenses, leading to higher take-up rates by their employees. Unlike in the case of wages, we found little evidence of a spillover effect of health benefits to noncovered firms. Retail workers comprised most of the workers who reported that they lacked health care coverage.

Living wage policies can have effects on workers' lives beyond the paychecks themselves. To probe for these effects, we included a series of questions concerning quality of life in the worker survey. These questions asked about any changes in time spent with their family, their vacation time, personal finances, hours worked in all jobs, housing situation, and health status. Relatively few workers reported improvements in the various quality of life categories. Workers not covered by the QSP, however, were much more likely to report declines in quality of life than those covered by the QSP. The differences were greatest for time spent with family, personal financial savings, and housing situation and smallest for vacation time and health status. Hours worked in all jobs increased somewhat among non-QSP-covered workers while remaining mainly unchanged among QSP covered workers.

These findings suggest that the QSP mandate arrested a significant deterioration in the quality of life among low-wage workers. This is especially notable because the late 1990s represented a period of reported increases in real wage rates for low-wage workers elsewhere in the United States. In the Bay Area, however, the pay of many ground-based airport service workers had not kept up with the rapid growth in housing costs, which generated a relatively high estimated self-sufficiency or basic needs budget (California Budget Project 2001).

5.   THE COSTS OF THE QSP

The direct cost of the QSP to employers consists of increased wages, payroll taxes, health benefits, paid time off, and training costs. These costs approximate $42.7 million a year. Including the spillover effects to other workers and employers at SFO adds $14.9 million to employers' costs. This cost estimate does not take into account any savings from increased productivity, reduced turnover, and other employer savings and is consistent with the cost estimates found in other prospective living wage studies. Who bears this cost?

Economic theory suggests that increased labor costs for airline service firms, and to a lesser extent the concessionaires, will be passed on to the airlines over time. Two-thirds of the airline service firms surveyed reported that all or part of the costs of the wage increases had been passed on to the airlines. These responses, coming one year after the wage increases, could be expected to vary depending on the structure of the contract between the airline and the services firm.

Where service contractors are paid for services delivered, the airline service firms could be expected to absorb more of the increased costs in the short run. Over time, as contracts are rebid and/or renegotiated, increased costs that are not offset by increases in productivity will be passed on to the airlines. Similarly, while costs of per-hour worker contracts will be fully passed through in the short run, the aggregate cost of these contracts might go down over time as contracts are rebid and savings from increased productivity are passed back to the airlines.

Increased costs to concessionaires that are not absorbed through lower profit, price increases, or productivity increases may lead to renegotiations to reduce terminal rentals over time. These rent reductions will effectively be passed on to the airlines in the form of increased landing fees. The airport is financed by rents and fees charged to users, which are held in an airport revenue fund, separately from the city and county general fund. In the case of SFO, transfers of airport revenues to the city for fire, policing, and other services are capped at 16 percent of concession revenue or $5 million per year, whichever is greater. Hence there is no mechanism to transfer reduced terminal rents to city taxpayers or the airport commission. The airport instead absorbs these reduced rents by increasing landing fees charged to the airlines.

Given that most of the costs are passed on to the airlines, are the airlines able to pass these costs on to the consumers? If the airlines passed the total costs directly to the customers, the cost increase would have averaged $1.42 per airline passenger in 2000. Their ability to do so depends, of course, on the price elasticity of demand for air travel in general and on the availability of substitutes for air travel through SFO in particular.

6. CHANGES IN THE LEVEL OF EMPLOYMENT AND AIRPORT ACTIVITY

A principal issue with wage mandates as broad as the QSP concerns whether any displacement of workers occurred as a result of the policies. Fewer workers might be hired if capital is substituted for more expensive labor or if cost increases reduce the level of airport activity. Either channel might result in fewer employed workers after the program than before.

To examine potential employment effects, we compared 1998 employment by occupation for selected (mainly low-wage) occupations and employers to mid-2001 employment for the same occupations and employers. The 1998 estimate is based on the airport commission's own economic impact study and provides a reliable baseline. The data for mid-2001 come from our own employer survey.

Ground-based employment among airlines and airline services firms rose 15.6 percent during the period in which the QSP was implemented. Over the same period, airport activity rose by 4 percent, indicating that employment grew faster than activity. The greater increase in employment most likely derives from the opening of the new international terminal in late 2000 and the associated expectations of increases in Pacific Rim traffic. International activity levels had already begun to grow substantially in 1999; the expansion in terminal capacity had generated optimistic forecasts of further sharp increases in passenger levels. Employers hired more workers during their migration from the old to the new international terminal and in anticipation of higher activity levels.

However, travel declined markedly from August 2000 to August 2001 in all categories at SFO, and across all U.S. airports, even before the dramatic events of September 11, 2001. These reductions in activity do not appear to be causally related to the QSP. Rather, this downturn in international travel and the absolute decline in domestic travel resulted from the broader decline in the Bay Area economy following the shakeout among technology firms as well as from the national recession. This correspondence is illustrated in figure 3.1, which tracks the relationship between growth in activity at SFO and at all U.S. airports from 1998, before the policy went into effect, through 2011.

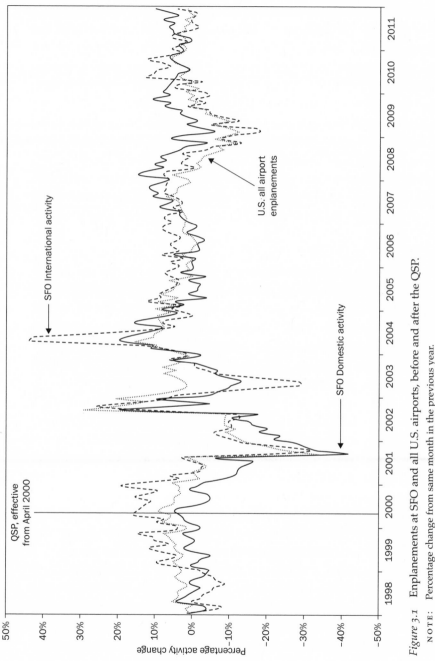

Figure 3.1 Enplanements at SFO and all U.S. airports, before and after the QSP.

NOTE: Percentage change from same month in the previous year.

SOURCE: San Francisco International Airport (www.flysfo.com); Bureau of Transportation Statistics T-100 Market data, Department of Transportation (http://www.rita.dot.gov/bts).

One carrier, Southwest Airlines, did cease operations at SFO in March 2001, after the QSP went into effect, relocating to Oakland, San Jose, and Sacramento. According to a Southwest Airlines official at the time, the airline was "not able to secure terminal facilities, and there is limited runway capacity at SFO." Southwest returned to SFO in 2007, the same year that Virgin America chose SFO as its hub airport.

The evidence thus does not suggest that the costs of the QSP derailed growth in passenger volumes at SFO. As noted above, even if all the costs of the QSP had been passed on to consumers, this would not have had a significant effect on ticket prices. Both international and domestic passenger growth declined primarily as a result of the downturn in the economy.

Changes in Employment of Low-Skilled Workers

What about labor-labor substitution? Standard economic theory predicts that mandated wage increases that are set above competitive equilibrium levels will lead to some employee displacement. In a perfectly competitive situation, the firm can no longer afford to employ low-skill (and hence low-productivity) workers and remain in business. Moreover, with a binding minimum wage, low-skill workers cannot accept lower pay in exchange for employer-provided training.

However, the standard economic theory makes very restrictive assumptions about the competitive character of labor markets. Airport labor markets—with their own distinctive social character and contained spatial reach—certainly depart from the competitive textbook model. Screener firms at SFO historically hired older workers, many of whom were recent immigrants from the Philippines and who were not able to compete for more skilled jobs. These workers tend to be highly educated, and many hold professional degrees that are not recognized in the United States. For these reasons, skill-based substitution would be unlikely.

The QSP mandated high school completion as a condition of hiring; this requirement was implemented by finding alternative employment positions at the airport for those without the required schooling. However, the mandate cannot entirely prevent displacement because firms could still use normal attrition to substitute more skilled workers.

A survey of baggage screeners conducted for the union, SEIU Local 790, provided additional information that allowed us to examine whether the QSP resulted in the displacement of less educated by more educated workers. We compared the education profile of those hired in the year before the implementation of the QSP (June 1999 to May 2000) and in the eighteen months between the implementation of the QSP until the implementation of the Airline Transportation Security Act (June 2000 to November 2001).

The proportion of screeners hired with only a high school diploma fell from 31.6 percent prior to the QSP to 23.1 percent immediately afterwards, while the proportion of screeners hired with high school plus some college rose from 16.5 percent to 23.1 percent. This change indicates a relatively small displacement effect for less educated workers, as the "some college" group includes workers that may have enrolled in as little as one college level class. Moreover, the change is not statistically significant.

Finally, we considered whether employers responded to the increased wage mandate by hiring workers with different demographic characteristics. The displacement of workers who are then unable to find work elsewhere would be an undesirable and unintended consequence of the policy. Using SFO Badge Office data, we find some evidence that the QSP did lead to slightly more hiring of men than women. Among all ground-based nonsupervisory workers (the survey population), the overall proportion of women hired did not change (32.3 vs 31.8 percent). Among low-wage occupations (customer service, ramp, cabin cleaners, screeners, wheelchair attendants, and skycaps only), the proportion of women hires fell from 33.4 percent to 30.3 percent. The proportion of workers in different racial/ethnic groups did not change with the implementation of the QSP. The proportion of young workers (those under the age of twenty-four) is higher among those hired after QSP implementation. However, there were no differences between the airline and airline service sectors with respect to age at hiring, suggesting that the change was not a result of the mandated wage increase. Rather, it is likely that our data reflect higher quit rates among young workers soon after being hired. In all, the only demographic shift attributable to the QSP was a small decline in the proportion of women hired.

7.   DYNAMIC ADJUSTMENT TO THE QSP

In this section we present evidence on the dynamic adjustments by firms and workers to the higher wage, benefit, and other employment mandates contained in the QSP. As the efficiency wage literature has emphasized, nonwage labor costs, such as turnover, can fall with wage increases; moreover, work effort and productivity can increase as a result of wage increases (Katz 1986). Dynamic adjustments to the QSP might therefore improve the benefit-to-cost ratio of the policies.

Turnover fell the most among the airline service firms, with smaller reductions in the airline and concession sectors. This pattern is expected, as most airline employees already received wages above the QSP mandated levels and generous benefits packages, while the QSP only indirectly influenced the concessions sector. Similarly, turnover fell dramatically for firms that experienced the greatest increases in wage costs. Among firms experiencing an increase in wage costs of 10 percent or more as a result of the QSP, turnover rates fell by approximately three-fifths (from almost 50 percent per year to 20 percent). In contrast, among firms experiencing wage cost increases of less than 10 percent, turnover fell between 14 and 17 percent.

Table 3.4 shows that on a job-specific basis larger wage increases are clearly associated with greater turnover reductions. For example, among ramp workers, entry-level wages increased 27 percent and turnover declined by 25 percent. Among screeners, wages increased by 69 percent and turnover declined by 80 percent. Among customer service agents, whose turnover was already low prior to the QSP, entry-level wages rose 26 percent and turnover declined by 5 percent. Unlike outsourced airline service jobs, these unionized positions with United Airlines had career advancement opportunities both within the job category and to other positions in the airline.

The Census Bureau's Quarterly Workforce Indicators (QWI) dataset provides some further confirmation of the positive effect of the QSP on turnover. The QWI measures the turnover rate as the ratio of half the number of accessions plus separations to the number of stable jobs per quarter. Data are published for counties (SFO is in San Mateo County)

Table 3.4   Change in Wages and Turnover Rates for Selected Job Titles

	Percent Increase		Percent Decrease
	ENTRY WAGE	AVERAGE WAGE	TURNOVER
Customer service			
n = 1,621	26	17	5
Baggage / ramp			
n = 1,484	27	18	25
Cabin cleaner			
n = 553	32	15	44
Screener			
n = 916	69	55	80

SOURCE: UCB-SFO Employer Survey, 2001, conducted by the authors.

NOTE: The pre- and post-QSP entry wage, average wage, and turnover rate are significantly different at the 99 percent level for each of the occupations reported here according to the paired sample t-test. Data cover April 2000 to June 2001.

and by industries, including scheduled air transportation (airlines) and support services for air transportation (air transport service firms). Unfortunately, the QWI does not allow separate identification of many of the jobs most affected by the QSP, such as airline catering and cleaning and concession services.

Table 3.5 displays annual employee turnover among air transportation support services for selected airports from 1997 to 2006. LAX (Los Angeles International Airport) and SFO both have living wage policies; the Los Angeles living wage was instituted in 1997, but was only fully implemented at LAX in 1999 after an amendment clarified the coverage of the ordinance (Fairris et al. 2005). DFW (Dallas–Fort Worth) is the airport most comparable in passenger traffic to LAX. LAS (Las Vegas) is most comparable to SFO. Neither of the comparator airports has living wage policies.

Turnover generally is subject to two main determinants: It tends to be higher among lower-wage firms and during economic expansions (but

Table 3.5   Turnover Rates at SFO and Other Large Airports

	LAX (3)	DFW (4)	LAS (8)	SFO (9)
1997	8.6	12.5	13.7	13.1
1998	11.7	12.4	13.7	13.5
1999	9.8	13.3	13.1	14.8
2000	8.0	12.8	13.6	11.1
2001	7.3	12.3	11.2	10.7
2002	10.2	11.9	14.3	*
2003	6.0	9.8	12.1	8.1
2004	7.0	13.5	12.9	7.1
2005	7.6	14.2	13.3	9.8
2006	7.4	12.2	14.5	11.1

* Excluded because of opening of new international terminal.

SOURCE: Quarterly Workforce Indicators.

NOTES: Turnover rates are shown for "Support services for air transportation" (NAICS 4881), county-level data for the fourth quarter of each year. SFO and LAX have living wage policies. Other airports are chosen for comparable size.

Numbers in parentheses indicate rank in passenger traffic among all U.S. airports in 2010, according to data from Airports Council International.

lower in recessions). Turnover rises during expansions because the number of new hires increases and because employee quit rates increase as workers are more likely to find better job opportunities elsewhere.

In line with this conventional wisdom, table 3.5 shows that employee turnover fell at both LAX and SFO when they instituted living wage policies and remained lower than at their comparator airports. Turnover also fell in all four airports during the economic downturn that occurred in 2001. During the subsequent expansionary period, turnover increased much less at the living wage airports than at the comparators. Although these results are based on small samples and are therefore only suggestive, they are consistent with the hypothesis that living wage policies at airports have reduced employee turnover.

The employer survey suggested that higher wages and better benefits at SFO also translated into improved worker performance. According to one longtime airport worker, "Before we could take more liberties. The job had less value; there was a lower threat of replacement. Now you have to be responsible, show up on time, look right, and do your job correctly." Employers were more likely to report an improvement than to report deterioration in overall worker performance (35 percent vs. 4 percent), morale (47 percent vs. 16 percent) and customer service (45 percent vs. 3 percent), as well as less absenteeism (29 percent vs. 5 percent) and fewer disciplinary issues (44 percent vs. 9 percent) or problems with equipment maintenance (29 percent vs. 4 percent). In all cases but one (equipment damage), the proportion reporting an improvement was statistically significantly higher than the proportion reporting a worsening of the condition.

For the most part, employers had not, at least by the time we surveyed them, adjusted to the costs of the mandated wage increases by changing employment practices. Only a few firms reported changes in shift schedules, job descriptions, skill requirements, or hiring practices following implementation of the QSP. Firms that were more heavily influenced by the QSP did report higher entry skill requirements and stricter hiring policies, reflecting the increases in entry-level skills that the QSP mandated. One-fifth (19.8 percent) of all employers reported a change in training. In every such case, employers commented that they increased the amount of initial or on-the-job training provided. Although this result is consistent with the increased training mandates of the QSP, it is not statistically significant.

Other anecdotal evidence in the employer survey points in the same direction. For example, one large employer reported a substantial improvement in the trainability of new hires. Another employer reported, "[The QSP] changed the way we do business. We are more proactive in getting good folks and keeping them trained. . . . If we have someone who isn't performing, we have no hesitation about letting them go. We've weeded out nonperformers, so the quality goes up considerably." Our findings from the worker interviews indicate that work in the QSP covered jobs did involve increased skill and more effort. QSP-covered workers reported that more skills are required of them (50 percent), that they were working harder at their jobs (44 percent), that that they have greater stress on the job (43 percent), and that the pace of work has increased (37 percent). In each case, the percentage reporting "more" was similar to the percentage reporting "no change" and greatly exceeded the percentage reporting "less."

8. CONCLUSIONS AND IMPLICATIONS

Unlike living wage policies in most other cities, which typically cover only a small number of workers and have limited spillover impacts on the local labor market, the QSP and related policies had a major impact on the labor market at SFO. About 8,000 of the 11,000 low-wage, ground-based, nonmanagerial workers received wage increases as a result of these policies. Other benefits to workers included new health benefits for approximately 2,000 workers and improved health packages or a wage premium for all 8,300 workers covered by the QSP. The living wage policies at SFO effectively established a binding minimum wage norm in this distinct labor market. These benefits reduced previous trends toward lower real wages in the airline service sector and significantly reduced the pay differential between in-house and contracted-out positions.

We calculated that the total costs of the wages, health benefits, leave, and employer-paid taxes that are directly or indirectly attributable to the living wage policies amount to $57.6 million per year. We argue that these costs are, for the most part, incurred by airlines operating at SFO. We also identify a series of dynamic adjustments by firms and workers that generated cost savings and improved productivity. Turnover declined markedly among jobs that received the largest wage increases. Both the worker interviews and the employer survey confirm that employees were working harder, whether this increased effort is "voluntary" or because employers are demanding more.

One concern with living wage laws is that they may lead to the displacement of intended beneficiaries of the policy. Data on airport activity levels show that they were not affected by the living wage policies. The living wage laws slightly changed hiring patterns of firms, specifically, the hiring of more male workers in some low-wage occupations. There is no evidence that the QSP changed hiring patterns by race and age. The QSP also entailed the intentional raising of education requirements for screeners, but this requirement was not used to displace any incumbent workers.

The impressive scale of the impacts at SFO reflects three distinct characteristics that differentiate this policy experiment from living wage policies enacted elsewhere. First, the wage policies at SFO were binding for a very large proportion of the workers in the airport labor market, unlike contractor-focused living wage ordinances that typically benefit only a small number of workers. The SFO experience consequently suggests that area-based living wage ordinances or local minimum wage ordinances may be able to deliver benefits to workers on a wider scale. Second, beyond simply improving wages and benefits, the SFO policies addressed a wider range of employment standards and regulations, notably hiring and training requirements, labor peace / card check provisions, and worker protection clauses. Such an institutional context might be more conducive to improved labor-management relations and to generating the observed efficiency wage-type effects. The design and enforcement of these regulations resulted from concerted organizing by labor, innovative policy making by public officials, and enlightened acceptance by key employers. Third, the policies were implemented in a context that maximized the likelihood that their costs would be borne by consumers rather than through reduced levels of business or contractor effort or through increased costs to taxpayers.

Living wage ordinances now apply to workers at several California airports (e.g., Los Angeles, San Jose, Oakland) and campaigns are under way in other airports. The living wage applied at LAX today most closely resembles the QSP in terms of coverage: a 2010 determination confirmed that the licensed airlines and leaseholders, as well as contractors, sublicensees, and subleaseholders, were covered by the living wage ordinance (Reamer 2010). Fairris et al. (2005) identified 9,600 jobs at LAX in firms that gave raises as a result of the citywide living wage ordinance, although they acknowledge that it is difficult to say precisely how many benefited directly from the policy or indirectly from the associated union organizing efforts. Enforcement may be more effective at SFO and in Los

Angeles, where offices devoted to enforcement handle confidential employee compliance complaints. In contrast, at Oakland International Airport there have been allegations of a lack of enforcement (Duncan 2012).

While living wage policies have extended to some other airports, the more generous wage mandates and related high road training and recruitment provisions have not been widely replicated. This probably reflects the post-9/11 changes in airports: a much more difficult organizing environment and, initially at least, the improved working conditions of security screeners hired under the Transportation Security Administration (TSA). Indeed, TSA represents, in essence, the widespread adoption of the employment model created by the QSP. Notwithstanding popular discourses about intrusive security procedures, TSA provides a trained, professionalized, and relatively well paid workforce. According to a TSA-sponsored blog, "Prior to 9/11, turnover in the industry was over 125 percent—today, TSA's turnover rate is 6.4 percent" (Blogger Bob 2011). Studies conducted by the Government Accountability Office also point to improved airport security training and performance by the middle of the decade (GAO 2005).

Although QSP-type policies have not been widely adopted at other airports, we have shown that they were able to raise pay and benefits for low-wage workers without adverse impacts on employment or business conditions. Instead, the demonstration effects of the QSP were more local, providing encouragement for further attempts in San Francisco to reverse the growing wage inequality that has characterized the U.S. labor market since the 1970s.

REFERENCES

Blogger Bob. 2011. "TSA 10 Years after 9/11." *TSA Blog*, http://blog.tsa.
gov/2011/08/tsa-10-years-after-911.html, accessed Apr. 22, 2012.
Brenner, Mark. 2005. "The Economic Impact of the Boston Living Wage
Ordinance" *Industrial Relations* 44, 1: 59–83.
California Budget Project. 2001. "Making Ends Meet: How Much Does It Cost to
Raise a Family in California?" Sacramento, CA.

Cappelli, Peter. 1985. "Competitive Pressures and Labor Relations in the Airline Industry." *Industrial Relations* 24, 3: 316–38.

Duncan, Lisl. 2012. "Port of Oakland and DLSE Actively Investigate Several Airport Concessionaires for Alleged Wage, Overtime, Anti-Union Violations," www.unioncounsel.net/developments/private_sector/port_of_oakland_and_dlse_actively_investigate.html, last accessed Aug. 29, 2012.

Fairris, David. 2005. "The Impact of Living Wages on Employers: A Control Group Analysis of the Los Angeles Ordinance." *Industrial Relations* 44, 1: 84–105.

Fairris, David, David Runsten, Carolina Briones, and Jessica Goodheart. 2005. *Examining the Evidence: The Impact of the Los Angeles Living Wage Ordinance on Workers and Businesses.* Los Angeles: Los Angeles Alliance for a New Economy. www.laane.org/whats-new/2005/05/26/examining-the-evidence-the-impact-of-the-los-angeles-living-wage-ordinance-on-workers-and-businesses-2005/.

Freeman, Richard. 2005. "Fighting for Other Folks' Wages: The Logic and Illogic of Living Wage Campaigns." *Industrial Relations* 44, 1: 14–31.

GAO. 2005. "Aviation Security: Screener Training and Performance Measurement Strengthened, but More Work Remains." Report GAO-05–457. Washington DC: Government Accountability Office.

Hall, Peter V. 2009. "Container Ports, Local Benefits and Transportation Worker Earnings." *GeoJournal* 74, 1: 67–83.

Katz, Lawrence. 1986. "Efficiency Wage Theories: A Partial Evaluation." *NBER Macroeconomics Annual* 1: 235–90.

Lester, T. William. 2012. "Labor Standards and Local Economic Growth: Do Living Wage Provisions Harm Economic Growth?" *Journal of Planning Education and Research* 32: 331–48.

Peoples, James 1998. "Deregulation and the Labor Market." *Journal of Economic Perspectives* 12, 3: 111–30.

QWI (Quarterly Workforce Indicators). 2012. QWI Online. US Census Bureau. http://lehd.did.census.gov/led/datatools/qwiapp.html.

Reamer, J. L. 2010. "Determination Regarding Application of the Living Wage Ordinance to All Airport Employees Providing Industry-Specific Services to or for the Los Angeles World Airports." Letter to LAWA, Feb. 26, 2010. www.lawa.org/uploadedFiles/LAWA/Business/LAWA%20LWO%20DETERMINATION%20022610.pdf.

Reich, Michael, Peter V. Hall, and Fiona Hsu. 1999. "Living Wages and the San Francisco Economy: The Benefits and the Costs" (in two releases). Report of the Bay Area Living Wage Research Group, Institute of Industrial Relations, UC Berkeley. http://iir.berkeley.edu/living wage/.

Reich, Michael, Peter V. Hall, and Ken Jacobs. 2003. *Living Wages and Economic Performance: The San Francisco Airport Model.* IRLE Monograph. www.irle. berkeley.edu/research/livingwage/sfo_mar03.pdf

———. 2005. "Living Wages Policies at the San Francisco Airport: Impacts on Workers and Businesses." *Industrial Relations* 44, 1: 106–38.

Rubery, Jill, Fang Lee Cooke, Jill Earnshaw, and Mick Marchington. 2003. "Inter-organizational Relations and Employment in a Multi-employer Environment." *British Journal of Industrial Relations* 41, 2: 265–89.

SFO. 1998. "The Economic Impact of the San Francisco International Airport." Study conducted by Martin Associates for the San Francisco Airport Commission.

———. 2009. "Quality Standards Program." San Francisco International Airport. www.flysfo.com/web/export/sites/default/download/about/rules/pdf/QSP.pdf.

FOUR Living Wages and Home Care Workers

Candace Howes

This chapter reports on the effects of living wages and employer-provided health insurance on job quality and workforce attachment among the home care workers in San Francisco who are employed through the Medicaid-funded In-Home Supportive Services (IHSS) program.

When they work directly for consumers in their home, both publicly funded and privately paid consumer-directed home care workers are classified as independent providers or contractors. As independent providers, they are covered neither by the National Labor Relations Act nor by state public employment law. Accordingly, they do not have the right to form a union or engage in collective bargaining (Smith 2008). By 2015, home care workers will be covered under the federal Fair Labor Standards Act, which guarantees payment of a minimum wage and overtime pay, reversing the previous view that they were primarily

97

providing "companionship" rather than compensable services (Smith 2008; Forhan 2010; Gross 2013).

In contrast, in the 1990s, California created quasi-governmental entities that could serve as the employer of record for IHSS workers, providing workers with the protection of employment and labor laws. The concomitant passage of the living wage mandate in San Francisco, combined with health care unions' solid footholds in segments of California's long-term care industry, provided a supportive environment for improving the quality of jobs in this sector and more generally in the low end of the wage distribution. The IHSS program in San Francisco had introduced an early model of an effective health insurance policy for low-wage workers in nontraditional work environments by 1999, which may well have served as a model for the Healthy San Francisco program that followed eight years later.

I argue that San Francisco has set the national standard for job quality in consumer-directed home care services, a standard that has diffused throughout a number of California counties and to other states. At least for a time, San Francisco has provided a good case study of how higher wages originating in publicly funded jobs can raise the standard of living and quality of care and diffuse better practices even to the private for-profit and not-for-profit industry, and even in an industry in which workers do not have traditional labor protections. An important synergy developed between the wage and benefit trends in IHSS and the other labor mandates in San Francisco. Just as San Francisco offers important lessons about the role of mandates, the story of IHSS in San Francisco offers lessons about the significant role that large publicly funded programs employing unionized workers can play in both modeling the potential and reinforcing the effects of mandates.

Moreover, the significance of the long-term care sector to the conditions of low-wage workers cannot be overemphasized. As a result of well-documented trends in family formation and demographics, the long-term care industry is among the fastest growing industries in the country. The home health and home care industries are the fastest growing segments of this industry, and home care worker (personal care aide) is the fastest growing occupation in the country, followed immediately by home health aide (BLS 2012). In San Francisco, with a workforce of about 476,000 (CA

EDD), the nearly 20,000 IHSS workers make up 4.2 percent of the entire workforce. They also make up 28 percent of low-wage workers, as measured by the bottom 15 percent of the wage distribution, and about half of the low-wage female workforce. When the private pay and largely unmeasured gray market segments of the industry are added, the significance of these jobs to the low-wage sector is even greater. Thus, the quality of jobs for low-wage workers with less than a college education is disproportionately affected by the quality of jobs in this sector.

California has been at the forefront of most of the trends in the long-term care sector, including the shift from institutional to home- and community-based care and, within home care, to consumer-directed care. It is on the verge of taking the next step, integrating long-term care into the provision of health care services for low-income persons through a managed care program. None of these steps can be made without substantially expanding the size and stability of the home care workforce. Whether or not the expanding industry provides good jobs for low-wage workers depends crucially on whether states, counties, and municipalities can raise the floor on the quality of jobs created in this industry. By doing just that, San Francisco has created the best consumer-directed home care jobs in the United States.

San Francisco and the contiguous California counties and other states to which the San Francisco model has spread offer important lessons on how to develop that future workforce, in particular lessons about the role of wages and benefits. In an industry in which much of the workforce labors in nontraditional work sites such as individuals' homes, San Francisco–like mandates play an important role.

1.   LONG-TERM CARE POLICY, THE LONG-TERM CARE INDUSTRY, AND HOME CARE

Long-term care is assistance provided to people over the age of eighteen who need help performing some activities of daily living (e.g., bathing, dressing, eating, transferring from bed to chair) due to physical or mental disabilities, chronic illnesses, or the effects of aging. Long-term care workers may also provide companionship and help with cooking, house-work, and transportation (IOM 2008). Eighty percent of all hours of long-term care assistance are still performed by unpaid caregivers in the home. But increasingly people are relying on paid care outside the home. They are relying on workers whose titles include nurse's aide, nursing assistant, personal care aide, home care aide, home health aide, certified nursing assistant, and direct support professional (PHI 2010).

Long-term care workers can be found in a variety of settings, from for-profit and not-for-profit nursing facilities, assisted living facilities, and continuing care retirement communities (CCRCs) to private households and group homes for people with psychological or developmental disabilities (NDSWRC 2008).[1] Some independent and self-employed providers work in very informal arrangements that are not included in standard labor force surveys. A little less than half of adult care workers in the United States currently report to a facility each workday in a traditional employer/employee arrangement (PHI 2010). Home health aides and home care workers, who make up about half of the long-term care workforce, work in home-based settings. They are employed either by agencies or directly by individuals or a fiscal intermediary.

Since long-term care is expensive and public funding is available only for persons whose household income is at or close to the poverty line, the industry is stratified by income level and payment source. Almost half of all financing for long-term care comes from Medicaid, and its rules and reimbursement policies substantially shape the industry (Kaye, Harrington, and LaPlante 2010). Over the past thirty years, program rules have gradually evolved to support more community-based and less institution-based care (Harrington et al. 2009). Most people with intellectual or developmental disabilities receive personal care services in community settings or family homes. More recently, states have begun to move or redirect older persons and adults with disabilities to home- and community-based services. Consumer preference, state fiscal crises,

[1] Assisted living facilities and continuing care retirement communities are rapidly growing, mainly private, for-profit, private pay establishments that cater to high-income elderly persons. As of 2006, about 700,000 people lived in assisted living and continuing care retirement communities (Spillman and Black 2008).

and the Supreme Court's Olmstead decision in 1999 all motivate states to "rebalance" their long-term care services to favor community over institutional care (Howes 2010, 2012; Gornick, Howes, and Braslow 2012a).

The formal sector of the fast-growing home health/home care sector includes Medicare- and Medicaid-certified home health care companies that supply services ranging from skilled nursing, home health care, and personal care to durable medical equipment. Some for-profit chains and smaller proprietary and nonproprietary firms limit their services to non-medical, limited personal care and homemaking (Seavey and Marquand 2011).

Within the home-based care segment, consumer-directed publicly funded home care is gaining ground in many states. Under this model, individuals hire providers of their own choice, supervise them, and either pay them directly using cash support from Medicaid or the provider is paid directly by the state or an intermediary such as a "public authority." Including California, twelve states now provide Medicaid personal care services under this model of "consumer-directed" care.

States' rebalancing projects combined with the demographic trends associated with aging baby boomers account for the very high rate of projected job growth in the home health and home care industries. Between 1989 and 2004, the workforce providing noninstitutional personal assistance and home health services tripled while the workforce providing similar services in institutional settings remained relatively stable (Kaye et al. 2006). Together, long-term care industries, which made up about 3.7 percent of all jobs in 2010, are projected to account for 10 percent of all expected new jobs between 2010 and 2020. Two-thirds of these jobs will be in home health and home care (BLS 2012).[2]

---

[2] Under the North American Industrial Classification System (NAICS), the following industries comprise the institutional/residential sector of the adult care: (1) home health care services (621600); (2) as part of the Social Assistance subsesctor, Services for the Elderly and Persons with Disabilities (624120), which "comprises establishments primarily engaged in providing nonresidential social assistance services to improve the quality of life for the elderly, persons diagnosed with mental retardation, or persons with disabilities. These establishments provide for the welfare of these individuals in such areas as day care, nonmedical home care or homemaker services, social activities, group support, and companionship" (NAICS 2010, www.census.gov/eos/www/naics/index.html).

Many states have expressed doubts about their ability to fill the new openings as they proliferate, concerned that low wages, poor working conditions, and a lack of affordable benefits will keep turnover rates high and fail to attract enough new workers.[3] States have also expressed concern that the cost of improving job quality, which is shared by states and the federal government, will put an unsustainable burden on state and county budgets.

2.   JOB QUALITY, RECRUITMENT, AND RETENTION

Considerable evidence indicates that many long-term care workers prefer to work in home-based settings. Long-term care workers are motivated to do this kind of work, as they frequently report, because they value the personal relationship with their clients and the opportunity to provide empathic care. Even though they earn lower pay and often experience more hazardous working conditions, home health and personal care aides enjoy more autonomy, discretion, and flexibility than workers employed in institutional settings. Having some control over the terms and conditions under which they care for their clients enhances their ability to provide high-quality, empathic care. However, while many home care workers find intrinsic satisfaction in their job, the low pay and poor working conditions often prompt them to leave (Howes 2008).

Turnover is a generally accepted indicator of job quality. Turnover is high across all sectors of the long-term care industry, related to problems of low wages, low morale, absenteeism, and burnout (Seavey and Marquand 2011). Certified nursing assistant (CNA) turnover averages 71 percent a year in nursing homes nationwide, and it reaches even higher levels in many states (Decker et al. 2003). An estimated 40 percent to 60 percent of home health aides leave after less than one year on a job, and 80 percent to 90 percent leave within the first two years (IOM 2008).

---

[3] In a 2007 survey of states, 33 of the 34 respondents ranked "direct care" vacancies and/or turnover as a "serious" or "very serious" issue. This figure represents a substantial increase from 2005, when 76 percent of respondents indicated that vacancies and turnover was a serious issue (PHI and DCWANC 2009).

There are no large-scale studies of turnover among home care workers, but small-scale studies have found that these turnover rates are lower than those in home health care and considerably lower than in nursing homes, suggesting that increased autonomy may offset some of the negative effects of low wages and benefits.[4] But there is a tipping point beyond which autonomy is not an adequate substitute for compensation.

The disruption that comes from turnover likely lowers the quality of care provided. When these personal relationships become temporary, workers have less incentive to invest in them. Further, frequent turnover requires existing care workers to work overtime, which makes them "susceptible to exhaustion, increased mistakes and decreasing quality of performance" (Hewitt and Lakin 2001). Turnover increases employer costs because of the need for continuous recruitment and training. The costs of long-term care worker turnover on the national level have been estimated to total $4.1 billion per year (Seavey 2004). State-level studies also yield high estimates (Leon, Marainen, and Marcotte 2001).

As I show in greater detail below, studies of home care workers in San Francisco and California demonstrate that turnover rates can be reduced with higher wages and benefits, even when a worker is significantly motivated by nonpecuniary rewards.

3. CALIFORNIA'S LONG-TERM CARE INDUSTRY AND IN-HOME SUPPORTIVE SERVICES

California is at the forefront of many of the trends in the industry. Close to 75 percent of Medicaid-funded long-term care recipients now receive

---

[4] A review of thirteen state and two national studies of in-home care for persons with intellectual and developmental disabilities found an average turnover rate of 65 percent (Hewitt and Larson 2007). A study of consumer-directed home care workers in one county in California found a turnover rate of 24 percent and for the entire state, a turnover rate of 27 percent in 2003 (Howes 2004, 2005). One intent-to-leave study showed that 37 percent of home care workers intended to leave their job in the following year (Brannon et al. 2007). One statewide study conducted over a two-year period found that 47 percent of agency-based home care workers intended to leave and that 46 percent actually did (Morris 2009). Staff turnover in assisted living facilities ranges from 21 percent to 135 percent, with an average of 42 percent (Maas and Buckwalter 2006).

their care in a home setting, compared to a national average of 50 percent. California has also favored consumer-directed over agency-directed home care.

Under the Medicaid program, in order to receive federal matching funds each state must have a state plan for the provision of long-term care. That plan must include nursing home care and may as an option include home- and community-based services, including home care. Home care can be offered as a State Plan option or through Waiver programs. IHSS is California's State Plan Personal Care Services Option (Gornick, Howes, and Braslow 2012a, 2012b).

The costs of the IHSS program, as with other Medicaid programs, are shared by the federal government and the state. Until recently, the federal matching share was 50 percent, but under certain provisions of the Affordable Care Act, the federal share has been increased to 56 percent. The federal funds are available to match the cost of wages and benefits up to twice the state minimum wage, or $16.00 per hour. In California, the state pays 65 percent of the nonfederal share up to a maximum combined wages and benefits of $12.10 ($11.50 for wages and $0.60 for benefits) and holds counties responsible for the remaining 35 percent of wages, benefits, and associated costs such as employment taxes (California WIC 12301.6). The state requires counties to pay the full nonfederal share of any wage and benefit costs beyond $12.10.

Tipping the balance toward the use of home- and community-based services has not only increased the choices and autonomy available to Medicaid consumers. It also has helped slow the growth of per capita costs in states. For example, in 2006, California and Rhode Island had similar levels of participation in Medicaid long-term care programs (13.8 per thousand and 13 per thousand in the population, respectively). Yet California, which had a far larger share of its Medicaid long-term care recipients in home care (69 percent of its participants, compared to 22 percent in Rhode Island), spent far less per capita on Medicaid long-term care services: $210 compared to Rhode Island's $323 (Gornick, Howes, and Braslow 2012).

The In-Home Supportive Services program in California, which served almost 450,000 individuals in August 2012 (CDSS 2012), is the largest consumer-directed home care program in the country, if not the world. Under this program, after consumers meet the income qualifications and a social worker assesses their need and authorizes them to receive a specified number of hours of service, consumers are permitted to hire their own provider. More than half of consumers hire family members or close relatives; 80 percent hire someone they already knew (Howes 2004).

Approximately 400,000 IHSS workers are employed under a unique arrangement devised in 1992 to create IHSS Public Authorities. The public authority is a quasi-governmental organization that has a consumer-majority advisory committee. The public authority model was first conceived in California by a coalition of union and consumer advocates (Boris and Klein 2012). In this model, the consumer hires the provider, the state pays the provider directly, and the public authority maintains a registry of providers, offers training for consumers and providers, and serves as the "employer of record" for the purposes of collective bargaining. With an employer of record, home care workers can be reclassified from independent contractor to employee status, which means they are covered by the National Labor Relations Act and can legally join unions, bargain collectively, and access group benefits such as worker compensation and health care (Smith 2008).

Following the passage in 1992 of a state law permitting their formation, San Mateo and Alameda were the first California counties to create public authorities in 1993; San Francisco passed an ordinance in May 1995 creating its IHSS Public Authority. As Boris and Klein (2012) report, San Francisco IHSS workers voted to join SEIU Local 250 in spring 1996. The County Board of Supervisors allocated $1.3 million for higher wages, giving IHSS workers their first, albeit small, raise in twenty years. In 1997, San Francisco became the first county in California to sign a union contract that covered independent providers. Legislation in 1999 required each California county to set up, by January 2003, an entity, such as a public authority, that could serve as the employer of record for IHSS workers (California WIC).

At the time of this writing, each county maintains a separate public authority or similar entity. In those counties where workers are represented by a union, the public authority negotiates a contract, usually of three years duration. Bargaining is limited by statute to wages and benefits. Providers are prohibited, also by statute, from striking or bringing grievances against their consumers (California WIC). In this decentralized system, in which each county negotiates separately with a union, wages and benefits vary considerably across counties. In those counties that have no contract or in which the union has been unable to win any wage increases, IHSS workers are paid the state minimum wage of $8.00 an hour and receive no health insurance or any other benefits. In other counties, including San Francisco and bordering Bay Area counties and in counties between San Francisco and Sacramento, wages have risen as high as $12.35 an hour and providers receive health insurance, dental insurance, and even paid time off.[5]

The IHSS program grew dramatically between July 1998 and July 2008. From an average annual growth rate of about 3.3 percent between July 1994 and July 1998, when the caseload grew from 175,000 to 200,000, the growth rate increased to an annual average of 8.1 percent for the ten-year period between 1998 and 2008 (CDSS Estimates Branch 2011). Program growth is not fully explained by the underlying demographic determinant of growth—the growth rate of the aged, blind, and disabled SSI/SSP caseload—which was far slower during the same period (CDSS Estimates Branch 2011). In all likelihood, rising wages and low-cost health insurance, for which most providers were eligible, and increased awareness of the program, which made it easier for eligible consumers to find qualified and willing providers, explain the rapid growth.

---

[5] This system will change over the next few years as counties transition under the new Coordinated Care Initiative (CCI), which was established as part of the enacted 2012–13 California state budget in June 2012 (Scan Foundation 2012). The CCI specifies, among other things, that long-term services and supports (LTSS), which includes nursing home care and in-home services, will be integrated into managed care plans for all Medi-Cal beneficiaries. Under the CCI, a statewide IHSS Public Authority will take over county-level public authorities' responsibilities for collective bargaining. While this does not necessarily mean there will be a statewide contract in which all workers are paid the same wage and benefits, there is likely to be considerably less variability across counties and wages are likely to rise on average.

4. SAN FRANCISCO MANDATES AND IHSS WAGE
    AND BENEFIT HISTORY

While the IHSS Public Authority is a discrete legal government entity that is separate and distinct from the City and County of San Francisco, it was created by the City, and wage rates for IHSS workers are ultimately set by the Board of Supervisors. IHSS workers are covered by the Minimum Compensation Ordinance, the city's living wage policy, at the nonprofit rate. The nonprofit rate was set at $9.00 an hour in 2000 and was not increased again until November 2007, when it was raised to $10.77 and then $11.03 an hour in January 2008.[6] The MCO allows employers to pay proportionally higher wages in lieu of providing twelve days of paid time off, which brings the total wage rate to $11.54 if paid time off is not provided. IHSS workers were not covered by the city's health care requirements, since the program has its own health plan. While IHSS workers were paid above the MCO nonprofit rate until it was increased in late 2007, there is a strong relationship between trends in IHSS wages and benefits and the requirements in San Francisco labor standards policies (fig. 4.1).

In the three years after the establishment of the IHSS Public Authority in 1995 but before the first collective bargaining agreement was signed, workers received only small increases, and wages remained at only $0.30 to $0.60 above the minimum wage. In July 1998, a full two years before the living wage ordinance was passed, the union bargained a significant wage increase, to $7.00 an hour. With that increase, the IHSS wage rose to $1.25 above the state minimum wage (Howes 2005).

In the year preceding the anticipated passage of the living wage ordinance in October 2000, the Board of Supervisors agreed to increase the IHSS wage to $9.00 an hour, $3.75 above the state minimum wage. Wages were again increased to $9.70 in July 2000. So by the time the living wage ordinance passed, wages had actually risen above the mandated

---

[6] While the MCO rate for for-profit firms and San Francisco's general minimum wage law are both indexed to the Bay Area CPI, the nonprofit MCO rate is not. Without further action by the Board of Supervisors, the minimum wage rate will become the floor for nonprofit workers, including IHSS.

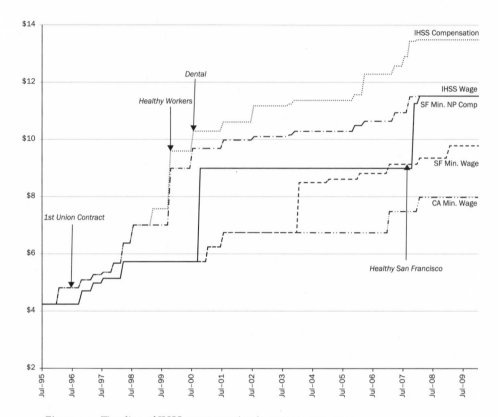

Figure 4.1 Timeline of IHSS compensation increases, 1995–2010.

minimum. The wage was increased to $10.00 an hour in July 2001 and
$10.10 in August 2002, when it stood at 23 percent above the 10th percen-
tile wage in the county and 12 percent above the nonprofit minimum
wage rate.[7] The pace of the increase in the San Francisco IHSS wage
slowed in subsequent years, rising by only 14 percent, to $11.54, by
December 2007, 15 percent above the 10th percentile wage at the time but
equal to the nonprofit MCO rate for entities that do not provide paid

[7] Wage data is from the California Management Information and Payrolling System
(CMIPS) dataset, which is an administrative dataset owned and maintained by the
California Department of Social Services; the 10th percentile wage is from California EDD.

time off, where it has remained.[8] The IHSS real wage, like the MCO non-profit rate, has declined in the past four years; it stood only 11 percent above the 10th percentile wage of $10.43 in the first quarter of 2011.

By March 1999, long before Healthy San Francisco was launched (July 2007), the Healthy Workers plan provided individual health insurance to any IHSS employee who had worked a minimum of two months and who worked at least twenty-five hours in one of those months (SF IHSS Public Authority). Because the eligibility requirements were so low, over 90 percent of providers were eligible, and within a few years nearly 60 percent of those eligible had signed up for the program (RTZ Associates 2005).

The cost of this plan greatly exceeded the $0.60 per hour cap on the costs for which the state was willing to contribute its share. But at its inception, the Public Authority, working with the union and county Board of Supervisors, devised a strategy to fund the plan out of savings in the county Medically Indigent Service Program (Community Health Network Sliding Scale Program) which was serving many IHSS providers (Howes 2002; RTZ Associates 2005; CHCF 2009). Dental benefits were added in January 2000, and all workers were automatically enrolled in the program. The San Francisco IHSS Public Authority contributed $1.95 per hour to the Healthy Workers fund in FY 2011. Eligible IHSS workers paid premiums of $3.00 per month.

San Francisco is effectively spending $1.35 more per hour for health insurance for IHSS providers than most counties. While the federal government pays 56 percent of the total cost, the state pays only 65 percent of the nonfederal share for the first $0.60 and none of the nonfederal share for the extra $1.35 per hour, leaving the balance to be paid by the county. Since IHSS independent providers delivered 20.9 million service hours in the 2010–11 fiscal year at a total cost in wages, benefits, and payroll taxes of $308.9 million, San Francisco spent about $41 million on health and dental benefits for IHSS workers. The federal government would have reimbursed the county $23 million, the state would have reimbursed $4 million, but the county paid $14 million,

[8] Author's calculations using the Occupational and Employment Statistics.

which was about $12 million above what it would have paid if it had kept hourly health insurance contributions at $0.60 (SF IHSS Public Authority).

San Francisco's practice stands in contrast to many counties that do cap their health care contribution at $0.60 an hour. In order to cover the costs of health insurance with such a small hourly contribution, the counties have limited eligibility to workers who work eighty or more hours per month and maintained enrollment caps that can keep eligible providers on a waiting list for years (CAPA).

Because its Healthy Workers health insurance plan is already part of the San Francisco Health Plan, IHSS does not contribute to Healthy San Francisco.[9] But the filial relationship between the two programs is evident. In fact, Healthy San Francisco could have been modeled after Healthy Workers. The Health Care Security Ordinance requires that an employer with 100 or more employees must make health care expenditures of at least $2.20 per hour worked; an employer with 20 or more employees, or nonprofits of 50 to 99 employees, must make health care expenditures of at least $1.46 per hour, up to 172 hours in a month, for providing health services (SF Living Wage Coalition). The money can be spent on health insurance, to create health savings accounts, to pay health care claims, or to contribute toward employees' participation in Healthy San Francisco (Katz and Brigham 2011; San Francisco Health Plan).[10]

The caseload in San Francisco grew at a rate of 10 percent annually between 1998 and 2008, slightly higher than the growth rate for the program statewide. Since 2008, caseload growth has been negligible. As of December 2012, nearly 22,000 San Francisco consumers received care

[9] Healthy Workers is one of four programs currently subsumed under or administered by the San Francisco Health Plan, a licensed community health plan, which includes Medi-Cal, Healthy Families, Healthy Children, and Healthy San Francisco (SFHP, SFIHSSPA). (The San Francisco Health Plan is also the third-party administrator for Healthy San Francisco.)

[10] All uninsured San Franciscans ages 18 to 64 are eligible for Healthy San Francisco if they meet one of two criteria: income and assets are no higher than 500 percent of the FPL, or their employer contributes to Healthy San Francisco through the employer spending requirement.

from approximately 18,000 providers. In sum, as Boris and Klein (2012, 196) have argued, "San Francisco developed the best conditions for homecare workers in the country."

5. SPILLOVER TO OTHER COUNTIES AND STATES

One measure of the relative success of the San Francisco model is the extent to which it has diffused to other states and California counties. Within five years, all surrounding Bay Area counties had passed ordinances to create public authorities. By 2010, all but two of California's fifty-eight counties had public authorities. Unionization followed in all Bay Area counties, and by 2005, IHSS workers were unionized in all but thirteen of California's counties. As of 2010, IHSS wages in all Bay Area counties were at least $11.50; Santa Clara County paid IHSS workers $12.35, and all of these counties offered health insurance. Also by 2010, all but twelve California counties paid wages higher than the state minimum wage of $8.00. Not all, however, have adopted health insurance benefits that are comparable to San Francisco in terms of eligibility and enrollment. As the next section shows, both wages and benefits have a measurable impact on turnover; however, the effect of health insurance benefits depends on making them broadly available to very part-time workers.

The model also spread quickly to Oregon and Washington (Boris and Klein 2012). States in the rest of the country have been slower to embrace consumer-directed care. But as they have, many states have created public authority–like entities either by ballot initiatives to amend the state constitution or by executive order or intergovernmental cooperative agreements (Smith 2008). As of this writing, twelve states have models similar to California. Connecticut passed a public authority law in 2012. Minnesota and Vermont both passed similar bills in 2013.

Until recently, whether home care workers were employed through a consumer-directed program or an agency, employers did not have to pay minimum wage and overtime because of the "companionship exemptions" to the Fair Labor Standards Act. After a two year wait on President Barack Obama's promise in December 2011 to change the rules, the

Department of Labor issued a final rule in September 2013 which will take effect beginning in January 2015 (USDOL/WHD). Nonetheless, San Francisco, like many other counties and 15 states, including California, has required employers to pay home care workers well in excess of the federal minimum wage (Gross 2013).

6.   MEASURING THE EFFECT OF WAGE AND BENEFIT INCREASES ON IHSS WORKER TURNOVER

In a 2004 study, I examined the effect of the large wage increases and the addition of health insurance on retention of IHSS workers between November 1997 and February 2002. During the period of analysis wages nearly doubled. The San Francisco economy was also expanding rapidly, and unemployment rates fell from about 3 percent to 2 percent by late 2000, so there were plenty of alternatives to IHSS jobs. In a survey I administered in 2004–5 in eight California counties, including San Francisco, I found that the majority of IHSS workers had previously worked or were concurrently working in other low-skill, low-wage jobs, including (private pay) home care; as clerks, wait staff, and cooks; in housekeeping, as maids and janitors; as factory workers; and as child care workers—all jobs that paid wages that put them near or below the 10th percentile of the wage distribution (Howes 2008). So how the IHSS wage compared to the wage at the 10th percentile of the wage distribution provided a good indicator of its relative worth.

In November 1997, San Francisco IHSS paid $5.75 per hour, which made the IHSS wage, at 83 percent of the 10th percentile wage in the San Francisco metro area,[11] uncompetitive. The one-year retention rate in 1998 was 78 percent for all providers but only 39 percent for new providers (Howes 2005).[12] Most providers would have reported, as many still

---

[11] Tenth percentile data are for San Francisco, Marin, and San Mateo Counties.

[12] Retention in this study was measured net of "natural turnover," the turnover that occurs when a provider and consumer enter and leave the program simultaneously. These are normally family providers or friends who have cared for one consumer only and do not intend to make a career of home care.

did in 2005, that they were doing IHSS work for reasons other than compensation, including family or friendship ties to the consumer or because they needed a job with flexibility. By 2002, the wage had risen to 123 percent of the 10th percentile wage, and the annual retention rate for all providers to 85 percent. But remarkably, the retention rate for new providers, at 74 percent, had nearly converged with that of all providers. In 2004, San Francisco IHSS providers were far more likely to report that wages and benefits were among the top three reasons that they were working in IHSS than were workers in any of the other lower-wage counties surveyed (Howes 2008).

After peaking at 126 percent in 2001, the relative wage declined slightly until August 2004 and then at a faster rate, from 120 percent in September 2004 to 113 percent in January 2007. It jumped up again to 120 percent with increases in the MCO nonprofit wage at the end of 2007. Thereafter, it continued a steady decline to 113 percent by November 2009. Of course, the 10th percentile wage has continued to rise since late 2007 because the San Francisco minimum wage is indexed to inflation, though the MCO nonprofit wage is not.

In a new analysis of the trends in San Francisco retention done for this chapter, I measured the probability of retention for all providers and for new providers, defined as the probability that a worker is still providing home care after one year, as a function of the relative wage, controlling for the unemployment rate, being a family provider, hours worked, and an array of demographic variables, covering the period from 2001 through 2009. I found that the retention rate of all providers and new providers continues to be similar and very high, averaging about 82 percent for all providers until late 2005, when it begins to decline, and falling to 77 percent by November 2008 (fig. 4.2).[13] In a logistic regression analysis of retention as a function, again, of the relative wage, the unemployment rate, and controlling for whether the provider is caring for a relative, number of hours worked per month, gender, ethnicity, and a measure of the functional limitations of the consumer, I found that the

[13] The analysis using data for 2001–9 is not an update of the earlier analysis as I was not able to link the post-2001 data to the earlier dataset that spanned the period 1997–2002.

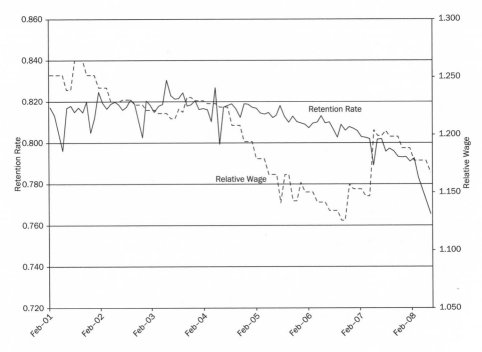

Figure 4.2   San Francisco retention rate and relative IHSS wage, 2001–2009.

relative wage had a statistically significant positive effect on retention. The model predicts that retention for all providers, holding all other variables at their mean, will be 76 percent when the relative wage is 0.8 and rise to 80 percent when the relative wage increases to 1.4.

Several other explanatory factors contributed to maintaining high retention rates, despite the decline of the IHSS wage relative to the 10th percentile wage. First, over the period of analysis, the percentage of family providers, who have substantially higher retention rates than nonfamily providers, has increased, in all likelihood because the wage is sufficient to justify substituting away from other jobs. Second, some ethnic groups have a substantially higher propensity to stay in the job, even controlling for whether or not they are family providers. In particular, the proportion of Chinese providers, who have higher than average retention rates, increased from 30 percent in 2001 to 39 percent by the end of 2009 while the share of white and African American providers, who have lower retention rates, declined. This change in composition contributed to keeping the retention rate high, even as the relative wage has declined.[14]

Howes (2004, 2005) provides evidence that San Francisco's IHSS health insurance policy, or policies similar to it in other counties, reduce turnover as well. But when counties limit enrollment by setting higher eligibility criteria or explicitly capping enrollment, there is no measurable effect of health insurance on turnover or retention. For example, in a cross-sectional study (Howes 2004), I estimated the determinants of turnover in all counties of California, as a function of wages and health insurance. Health insurance was measured as a categorical variable with three categories: "good" insurance, where providers were eligible if they worked as few as 25 to 35 hours per month and there were no caps on enrollment; "poor" health insurance, where enrollment was capped and the minimum monthly hours of work required for eligibility ranged from 80 to 100; and "no health insurance." I found that health insurance depressed turnover rates only in counties that had "good" health insurance policies. There was no measurable difference between having "poor" health insurance and no health insurance.

In the time-series and cross-sectional model I estimated (Howes 2009), using data from eight counties, I found that health insurance reduced turnover but, again, only in counties with "good" health insurance. Of the eight counties in the sample used to estimate the relative wage and health insurance elasticity of turnover, one county had a "good policy," three had a "poor policy," and three offered no health insurance. Enrollment as a percent of the workforce was below 20 percent in the counties with "poor" health insurance policies and as high as 66 percent in the county with a "good" policy. There was, again, no difference in the effect of health insurance in counties with "poor" and "no" policies. Only in the county with "good" health insurance, in which two-thirds of

[14] The IHSS caseload grew at a steady pace of 10 percent annually between 2001 and 2008 and then leveled off to about 1 percent a year. Therefore, changes in the rate of caseload growth do not explain trends in turnover.

providers were enrolled, was there a measurable effect on the average turnover rate.

What these studies suggest is that at least in this sector, the floor on wages and benefits that has been constructed in San Francisco as a consequence of unionizing the workforce and especially in a county that has systematically tried to improve the wages and benefits for all workers at the bottom of the income distribution has improved the quality of these jobs. Turnover, or retention, controlling for the effect of other influences beyond the immediate scope of county policies, such as unemployment, is the most direct measure of whether the jobs are better from the workers' perspective.

7. CONCLUSION

The intertwined history of compensation in the San Francisco IHSS program and the San Francisco mandates seems to suggest that IHSS paved the way, whether explicitly or not, for the San Francisco ordinances. Since the County Board of Supervisors was the decision-making entity in both cases, however, the similar outcomes were probably not accidental. Beginning with SEIU's unionization drive in the early 1990s, the passage of the San Francisco Public Authority ordinance in 1995, and the workers' vote to join SEIU 250 in spring 1996, there was a concerted effort to make IHSS jobs in San Francisco the best consumer-directed home care jobs in the country. San Francisco's mandates raised the floor on compensation for all workers with less than college educations in the city. As a consequence, individuals can now choose to work in IHSS, not because it is the best paid low-wage job in the city, and possibly the only one that offers health insurance, but rather because it is the kind of work they want to do. Turnover, the best metric, short of interviewing workers directly, to measure job satisfaction has remained low even as compensation in jobs requiring similar levels of education has risen relative to IHSS jobs.

Poor job quality in long-term care leads to poor care quality. As this chapter has argued, San Francisco's high road strategy offers a particularly high payoff in the rapidly growing care sector of the economy, especially in relatively poorly paid long-term care jobs. The labor process in these jobs is typically improved by development of long-term relationships among workers and between workers and care recipients. Better pay, benefits, and working conditions could help strengthen the intrinsic motivation that brings many into this field of employment, reducing turnover and mitigating worker burnout. Consumers and care recipients would benefit from resulting enhancements in care quality.

Once jobs move out of the institutions into the more informal setting of the home, the opportunity for developing a caring relationship increases, but other problems arise. Some institutional arrangements are better for simultaneously protecting the caring relationship between the worker and recipient and the labor rights of workers. With agency-based home care, workers are likely to be deployed to maximize the profit of the firm, without regard for how that affects the quality of the relationship between the consumer and the care worker. Consumer-directed care, on the other hand, puts consumers and workers in control of the care plan but at some risk that those workers' rights will not be enforced.

With third party intermediaries acting as the employer of record, workers are far more likely to see their rights enforced, including entitlement to contributions to the social security fund and to overtime and minimum wage payments. When consumer-directed workers can join unions, higher than average wages, higher levels of employer-provided health insurance, and much lower than average turnover rates have resulted. But when consumer direction and unionization are backed by broad local mandates that constrain competition over compensation within the low end of the wage distribution, workers have real choices.

One of the ironies of care work in the United States is that it has created opportunities for women and blacks to advance in professional care occupations where they can earn high wages. But this has been possible, in large part, because weak labor market regulations and open immigration policies have helped create an extremely low-wage labor market in which many women work in care jobs that release other women from performing household labor. San Francisco's experiment in raising the floor on labor standards at the bottom of the wage distribution provides a useful example of how public monies can be leveraged to solve some of the intractable problems of the low-wage work that cannot be addressed in the workplace alone, especially when the workplace is someone's home.

REFERENCES

Brannon, Diane, Teta Barry, Peter Kemper, Andrea Schreiner, and Joe Vasey. 2007. "Job Perceptions and Intent to Leave among Direct Care Workers: Evidence from the Better Jobs Better Care Demonstrations." *The Gerontologist* 47, 6: 820–29. doi:10.1093/geront/47.6.820.

Boris, Eileen, and Jennifer Klein. 2012. *Caring for America: Home Health Workers in the Shadow of the Welfare State.* New York: Oxford University Press.

Bureau of Labor Statistics (BLS). 2012. "January 2012 Employment Outlook: BLS Employment Matrix 2010–2020." www.bls.gov/emp/ep_table_203.htm; www.bls.gov/opub/mlr/2012/01/art4full.pdf.

California Association of Public Authorities (CAPA). Various dates. CAPA IHSS Wage Information. [Provided to author by Karen Keeslar, executive director of CAPA, 915 L St., Suite 1435, Sacramento, CA 95814.]

California Department of Social Services. Estimates Branch. 2011. "Caseload Projections: November Subvention." www.cdss.ca.gov/cdssweb/entres /localassistanceest/Jan12/Caseload.pdf. Accessed October 14, 2012.

California Department of Social Services. 2012. "State of California In-Home Supportive Services Management Statistics Summary, August. Run date: 9/10/2012." www.cdss.ca.gov/agedblinddisabled/res/MgmtStats /2012AugMgmtStats.pdf. Accessed October 13, 2012.

California Employment Development Department (EDD). 2012. OES Employment and Wages by Occupation. www.labormarketinfo.edd.ca.gov /Content.asp?pageid = 152. Accessed December 1, 2012.

California Health Care Foundation (CHCF). 2009. "County Programs for the Medically-Indigent in California." Fact Sheet, October. www .chcf.org/~/media/MEDIA%20LIBRARY%20Files/PDF/C/PDF%20 CountyIndigentPrograms.pdf. Accessed December 8, 2012.

California Welfare Institutions Code. Division 9, Part 3, Chapter 3, Article 7. "In-Home Supportive Services." Section 12300–12330. www.leginfo.ca.gov

/cgi-bin/displaycode?section = wic&group = 12001–13000&file = 12300–
12330. Accessed May 8, 2013.

Decker, Frederic H., Peter Gruhn, Lisa Matthews-Martin, K. Jeannine Dollard,
and Anthony M. Tucker. 2003. "Results of the 2002 AHCA Survey of Nursing
Staff Vacancy and Turnover in Nursing Homes." Health Services Research
and Evaluation, American Health Care Association, Feb. 12. www.ahcancal.
org/research_data/staffing/Documents/Vacancy_Turnover_Survey2002.
pdf. Accessed June 1, 2011.

Forhan, Lisa. 2010. "Summary of Comments Regarding Department of Labor
Proposed Amendments to 29CFR Part 552." Application of the Fair Labor
Standards Act to Domestic Service. Manuscript. Center for Public Policy and
Administration, University of Massachusetts, Amherst.

Gornick, Janet, Candace Howes, and Laura Braslow. 2012a. "Care Policy in the
United States." In For Love and Money: Care Provision in the U.S., ed. Nancy
Folbre, 112–39. New York: Russell Sage Foundation.

———. 2012b. "Care Policy across the States." In For Love and Money: Care
Provision in the U.S., ed. Nancy Folbre, 140–82. New York: Russell Sage
Foundation.

Gross, Jane. 2013. "The Long Wait for Wage Protections." New York Times, Apr.
30. http://newoldage.blogs.nytimes.com/2013/04/30/the-long-wait-for-
wage-protections/?hp. Accessed May 6, 2013.

Harrington, Charlene, Terence Ng, Stephen H. Kaye, and Robert Newcomer.
2009. "Home and Community-based Services: Public Policies to Improve
Access, Costs, and Quality." UCSF, PAS, January. www.pascenter.org/docu-
ments/PASCenter_HCBS_policy_brief.pdf. Accessed Feb. 3, 2010.

Healthy San Francisco. www.healthysanfrancisco.org.

Hewitt, Amy, and K. Charley Lakin. 2001. "Issues in the Direct Support
Workforce and Their Connections to the Growth, Sustainability and Quality
of Community Supports." A Technical Assistance Paper of the National
Project: Self-Determination for People with Developmental Disabilities, May.
Minneapolis, MN: University of Minnesota, Research and Training Center
on Community Living. http://rtc.umn.edu/docs/hcfa.pdf. Accessed Feb.
21, 2012.

Hewitt, Amy S., and Sheryl A. Larson. 2007. "The Direct Service Workforce in
Community Supports to Individuals with Developmental Disabilities:
Issues, Implications, and Promising Practices." Mental Retardation and
Developmental Disabilities Research Reviews 13: 178–87.

Howes, Candace. 2002. The Impact of a Large Wage Increase on the Workforce
Stability of IHSS Home Care Workers in San Francisco County. Berkeley:
University of California, Berkeley, Labor Center. http://laborcenter.berkeley.
edu/homecare/Howes.pdf. Accessed Aug. 5, 2004.

———. 2004. "Upgrading California's Home Care Workforce: The Impact of Political Action and Unionization." *The State of California Labor* 4:71–105. Accessed May 21, 2011. http://www.irle.ucla.edu/research/scl/2004.html.

———. 2005. "Living Wages and Retention of Homecare Workers in San Francisco." *Industrial Relations* 44, 1: 139–63.

———. 2008. "For Love, Money or Flexibility: Why People Choose to Work in Consumer-Directed Homecare." *The Gerontologist* 48, Special Issue 1: 46–59.

———. 2009. "Declaration of Candace Howes." In Martinez v Schwarzenegger, N.D. Cal. Case No. C 09–02306 CW, June 4.

———. 2010. "The Best and Worst State Practices in Medicaid Long-term Care." Policy Brief No. 3, Direct Care Alliance. Apr. 2010. Accessed May 21, 2011. http://blog.directcarealliance.org/wp-content/uploads/2010/03/Howes-Medicaid-Policy-Brief_final.pdf.

———. 2011. "Homecare Workers and the Immigrant Workforce in the U.S." Paper presented at the Feminist Economics Workshop on Migrant Labor, Bilbao, Spain, Mar. 11–12, Department of Economics, Connecticut College.

———. 2012. "Wages, Unemployment, and Turnover among Family and Non-Family Homecare Providers." Paper presented at the Gerontological Society of America Annual Meeting, San Diego, CA, Nov. 15.'

Howes, Candace, Carrie Leana, and Kristin Smith. 2012. "The Care Workforce." In *For Love and Money: Care Provision in the U.S.*, ed. Nancy Folbre, 65–91. New York: Russell Sage Foundation.

IOM (Institute of Medicine). 2008. *Retooling for an Aging America: Building the Health Care Workforce*. Committee on the Future Health Care Workforce for Older Americans, Institute of Medicine. www.nap.edu/catalog/12089.html. Accessed May 2, 2010.

Katz, Michael, and Tangerine Brigham. 2011. "Transforming a Traditional Safety Net into a Coordinated Care System: Lessons from Healthy San Francisco." *Health Affairs* 30, 2: 237–45. doi:10.1377/hlthaff.2010.0003.

Kaye, H. Stephen, Susan Chapman, Robert J. Newcomer, and Charlene Harrington. 2006. "The Personal Assistance Workforce: Trends in Supply and Demand." *Health Affairs* 25, 4: 1113–20.

Kaye, H. Stephen, Charlene Harrington, and Mitchell P. LaPlante. 2010. "Long-Term Care: Who Gets It, Who Provides It, Who Pays and How Much?" *Health Affairs* 29, 1: 11–21.

Leon, J., J. Marainen, and J. Marcotte. 2001. "Pennsylvania's Frontline Workers in Long Term Care: The Provider Organization Perspective: A Report to the Intergovernmental Council on Long Term Care." Polisher Research Institute at the Philadelphia Geriatric Center, Philadelphia, PA.

Maas, Meridean, and Kathleen Buckwalter. 2006. "Providing Quality Care in Assisted Living Facilities: Recommendations for Enhanced Staffing and Staff Training." *Journal of Gerontological Nursing* 32, 11:14–22.

Morris, Lisa. 2009. "Quits and Job Changes among Home Care Workers in Maine." *The Gerontologist* 49, 5: 635–50.

NDSWRC (National Direct Service Workforce Resource Center). 2008. "A Synthesis of Direct Service Workforce Demographics and Challenges across Intellectual/Developmental Disabilities, Aging, Physical Disabilities and Behavioral Health," by Amy Hewitt, Sheryl Larson, Steve Edelstein, Dorie Seavey, Michael A. Hoge, and John Morris. http://rtc.umn.edu/docs/Cross-DisabilitySynthesisWhitePaperFinal.pdf. Accessed Jan. 11, 2010.

PHI and DCWANC (Direct Care Workers Association of North Carolina). 2009. *The 2007 National Survey of State Initiatives on the Direct Care Workforce: Key Findings.* December. http://directcareclearinghouse.org/l_art_det.jsp?res_id=297910. Accessed Apr. 3, 2010.

PHI. Facts 3. 2010. "Who Are Direct Care Workers? February Update." www.directcareclearinghouse.org/download/NCDCW%20Fact%20Sheet-1.pdf. Accessed May 15, 2010.

RTZ Associates. 2005. *The State of IHSS Health Benefits in California: A Survey of Counties.* Rtzassociates.com.

San Francisco Administrative Code, Section 70.11. www.amlegal.com/nxt/gateway.dll/California/administrative/administrativecode?f=templates$fn=default.htm$3.0$vid=amlegal:sanfrancisco_ca$sync=1.

San Francisco Health Plan. www.sfhp.org/.

San Francisco In-Home Supportive Services (IHSS) Public Authority. www.sfihsspa.org/content.asp?CT=6&CC=0.

San Francisco Living Wage Coalition. www.livingwage-sf.org/summary-of-wages-and-benefit-laws/summary-of-wage-and-benefit-laws.html.

The Scan Foundation. 2012. "California's Coordinated Care Initiative: Background and Overview: Fact Sheet." www.thescanfoundation.org/sites/thescanfoundation.org/files/ca_coordinatedcareinitiative_sep2012_fs_0.pdf. Accessed Oct. 13, 2012.

Seavey, Dorie. 2004. "The Cost of Frontline Turnover in Long-Term Care." In *A Better Jobs, Better Care Practice and Policy Report.* Washington DC: Institute for Aging Services, American Association of Homes and Services for the Aging. www.directcareclearinghouse.org/download/TOCostReport.pdf. Accessed Feb. 17, 2012.

Seavey, Dorie, and Abby Marquand. 2011. "Caring in America: A Comprehensive Analysis of the Nation's Fastest Growing Jobs—Home Health and Personal Care Aides." PHI National, New York. www.directcareclearinghouse.org/download/caringinamerica-20111212.pdf. Accessed Feb. 20, 2012.

SEIU-UHW West Collective Bargaining Agreement with SF Public Authority. www.sfihsspa.org/documents/3686487.pdf.

Smith, Peggie R. 2008. "The Publicization of Home-Based Care Work in State Labor Law." *Minnesota Law Review* 92: 1390–1423.

Spillman, Brenda, and Kirsten Black. 2008. "The Size of the Long-Term Care Population in Residential Care: A Review of Estimates and Methodology." Urban Institute, Washington DC. www.urban.org/health_policy/url. cfm?ID=1001202. Accessed May 25, 2011.

U.S. Department of Labor. Wage and Hour Division. (USDOL/WHD) 2013. "29 CFR Part 552. Application of the Fair Labor Standards Act to Domestic Service; Final Rule." *Federal Register*, 78 (190):60454-557. Tuesday, October 1. Accessed Oct. 21, 2013 at http://webapps.dol.gov/FederalRegister/ PdfDisplay.aspx?DocId=27104.

PART TWO   The Benefit Mandates

FIVE Health Spending Requirements in San Francisco

Carrie H. Colla, William H. Dow, and Arindrajit Dube

1. INTRODUCTION

In 2006, San Francisco adopted a major health care reform and became the first city in the United States to implement a pay-or-play employer health-spending mandate. It also created Healthy San Francisco, a "public option" to promote affordable universal access to care. In this chapter,

*Portions of this chapter are based on or appeared in the following articles: Carrie H. Colla, William H. Dow, et al., "How Do Employers React to a Pay-or-Play Mandate? Early Evidence from San Francisco," *Forum for Health Economics & Policy* 14, 2 (2011): 1–43, www.degruyter.com/view/j/fhep; Carrie H. Colla, William H. Dow, et al., "The Labor Market Impact of Employer Health Benefit Mandates: Evidence from San Francisco's Health Care Security Ordinance" (2011), www.nber.org/papers/w17198; Carrie H. Colla, William H. Dow, et al., "San Francisco's 'Pay or Play' Employer Mandate Expanded Private Coverage by Local Firms and a Public Care Program," *Health Affairs* 32, 1 (2013): 169–77.

we examine the effects of this mandate on employers, costs, earnings, and employees. To examine the effects of the Health Care Security Ordinance (HCSO) on health care benefits we use the Bay Area Employer Health Benefits Survey; and to investigate the effect of the HCSO on jobs and wages, we use the Quarterly Census of Employment and Wages (QCEW). We find that most employers (76 percent) had to increase health spending to comply with the law, yet most (61 percent) are supportive of the law. There is substantial employer demand for the public option, with 18 percent of firms using Healthy San Francisco for at least some employees, yet there is little evidence of firms dropping existing insurance offerings in the first year after implementation. To date, the health-spending requirement has had little discernible impact on employment or earnings in affected sectors. We do find, however, that part of the increased cost was passed on to consumers through surcharges.

Our chapter proceeds as follows. We start with a description of the law itself and its place in the context of broader health care reform. Next we lay out the conceptual framework that informs our research. Following this, we describe our data and methods and report our results. In the conclusion we discuss lessons for other jurisdictions.

On July 18, 2006, San Francisco substantially expanded efforts to achieve universal health care coverage in the city by passing the Health Care Security Ordinance into law. Part of this reform was a pay-or-play type of minimum employer health spending requirement. This requirement, which became effective in 2008, covers all private sector employers hiring twenty or more workers. Employers can meet their spending requirement by providing insurance to workers, by paying into Health Savings Accounts (HSAs) or Health Reimbursement Accounts (HRAs), or by paying into the public Healthy San Francisco program.

Operated by the San Francisco Department of Public Health, Healthy San Francisco was launched in July 2007 and offers affordable access at select public and private facilities within the city of San Francisco for uninsured San Francisco residents. It constitutes a low-cost health access plan that strengthens the safety net and provides a public "pay" option for employers to fulfill their health spending requirement. Although this public option is not formally considered insurance, it is tantamount to a generous public insurance policy, with the significant caveat that it is restricted to a network of providers located only within San Francisco (Katz 2008; Katz and Brigham 2011).

The HCSO is similar to pay-or-play mandates that have been widely discussed in the context of national- and state-level health reform debates. In 2013, the employer spending requirement in San Francisco amounts to about $4,846 annually for a full-time employee in a large firm, up from $3,633 in 2008. This is a relatively stringent requirement; according to the 2012 Kaiser/HRET Employer Health Benefit Survey, premiums for single coverage averaged $5,615 in 2012.

Employer health insurance mandates have garnered increasing attention as Massachusetts implemented state-level health reform and then the federal health insurance reform was enacted, which also included a variant of a pay-or-play employer mandate. Hawaii also has a mandate for firms to provide health insurance, in place since the 1970s. There are many unresolved questions as to how employer mandates perform in practice and little evidence to inform debates about their potential effects, particularly at the employer level. When given different compliance options, which do employers most commonly choose? If one of these options is paying into a public program, how many and what type of employers opt to "pay" into a public plan, as opposed to "play," that is, meet the spending requirement by providing employees with insurance or health accounts? To what extent do employers support such mandates? What are the effects on wages and employment? Using the unique policy innovation implemented in San Francisco, we provide initial evidence on these questions.

The San Francisco reforms offer an unusual opportunity to advance our understanding of the effects of these types of reforms. First, the surrounding Bay Area counties offer natural comparison groups that allow for a stronger research design than has been possible for Hawaii and Massachusetts. Second, the nature of the policy allows us to address questions that were not possible to answer using either or both of the other policy interventions. For example, the use of a public plan in the pay option in San Francisco allows us to evaluate demand for a kind of public option. Third, given the minimal nature of the fee paid by nonoffering employers in Massachusetts, inferences from that state may be difficult to generalize to more stringent pay-or-play mandates such as those under the federal reform. Fourth, we can address questions for which there is little evidence: how employers change their health plans in response to a mandate, how employers choose to comply with a mandate, the role of Health Reimbursement Accounts and Health Savings Accounts, and the effects of the mandate on wages and employment.

The San Francisco Health Care Security Ordinance

The HCSO took effect on January 9, 2008, first covering for-profit employers with 50 or more employees. For-profit employers with 20 to 49 employees and nonprofit employers with 50 or more employees were subject to the mandate beginning on April 1, 2008. Although San Francisco adopted the ordinance in 2006, the HCSO was challenged under the Employee Retirement Income Security Act (ERISA) by the Golden Gate Restaurant Association. Court challenges were not resolved until June 2010, when the Supreme Court rejected a request to review the ordinance.

The employer spending requirement varies by employer size and profit status. In 2008, the ordinance required employers in San Francisco with 20 to 99 workers nationwide to meet a minimum spending requirement of $1.17 per hour for health care services for each worker. Employers with 100 or more workers nationwide were required to spend $1.76 per hour per worker. These rates have grown annually; in 2013, these rates were $1.55 per hour for employers with 20 to 99 employees and $2.33 for firms with 100 or more employees. For-profit employers with fewer than 20 employees and nonprofit employers with fewer than 50 employees are exempt from the spending requirement (about 25 percent of San Francisco workers at for-profit firms are employed at exempt firms).[1] There are no specific requirements to provide health benefits to family members. The HCSO specifies that employers must spend this minimum

---

[1] Author calculations from Dun and Bradstreet database, provided by Survey Sampling, Inc.

amount not as an average percent of payroll but rather for each and every nonexempt employee.

Employers may choose to spend the funds on a third-party health provider (including medical, dental, and vision insurance), reimburse employees directly for their health expenses, create Health Savings or Health Reimbursement Accounts, or pay the funds to the City for their employees' access to health care through participation in Healthy San Francisco. Some limited classes of workers are exempt from the mandate: managerial, supervisory, and confidential employees who earn over $84,051 per year, employees who are eligible for Medicare and/or CHAMPUS/TRICARE, and employees working less than eight hours per week. Finally, workers who verify that they receive dependent coverage from another employer may opt out voluntarily.

Healthy San Francisco

Healthy San Francisco encourages access to primary and preventive care by providing a medical home (a team of providers in one location that coordinates care for a patient across the continuum) and a primary physician to each program participant, as well as specialty care, urgent and emergency care, laboratory services, in-patient hospitalization, radiology, and pharmaceuticals. Quarterly program participation fees range from $0 to $450 on a sliding scale and are community rated. Employees at firms who choose to contribute to the City option, Healthy San Francisco, receive a 75 percent discount on these program participation fees if they qualify for Healthy San Francisco. San Francisco residents with an income at or below 500 percent of the federal poverty level (for one person, $55,860; for a family of four, $115,260) are eligible to enroll in Healthy San Francisco as long as they have been uninsured for ninety days, are between the ages of eighteen and sixty-four, and are not eligible for other public programs. Healthy San Francisco is free if an enrollee is below 300 percent of the federal poverty line and his or her employer contributes to the program. Employees must themselves enroll in Healthy San Francisco after the employer makes a contribution on their behalf, but they can enroll at any time and often enroll only when they seek care (Healthy San Francisco 2010).

2.   CONCEPTUAL FRAMEWORK

Under the HCSO, firms must decide whether to continue or to start to offer private health benefits, pay into the public plan, or pay into an HRA. In a competitive labor market with profit-maximizing firms, if the value employees place on health insurance is equivalent to the employers' costs of providing insurance, we would expect employers to shift the cost of the mandate to employees in the form of lowered wages (Rosen 1986). If, however, employees are near minimum wage or firms have other institutional constraints such as union rules or norms, then it may not be possible for wages to adjust in the short run (Baicker and Chandra 2006). Instead, employers may reduce the number of workers or their hours, or where possible they may pass on the costs to consumers in the form of higher prices.

Pay-or-Play Decision

When there is no mandate to provide coverage, an employer is expected to offer a private benefit package if the sum of the value that employees in the firm place on this benefit package is greater than the cost to the employer offering the benefit. Under a pay-or-play mandate with a per-hour spending requirement, the choice becomes whether to offer private coverage or to pay into the public option, Healthy San Francisco. Theory predicts that firms hiring workers with weak preferences for private health insurance and firms whose costs of providing coverage are higher will be less likely to offer private health benefits.

Among firms that choose to offer private coverage, the high spending requirement implies that insurance policies may be more generous than in the absence of the mandate, with less employee cost-sharing (thus lower employee-paid premiums, deductibles, etc.). Note that in the San Francisco case, the health spending requirement is based on the number of hours each employee works rather than a fixed cost. Since private health benefits usually have some fixed costs, in many cases it may be cost-minimizing for firms to pay into Healthy San Francisco. Historically, the firms least likely to offer coverage or other benefits are those with fewer employees, lower-wage workforces, greater turnover, no unions, and a large proportion of part-time employees (Gabel, Claxton, et al. 2003). Employers are more likely to offer private benefits and to make greater contributions in communities with tighter labor markets, less concentrated labor purchasers, greater union penetration, and a greater share of workers in large firms and a small share in regulated industries (Marquis and Long 2001).

Crowd-Out

Under an employer mandate with a public option, some firms may choose to drop their private coverage policies if they feel that the public option and private coverage are substitutes to employees and the public option is less expensive (Cutler and Gruber 1996). In this case, Healthy San Francisco and private health insurance are not likely to be perceived as substitutes: Healthy San Francisco has a limited provider network, there may be stigma associated with public programs, enrollment may be perceived as difficult, and Healthy San Francisco may be perceived as temporary or not meeting standards under the new federal law. In addition, enrollees must be uninsured for ninety days to be eligible for Healthy San Francisco.

All of these factors may reduce the value of the public option to employees. Healthy San Francisco premiums are community rated, so firms with higher risk profiles may find significant cost savings in Healthy San Francisco compared to the private market. Workers in these categories may place higher value on Healthy San Francisco benefits, and firms with more part-time, low-wage, or high-risk employees may be more likely to choose the public option. However, due to the considerations above, along with the rule that residents must be uninsured for ninety days to be eligible for Healthy San Francisco, we do not expect many workers who have the option of private insurance to drop it in favor of Healthy San Francisco.

Health Reimbursement Accounts

In addition to traditional private insurance and Healthy San Francisco, employers have the option of putting the required funds in a Health Reimbursement Account for the employee. HRAs are attractive to employers because the employer owns the account and, until 2012, the employer could take back unused funds at the end of the year or upon termination of employment (after 2012 contributions must remain available to the employee for twenty-four months from the date of contribution). Anecdotally, benefits consultants in San Francisco have suggested to businesses that HRAs may be the lowest-cost strategy for meeting the requirement; thus it is of interest to measure how commonly this strategy was adopted.

Effects on Wages and Employment

Economic theory and previous research suggest that in demographically identifiable groups who value a benefit at its cost, the incidence of a mandate is likely to affect workers through reductions in wages or jobs (Summers 1989; Gruber 1994). Wage adjustment and employment effects hinge on employee valuation of the benefit and features of the labor market, such as the minimum wage or collective bargaining agreements. In addition to being of interest at a theoretical level, the impact of an employer mandate to provide health benefits has policy relevance, as the likely effect of the Affordable Care Act on jobs has been politically controversial (Pear 2011).

The presence of a citywide minimum wage law in San Francisco—$10.24 in 2012—suggests that wages may not be able to adjust easily to compensate for the employer health spending requirement. The employer spending requirement in San Francisco amounts to about $3,224 annually for a full-time employee in a medium-size firm (20–99 employees) and $4,846 annually for a full-time employee in a large firm (≥100 employees). This requirement thus represents a substantial increase in compensation today: 15 percent for a minimum wage worker in a medium-size firm and 23 percent for a minimum wage worker in a large firm. However, it is illegal for employers to explicitly lower wages due to the Health Care Security Ordinance (SF DPH and OLSE 2010). In addition, all employers in San Francisco must provide paid sick leave to each employee. If workers' productivity does not equal the minimum wage plus the cost of benefits, including health insurance and paid sick leave benefits, these workers risk becoming unemployed or having their hours reduced (Bundorf 2002). While we may not expect nominal wages to fall among previously employed workers (Kahn 1997), in a competitive market the real wage could fall over time through slower wage growth for the existing workforce and lower wages for new employees.

To the extent that workers do not value the benefit at its cost or if the minimum wage is binding, the entire cost of the benefit will not be passed through to wages. Employees must themselves enroll in Healthy San Francisco after the employer makes a contribution on their behalf. If the employee does not enroll or does not attribute the reduced participation fees to the employer, they will not perceive any value from the benefit, and employers will be less able to pass on any of the costs to wages. Evidence through 2010 indicates that among employees whose employers are paying into the program on their behalf, 32 percent were not yet receiving Healthy San Francisco benefits (SF DPH and OLSE 2010).

At the minimum wage, the joint (employer and employee) surplus from paying into the City option is positive for most workers, due to the subsidies up to 300 percent of the federal poverty limit. For higher-wage workers, increased program fees make the subsidy smaller. Therefore, we might expect the largest amount of wage pass-through to occur for jobs paying somewhat higher than the minimum wage. If a wage adjustment is not sufficient to offset the cost of the spending mandate, employers may reduce the number of employees or work hours, though the latter is less likely due to fixed employment costs. Thus, neoclassical economic theory predicts some combination of slower wage growth and decreased employment.

Effects on Consumer Prices

Finally, in local service industries like restaurants, firms may be able to pass the additional labor costs on to consumers through price increases.

The ability of restaurants to pass through additional costs to consumers depends partly on how much the demand for restaurants changes when prices increase—that is, the price elasticity of demand for restaurants. Given transportation costs, driving outside of the city to buy a restaurant meal or to go to the grocery store is not a sensible decision for many consumers facing a moderate increase in meal price. Such transaction costs allow some prices in San Francisco to rise in response to the mandate.

3. STUDY DATA AND METHODS

To examine the effects of the HCSO on health care benefits we use the Bay Area Employer Health Benefits Survey, conducted in 2008 by the University of California, Berkeley. National Research, LLC, was contracted to conduct telephone interviews with employee benefit managers from 526 for-profit San Francisco firms with more than twenty employees and 310 for-profit firms with more than twenty employees from areas surrounding San Francisco to serve as a control group. Firms were asked about their health benefit offerings in 2007 before the employer spending requirement went into effect, in addition to 2008 changes in benefits, in order to measure both baseline offerings and post-implementation changes. The details of the survey and means of our sample groups are described in prior work (Colla, Dow, et al. 2011a).

This survey enables us to categorize firms based on the change they would have to make to their health benefit spending to comply with HCSO. To calculate how many employees would need to be offered new coverage and how many would need to have their coverage increased, we estimate the proportion of workers exempt due to being part-time or new employees, the number of employees not taking up offered insurance, and the average payment for health benefits across those with existing plans. The "contribution gap" is based on the difference between post-HCSO mandated spending levels and pre-HCSO reported employer total health benefit spending in 2007. The construction of these measures is described in greater detail in prior work (Colla, Dow, et al. 2011a).

A different set of analyses examines various strategies that San Francisco firms have reported adopting by 2008 or are highly likely to adopt for 2009. These include the proportion contributing to the Healthy San Francisco public option, the proportion expanding private coverage in various dimensions, and the proportion contracting private coverage. To investigate the extent to which health benefit changes were likely caused by HCSO and did not reflect other local trends, we next report regression-adjusted comparisons of health benefit changes in San Francisco firms compared to similar firms in surrounding Bay Area counties not subject to the HCSO mandate using a difference-in-difference framework. This method controls for common trends in the local area (i.e., San Francisco and adjacent counties) and trends that vary by firm characteristics. Existing research shows that this type of local comparison produces a valid counterfactual (Holmes 1998; Dube, Lester, et al. 2010). Migration from more regulated to less regulated counties takes time to plan and so is unlikely to bias our sample in this initial year following implementation. Moreover, analysis of the National Establishment Time Series (NETS) database shows that only 0.4 percent of firms left San Francisco in 2008 to relocate to another county, so this phenomenon would not be expected to affect our results.

In order to investigate the effect of the HCSO on jobs and wages, we use the Quarterly Census of Employment and Wages, which is a near census of the working population. We compare employment and weekly earnings trends in San Francisco to those of neighboring counties and to other large metropolitan statistical areas (MSAs) in the United States that did not implement any comparable new employer mandate. We term San Francisco the "center" county and used data on four "periphery" counties surrounding San Francisco as a local control group (Alameda, Contra Costa, Marin, and San Mateo Counties). We similarly constructed center and periphery counties in other comparable MSAs based on Core Based Statistical Area (CBSA) definitions for the twenty-five largest MSAs in the United States. We chose to use the twenty-five largest MSAs because San Francisco is the thirteenth largest in the country, producing an equal number of MSAs in the sample that are larger and smaller than San Francisco. We define a "center county" as one that encompasses the urban center of the MSA. A list of MSAs, the number of counties by MSA, and definitions of the center counties can be found in previous work (Colla, Dow et al. 2011b).

Our two primary outcome measures are total employment and average earnings. The earnings measure is the average rate of weekly pay for workers by industry. The QCEW does not report hours worked. However, we can partly address the possibility of an hour reduction, such as that claimed by the Golden Gate Restaurant Association (Mandelbaum 2009), by examining weekly earnings. In order to account for trends in the housing industry in different areas, we control for median housing price and housing sales, contemporaneously and lagged one year, using data purchased from Dataquick. We also use population data from the U.S. Census. We control for the relevant county-level minimum wage, based on national, state, and local minimum wage data from the Department of Labor. This helps us identify the San Francisco mandate effects separately from minimum wage changes.

Finally, we asked all firms in the 2009 Bay Area Employer Health Benefits Survey whether customers have to pay a price surcharge specifically attributed to health benefits. We interviewed an additional sample of 217 restaurants (64 percent response rate) by telephone in 2009 and 2010 to quantify the prevalence and magnitude of health-specific surcharges.

4.   RESULTS

Baseline Insurance Benefit Offering in San Francisco

Prior to the enactment of HCSO, most targeted firms already were offering health benefits to some employees but not to all employees covered by the mandate. In San Francisco, 92 percent of firms with twenty or more employees offered health insurance to some employees in 2007 before the employer mandate was implemented, though this finding differed somewhat by firm size (fig. 5.1). These statistics are similar to national averages: 91 percent of U.S. firms with twenty or more employees offer health benefits, and the rate rises to 93 percent if we limit the sample to this size group in urban areas (Kaiser Family Foundation and Health Research & Educational Trust 2008). Among firms in San Francisco, restaurants were

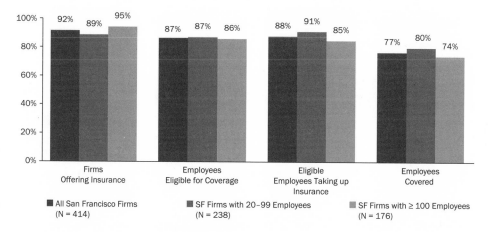

Figure 5.1   Health benefit statistics, 2007.
SOURCE: 2008 Bay Area Employer Health Benefits Survey.

significantly less likely to offer health benefits at baseline, as were smaller firms with twenty to fifty employees. Firms with unionized workers were significantly more likely to offer health benefits.

After adjusting for firm characteristics, the offer rate for San Francisco firms with twenty or more workers was statistically similar to that of comparison firms outside of San Francisco (94 percent overall) but greater than the offer rate in small San Francisco firms not subject to the mandate (80 percent).

As mentioned above, the mandate is per each worker in the firm. Thus, while most firms offered insurance to some employees, initial eligibility and take-up rates are also important for measuring how binding the policy was for affected firms. In San Francisco firms that offered insurance, about 87 percent of workers were eligible for benefits (82 percent in comparison firms, difference not significant after controlling for firm characteristics). Due to other forms of coverage or coverage refusal, 88 percent of eligible employees in San Francisco took up coverage (82 percent in comparison firms). This resulted in coverage for 77 percent of employees in San Francisco firms that offered health benefits (69 percent in comparison firms outside the city). On average, San Francisco firms required a minimum of 29.6 hours of work per week to qualify for

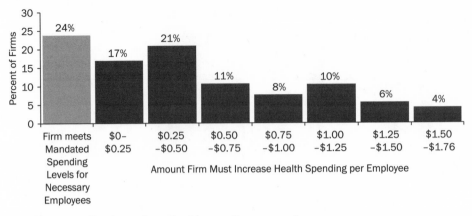

Figure 5.2   Gap in employer health spending per employee.
SOURCE: 2008 Bay Area Employer Health Benefits Survey.

benefits in 2007. Under the first year of implementation of the HCSO, any employee who worked ten hours per week or more on average needed to be paid health benefits. In 2009, workers who worked less than eight hours per week on average were exempt.

Baseline Offering and Spending Gaps Relative to Mandate

Many plans offered in San Francisco at baseline did not meet the minimum health spending requirements of the mandate. Figure 5.2 shows our measure of the gap in health care spending for San Francisco firms at baseline before HCSO went into effect—based on eligibility, coverage, and enrollment-weighted payments for health benefits across all plans the firms offer. At baseline, about 56 percent of firms were in compliance with eligibility requirements, 33 percent were in compliance with coverage requirements, and 24 percent were in compliance with coverage and spending requirements. The gap figure describes how much an employer needs to pay in addition to 2007 spending per worker-hour after the mandate assuming that the employer keeps existing plans in place and there is no redistribution from more generous plans to less generous plans.[2]

_____

[2] The estimate of 24 percent in compliance relies on several assumptions. If we assumed that half of the workers hired in the past year were hired in the past ninety days and all of

Firms with more low-wage, part-time (nonexempt), and temporary workers and smaller firms were significantly more likely to have gaps in eligibility, coverage, and generosity of benefits (as measured by the gap in per worker-hour spending at baseline). San Francisco restaurants were also more likely to have gaps in benefits, conditional on other covariates.

Changes in Health Benefits in San Francisco after Mandate Implementation (2008)

San Francisco firms used a variety of strategies to comply with the mandate (fig. 5.3). About 18 percent of firms paid into Healthy San Francisco, about one-third of which also reported some other benefit change as well. Many of the firms who made a change to their health benefits did so by adding a new health insurance offering (29 percent). The new health insurance offering might include a Health Reimbursement Account (14 percent), a new high deductible health plan (10 percent), or a mini-medical plan (10 percent). Although not shown in the figure, all of these changes were statistically significant at least at the 10 percent level. A mini-medical plan is a limited benefit plan with a very low maximum annual payout (often $10,000 or less). These plans often pay for a fixed number of physician visits, lab tests, or prescription drugs but do not offer any insurance against catastrophic events (Fuhrmans 2006). In San Francisco, some employers were setting up plans to just meet the health spending requirement.

Figure 5.3 shows the overall proportion of San Francisco firms adopting each strategy, along with the proportions among the least impacted (those who were already in compliance at baseline according to our best point estimate), the most impacted (those with a spending gap of at least $0.50 per worker) and low-wage firms (those firms who have employees earning under $10 per hour). Those most heavily affected by the HCSO

---

those who were eligible for insurance in 2007 but did not take up benefits sign voluntary waivers, then the estimate would rise to 43 percent. Alternatively, baseline compliance would have been estimated as low as 18 percent if we assumed every employee needed to be covered under the health spending requirement (i.e., assuming no part-time or new employees and no waivers).

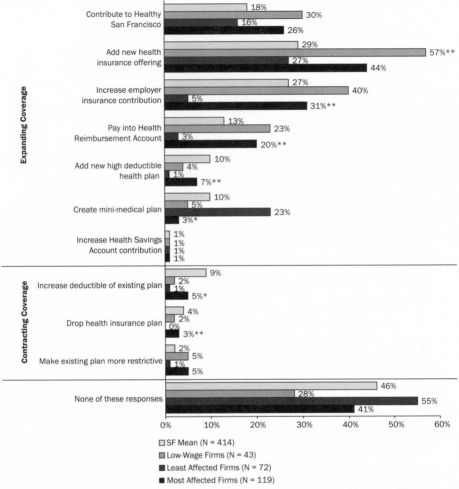

For the low-wage firms and most affted firms **,* indicates a significant difference between this category of firms and the rest of the smaple at the 5% and 10% levels, respectively.

Figure 5.3   San Francisco employer responses to HCSO.

were significantly more likely to create a new high deductible plan (7 percent), pay into an HRA (20 percent) or increase the employer insurance contribution (31 percent) than the least affected firms. Low-wage firms were significantly more likely to add a new health insurance offering (57 percent) than other firms.

The demand for Healthy San Francisco has been significant, with about one-fifth of firms paying into this public option for at least some employees in 2008. Of San Francisco firms in our 2008 sample, 18.3 percent responded that they were paying into Healthy San Francisco for their employees. A large majority (92 percent) of those contributing to Healthy San Francisco paid into the program for only some of their employees, not all employees. This evidence suggests that employers were using the Healthy San Francisco public option for workers who are not eligible or taking up coverage at baseline. Only 8 percent of employers who contributed to Healthy San Francisco in 2008 did so for all of their workers. This proportion remained consistent in the 2009 Bay Area Employer Health Benefits Survey (22 percent).

Administrative estimates of public option demand are quite similar to our survey-based estimates: as of August 2008, 950 employers had elected to pay into the public option, about 20 percent of the approximately 4,500 total covered employers (Healthy San Francisco 2008; U.S. Census Bureau 2008). The 2008 HCSO Annual Reporting Form, which businesses are required to submit, indicates that 20.5 percent of firms contributed to Healthy San Francisco for at least some employees in the fourth quarter of 2008, remarkably close to our survey-based estimates.

To analyze more systematically the determinants of the pay-or-play decision, we use a set of firm characteristics to estimate a probit model of whether the firm contributes to Healthy San Francisco (results reported in Colla, Dow, et al. 2011a). Firms with low-wage workers (those earning less than $10/hour) and firms with more temporary workers were more likely to contribute to Healthy San Francisco. Perhaps surprisingly, conditional on other characteristics, smaller firms (firms with 20–50 and 50–100 employees) were less likely to use the public option to meet the mandate. We extend two possible explanations for this phenomenon. First, the odds of a firm deciding to put at least one worker on Health San Francisco rise with firm size. Second, smaller firms were more likely to have to redesign their benefits package substantially; larger firms may have been close enough to their "optimal plan" that they put the remaining workers on the public plan.

Comparison of Changes in Health Benefits with Neighboring Counties

Table 5.1 reports regression-adjusted estimates of the effect of the Health Care Security Ordinance on new insurance offering among baseline nonofferers. Firms in San Francisco were 33 percentage points more likely to report that they planned to begin offering insurance in 2008 compared to Bay Area firms not subject to the HCSO, a statistically significant difference. About half of nonoffering firms subject to the mandate reported that they were likely to begin offering insurance after the 2008 implementation of the mandate, as opposed to 8 percent of comparison firms (but the sample size is small, with only forty-two nonoffering firms). The difference among low-wage firms was even more dramatic, with low-wage San Francisco firms 51 percentage points more likely to begin offering insurance than their low-wage counterparts in the Bay Area.

San Francisco firms were also significantly more likely than their Bay Area counterparts to begin offering an HRA after the mandate. HRAs are attractive to employers because (a) employers can deposit the exact amount of the mandate for each worker into the account and (b) the employer owns the account and until 2012 could take back unused funds at the end of the year or upon termination of employment. Further, employees who live outside San Francisco are not eligible for Healthy San Francisco, which makes HRAs more attractive from their perspective. After adjusting for firm characteristics, firms subject to the mandate were more likely to offer a new HRA in 2008 (13 percent of San Francisco firms, as opposed to 5 percent of Bay Area firms). In the group most affected by the HCSO, 21 percent more firms in San Francisco planned to begin offering an HRA; among low-wage firms only, the gap

Table 5.1   Effect of Mandate on Health Benefits (%)

2008 Health Benefit Change	Full Sample			Low-Wage Firms	Most Affected Firms
	SAN FRANCISCO	REGRESSION-ADJUSTED COMPARISONS	DIFFERENCE (SE)	DIFFERENCE (SE)	DIFFERENCE (SE)
Plan to start offering insurance (of firms currently not offering)	41.72	8.46	33.25* (17.95)	50.53* (25.21)	33.25* (17.95)
New Health Reimbursement Account (among firms that did not offer an HRA in 2007)	12.77	4.90	7.87* (4.02)	20.04** (9.62)	20.64** (7.00)
Reduced some health benefits (includes increasing employee premium, raising deductible, dropping coverage, or restricting benefits).	10.57	17.48	-6.91* (3.82)	-25.98** (10.82)	3.35 (9.09)

*,** Indicates significance at the 5% and 10% level respectively using heteroskedasticity-robust SEs. Firms are low-wage if they have workers earning <$10/hour. Most affected group includes firms with a spending gap of ≥$0.50 per worker.

SOURCE: 2008 Bay Area Employer Health Benefits Survey.

NOTES: Results are weighted and adjusted for firm size, industry, and whether the firm is part of a chain. Difference is marginal effect from probit regression except in models with small samples (firms that do not offer insurance and low-wage firms).

was 20 percent. San Francisco firms likely to offer an HRA were dispro-portionately in the restaurant industry and were characterized by a greater proportion of female workers and a greater proportion of tempo-rary workers (results not shown).

Relative to comparison firms outside of San Francisco, a smaller por-tion of firms in San Francisco cut back employer-sponsored health ben-efits during this time. To investigate further, we created a composite dichotomous measure called "reduced some health benefit," which is equal to one if a firm raised employee health insurance premiums by 25 percent or more, raised the deductible on a popular plan, dropped coverage, or restricted benefits. After adjusting for firm characteristics, fewer firms in San Francisco (11 percent) reduced at least one of these benefits than we predicted, absent the mandate (17 percent).

Employer Attitudes toward the Mandate

After six months to a year into implementation, only 15 percent of firms subject to the mandate were unaware of the regulation (fig. 5.4). Most of those that were unaware of the HCSO already offered health benefits to workers (80 percent, not shown in figure). This high awareness is likely due in part to the City's aggressive employer outreach efforts, which include mailing notices to employers, distributing brochures in six lan-guages, doing merchant walks, airing radio public service announce-ments, running bus shelter and print advertisements, and making pre-sentations to employer and employee associations.

Regarding employer expectations of the mandate, 39 percent of San Francisco employers felt it was very likely that the health spending requirement would still be in place in one year, while about 9 percent felt it was not likely. At the time of the survey, there was still consider-able uncertainty about the outcome of the legal challenges to the employer mandate; thus some employers may have refrained from planning major benefit changes in response to the mandate in its first year. Since the Healthy San Francisco public option may have been the simplest alternative for many employers, this uncertainty may have increased the use of the public option over what it might otherwise have

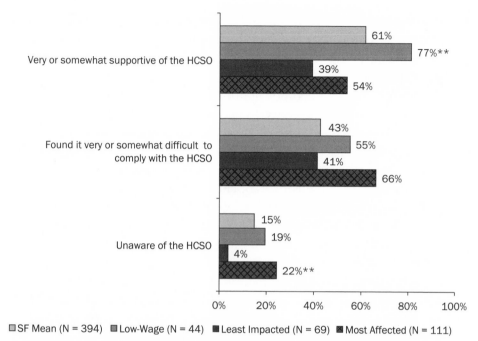

For the low-wage firms and most affected firms **, * indicates a significant difference between this category of firms and the rest of the sample at the 5% and 10% levels, respectively.

Figure 5.4 Employer sentiment regarding Health Care Security Ordinance.

been. But the uncertainty may also have restrained other employers from dropping insurance coverage in favor of the public plan. Longer-term follow-ups will be needed to better understand these competing effects of the uncertainty.

Most employers said it was not difficult to comply with the mandate, while 19 percent thought it was very difficult to comply and 24 percent found compliance somewhat difficult, for a total of 43 percent reporting some difficulty with compliance. Among San Francisco restaurants surveyed, about 85 percent found it difficult to comply with the HCSO; and 66 percent of those that were most affected found it difficult to comply. We also estimated a probit model of predictors of compliance difficulty using the same vector of firm characteristics. Restaurants, retail establishments, firms with a greater proportion of female workers, and those with more part-time workers found it more difficult to comply with the mandate. Firms with a greater proportion of workers over age sixty-five and smaller firms also found it less difficult to comply.

Despite the large proportion of firms that needed to make changes to become compliant, the majority (61 percent) were very or somewhat supportive of the mandate. Surprisingly, the proportion that was supportive was somewhat higher among low-wage firms (77 percent). Although not reported in the figure, the level of support was similar among restaurants (61 percent), whose industry association was most vocally against the HCSO. The proportion of firms in support was also greater among firms that are most affected by the HCSO (54 percent) than those that were the least affected (39 percent), while it was only slightly lower (52 percent) in the small subset of firms that did not offer health insurance in 2007 at all. Overall, the evidence does not indicate that the relatively high degree of support for the ordinance is driven by firms that were largely in compliance already (i.e., firms that might benefit if competitors' costs rose due to the ordinance).

Effects on Employment and Wages

Figure 5.5 provides evidence on the impact of the Health Care Security Ordinance on employment and earnings trends in San Francisco. For the most part, the figure displays similar trends in San Francisco and periphery Bay Area counties over the pre-period, and especially in highly affected sectors such as retail and restaurants. Moreover, during this period there was no evidence of any systematic trend between center and periphery counties in the other twenty-four MSAs, which suggests that, on average, peripheries were good control groups for centers.

Table 5.2 shows changes in outcomes in San Francisco vis-à-vis its neighbors (difference in difference) and a "triple difference" calculation that further adjusts for any trends between center and periphery counties within MSAs. Overall private sector employment in San Francisco was 3.4 percent higher between January 2008 and March 2010

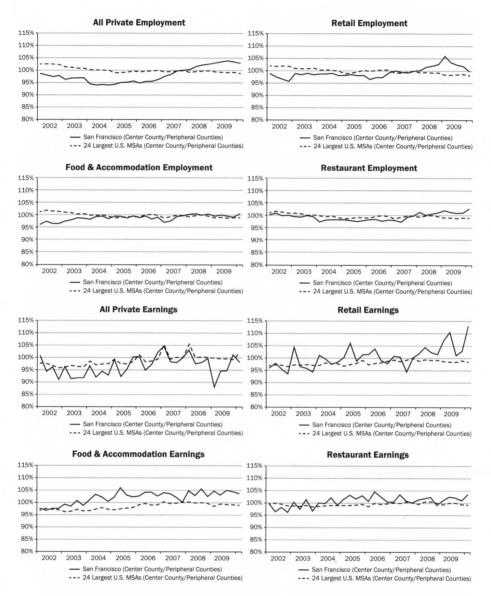

Figure 5.5 Ratio of center county employment and wages to periphery counties in San Francisco and 24 other MSAs, 2002–2010.

Table 5.2   Employment Trends in the Bay Area and Large MSAs

Log of Employment		*All Private*				*Retail*		
	SF	SF PERIPHERY	MSA CENTERS	MSA PERIPHERY	SF	SF PERIPHERY	MSA CENTERS	MSA PERIPHERY
Post	13.04	12.77	14.00	12.22	10.65	10.70	11.81	10.27
Pre	13.01	12.80	14.02	12.23	10.68	10.76	11.84	10.29
Diff	3.4%	-3.0%	–2.2%	–1.5%	–2.6%	–6.2%	–3.4%	–2.3%
Diff-in-Diff		6.5%		–0.8%		3.7%		–1.1%
Diff-in-Diff-in-Diff			7.2%					4.7%

		Accommodation & Food Services				*Restaurants*		
	SF	SF PERIPHERY	MSA CENTERS	MSA PERIPHERY	SF	SF PERIPHERY	MSA CENTERS	MSA PERIPHERY
Post	11.09	10.37	11.64	9.84	10.75	10.24	11.48	9.75
Pre	11.02	10.31	11.60	9.79	10.66	10.18	11.44	9.69
Diff	7.2%	5.5%	4.0%	5.3%	9.1%	6.6%	4.8%	5.9%
Diff-in-Diff		1.7%		–1.2%		2.5%		–1.0%
Diff-in-Diff-in-Diff			2.9%					3.6%

(continued)

(post-intervention) as compared with 2002 to 2007 (pre-intervention), while employment in San Francisco's neighboring counties (Alameda, Contra Costa, Marin, and San Mateo) shrank by 3.0 percent compared to the pre-period (table 5.2). Neither the difference in difference (6.5 percent) nor the triple difference (7.2 percent) suggest employment loss. Indeed, for all four industry groups, the simple, double, and triple difference estimates are either small (at most a 0.5 percent reduction) or positive, pointing away from employment or wage loss. Although not shown in the table, these estimates are all indistinguishable from zero at the 90 percent level.

Table 5.2 (continued)

Log of Earnings	All Private				Retail			
	SF	SF PERIPHERY	MSA CENTERS	MSA PERIPHERY	SF	SF PERIPHERY	MSA CENTERS	MSA PERIPHERY
Post	7.24	7.03	6.88	6.74	6.61	6.42	6.29	6.23
Pre	7.22	7.02	6.87	6.74	6.64	6.51	6.35	6.30
Diff	2.2%	1.1%	1.1%	–0.4%	–3.2%	–8.8%	–6.5%	–6.8%
Diff-in-Diff		1.0%		1.5%		5.6%		0.2%
Diff-in-Diff-in-Diff			–0.5%					5.4%

	Accommodation & Food Services				Restaurants			
	SF	SF PERIPHERY	MSA CENTERS	MSA PERIPHERY	SF	SF PERIPHERY	MSA CENTERS	MSA PERIPHERY
Post	6.23	5.88	5.88	5.73	6.03	5.83	5.79	5.68
Pre	6.21	5.89	5.88	5.74	6.02	5.84	5.79	5.69
Diff	1.9%	–1.1%	–0.5%	–1.2%	1.2%	–0.3%	–0.4%	–0.5%
Diff-in-Diff		3.0%		0.7%		1.5%		0.1%
Diff-in-Diff-in-Diff			2.2%					1.4%

SOURCE: Author analyses of Quarterly Census of Employment and Wages, Bureau of Labor Statistics.

NOTES: "Post" is January 2008 to March 2010. "Pre" is January 2002 to December 2007. "Diff" refers to the difference (Post – Pre) in each of the four geographic groups. "Diff-in-Diff" is difference of center minus difference of periphery, in SF and other MSAs. "Diff-in-Diff-in-Diff" is Diff-in-Diff of SF minus Diff-in-Diff of other MSAs. Multicounty estimates are weighted by county population. Earnings refer to average weekly earnings. All series are seasonally adjusted.

Overall, our results provide evidence that over the first twenty-seven months of the enactment of the policy, there was no discernible reduction in employment or earnings in San Francisco. More sophisticated regression-adjusted estimates are presented in previous work (Colla, Dow, et al. 2011b); these results reinforce simple comparisons and plots reported in this chapter.

Effects on Consumer Prices

We found that overall less than one percent of nonfood industries instituted a surcharge, while 25 percent of restaurants in our completed
2009 sample (standard error of 3.7 percent) and 27 percent of restaurants
in our completed 2010 sample (standard error of 4.2 percent) had
instituted a surcharge on their bills specifically attributed to health benefit costs. Although the extent and form of the surcharge varied, most
firms reported a charge of 4 percent on the bill, which was the mean,
median, and mode for firms using proportional charges in 2009 (the
majority).

We investigated the surcharges because they are the most easily measured form of pass-through to consumers. Firms that did not impose a
line item surcharge may have still adjusted their menu prices upward;
we have not investigated this type of response. We have, however, been
able to use data from the 2008 Bay Area Employer Health Benefits Survey
to calculate that 68 percent of the restaurants that have instituted these
surcharges already offered health benefits in 2007, prior to the implementation of the Health Care Security Ordinance. Thus it could be that some
firms that wanted to increase prices for other reasons did so as a surcharge under the guise of the health mandate, believing that demand
elasticity responses to health-linked surcharges might be smaller than
unexplained menu price increases. However, as mentioned above, even
among firms offering health insurance at baseline, most were required to
expand health spending to meet the mandated spending levels. Thus it
is not surprising that many restaurants opted to raise product prices.

5.   CONCLUSIONS AND DISCUSSION

San Francisco firms subject to a mandated health spending requirement
have altered their behavior compared to Bay Area comparison firms not
subject to mandated spending, yet we have not observed significant
changes in wages or employment levels in the early years of mandate
implementation. About one-fifth of employers responded to the spending

requirement by paying into the Healthy San Francisco public option for some employees. While comparison firms outside San Francisco increased employee contributions and switched to high deductible health plans, San Francisco firms subject to the mandate added new health insurance options. After one year there was little evidence of crowd-out due to the mandate, such as ceasing to offer insurance or restricting the generosity of benefits for some workers. There is some evidence that San Francisco firms are more likely to increase HRA offerings in response to the mandate.

Using the Quarterly Census of Employment and Wages to study the labor market effects of the Health Care Security Ordinance, we do not find evidence indicating substantial job losses or real earnings reductions from the employer spending requirement during the first few years the mandate was in place. This was true for the private sector overall, as well as for highly affected sectors including restaurants, food and accommodation establishments, and retail establishments.

Employer behavioral responses may also depend on uncertainty about future expected enforcement patterns. To the extent that there was uncertainty about whether the HCSO would be overturned in court or beliefs that there would be lax enforcement or only small penalties for violations, employer responses in this early period may have been muted. However, results from the 2009 Bay Area Employer Health Benefits Survey confirm the findings reported here based on 2008 survey data (Colla, Dow, et al. 2013). In addition, this type of uncertainty is likely to accompany implementation of similar employer mandates. The City of San Francisco worked aggressively to educate employers about the HCSO employer mandate (reflected in the fact that 85 percent of employers surveyed in 2008 were aware of it) but did not proactively audit for noncompliance. Enforcement activity has been primarily in response to employee complaints and has consisted mainly of further employer education and assistance rather than large fines. As of July 2012, the Office of Labor Standards Enforcement (OLSE) had opened 420 compliance cases and assessed penalties of about $135,000 (SF OLSE 2012).

How relevant are these findings to the national context or to other local jurisdictions? Given the limited evidence available from other settings it is important to study San Francisco's experience carefully. In doing so, we must bear in mind a number of features of the San Francisco setting that are unique and could limit generalizability, such as its geographic and political characteristics and specific parameters of the employer health spending mandate. First, San Francisco has the unique trait of being a city and a county, giving it broader municipal powers than many other municipalities. Second, the residents of San Francisco are disproportionately high income (median household income in 2008 was $73,798) and well educated (81 percent high school, 45 percent bachelor's degree or higher (DeLeon 2002; Advmeg 2010). Third, San Francisco is a peninsula, which increases the segmentation of its product markets—although this makes it, if anything, more relevant for understanding the impact of a national-level policy change. Finally, it is important to bear in mind that San Francisco's HCSO is on a per worker-hour basis; thus more firms may have had to expand health spending than if the health spending requirement were as a percentage of payroll or if more workers were exempt due to part-time hours. Similarly, the broad coverage of the mandate to include many temporary and part-time workers contributed to the fact that the majority of firms were required to expand spending in response to the mandate in San Francisco.

Employer behavioral responses to any pay-or-play mandate will also depend on the costs and perceived benefits of the "pay" option, in this case the Healthy San Francisco public option. Healthy San Francisco is in many ways a repackaging of the relatively generous set of safety net health services previously available in San Francisco, although that is changing as private providers such as Kaiser have also become care delivery options for program enrollees. Safety net usage may also be perceived as more legitimate now that it has clear copayments and authorizations, as well as medical homes for enrollees. But the fact that access is limited only to San Francisco suggests that Healthy San Francisco will necessarily be perceived as an inferior option for many employers and employees, and therefore crowd-out is likely to be lower here than if a true federal "public option" were introduced at the national level. Nevertheless, it will be interesting to see if the use of Healthy San Francisco by employers rises or falls with time and development of the program.

Lessons from the San Francisco mandates can help policy makers determine what to expect with implementation of a benefit mandate. First, pay-or-play mandates of this size are feasible; employers in San Francisco have been able to absorb the extra cost of providing health benefits without significant negative effects on employment or earnings. Some firms in industries where most competitors are also subject to the mandate, such as restaurants, have passed costs of the mandate to consumers. Second, many employers may choose the lowest-cost option available for newly insured employees. In the San Francisco case, this has largely played out through use of HRAs, Healthy San Francisco, and mini-medical plans, which are designed to just meet the health spending requirement. And third, despite most employers having to make changes in their benefit policies to comply with the mandate, most employers are supportive of the Health Care Security Ordinance. This may be because the pay-or-play mandate was bundled with Healthy San Francisco, offering firms a low-cost way to provide benefits to workers. Finally, the San Francisco policy is occurring in a single city. Multiestablishment firms with locations outside the city may respond differently when confronted with a mandate in one of many locations, as opposed to a national mandate. San Francisco also has one of the highest minimum wages in the country (though the difference is less striking after adjusting for the high general cost of living). The higher overall labor costs may influence the effects of the mandate, although a priori it is not clear in which direction. On the one hand, the additional costs due to the mandate may represent a smaller increase in overall costs. They also represent a smaller fraction of compensation, making it somewhat easier to absorb through lower-wage income. On the other hand, coming on the heels of other mandates (such as the high minimum wage and paid sick days requirements) might make it more onerous for businesses than would be the case nationally.

Although we should be cautious about inference from a single policy change, evidence from the early years of implementation suggests that San Francisco expanded coverage and access to health care under an employer mandate, yet we did not find evidence of significant decreases in employment or wages.

REFERENCES

Advmeg, I. 2010. "City-data.com." www.city-data.com/.

Baicker, Kate, and Amitabh Chandra. 2006. "The Labor Market Effects of Rising Health Insurance Premiums." *Journal of Labor Economics* 24, 3: 609–34.

Bundorf, M.Kate. 2002. "Employee Demand for Health Insurance and Employer Health Plan Choices." *Journal of Health Economics* 21, 1: 65–88.

Colla, Carrie H., William H. Dow, et al. 2011a. "How Do Employers React to a Pay-or-Play Mandate? Early Evidence from San Francisco." *Forum for Health Economics & Policy* 14, 2: 1–43. www.degruyter.com/view/j/fhep.

———. 2011b. "The Labor Market Impact of Employer Health Benefit Mandates: Evidence from San Francisco's Health Care Security Ordinance." N.W.P.N. 17198; and www.nber.org/papers/w17198.

———. 2013. "San Francisco's 'Pay Or Play' Employer Mandate Expanded Private Coverage by Local Firms and a Public Care Program." *Health Affairs* 32, 1: 169–77.

Cutler, David M., and Jonathan Gruber. 1996. "Does Public Insurance Crowd out Private Insurance?" *Quarterly Journal of Economics* 111, 1: 391–430.

DeLeon, Rich. 2002. "Only in San Francisco? The City's Political Culture in Comparative Perspective." *SPUR [San Francisco Planning + Urban Research Association] Newsletter* (Nov.–Dec.). www.spur.org/documents/pdf/01101_article_01.pdf.

Dube, Arindrajit, T. William Lester, et al. 2010. "Minimum Wage Effects across State Borders: Estimates Using Contiguous Counties." *Review of Economics and Statistics* 92, 4: 945–64.

Fuhrmans, Vanessa. 2006. "More Employers Try Limited Health Plans." *Wall Street Journal*, Jan. 17.

Gabel, Jonathan, Gary Claxton, et al. 2003. "Health Benefits in 2003: Premiums Reach Thirteen-Year High as Employers Adopt New Forms of Cost Sharing." *Health Affairs* 22, 5: 117–26.

Gruber, Jonathan. 1994. "The Incidence of Mandated Maternity Benefits." *American Economic Review* 84, 3: 622–41.

Healthy San Francisco. 2008. "Healthy San Francisco: Program Update. San Francisco Health Commission, August 19, 2008." www.healthysanfrancisco.org/files/PDF/August_2008_Program_Update.pdf.

———. 2010. "Who Qualifies for Healthy San Francisco?" www.healthysan-francisco.org/visitors/Who_Qualifies.aspx.

Holmes, Thomas J. 1998. "The Effect of State Policies on the Location of Manufacturing: Evidence from State Borders." *Journal of Political Economy* 106, 4: 667–705.

Kahn, Shulamit. 1997. "Evidence of Nominal Wage Stickiness from Microdata." *American Economic Review* 87, 5: 993–1008.

Kaiser Family Foundation and Health Research & Educational Trust. 2008. "Employer Health Benefits Survey." http://kff.org/health-costs/report /employer-health-benefits-annual-survey-archives/.

Katz, Mitch H. 2008. "Golden Gate to Health Care for All? San Francisco's New Universal-Access Program." *New England Journal of Medicine* 358, 4: 327–29.

Katz, Mitch H., and Tangerine M. Brigham. 2011. "Transforming a Traditional Safety Net into a Coordinated Care System: Lessons from Healthy San Francisco." *Health Affairs (Millwood)* 30, 2: 237–45.

Mandelbaum, Robb. 2009. "Is the Employer Mandate a Job Killer? Not in San Francisco." *New York Times*, Sept. 18. http://boss.blogs.nytimes. com/2009/09/18/is-the-employer-mandate-a-job-killer-not-in-san-francisco/.

Marquis, M. Susan, and Sharon H. Long. 2001. "Employer Health Insurance and Local Labor Market Conditions." *International Journal of Health Care Finance and Economics* 1, 3–4: 273–92.

Pear, Robert. 2011. "Political Focus on Jobs in Health Fight." *New York Times*, Jan. 5.

Rosen, Sherwin. 1986. "The Theory of Equalizing Differences." In *Handbook of Labor Economics*, ed. O. Ashenfelter and R. Layard, vol. 1, 641–91. Amsterdam: Elsevier/North Holland.

San Francisco Department of Public Health and the Office of Labor Standards Enforcement (SF DPH and OLSE). 2010. "Status Report on the Implementation of the San Francisco Health Care Security Ordinance." www.healthysanfrancisco.org/files/PDF/January_2009_Bos_Report.pdf.

San Francisco Office of Labor Standards Enforcement (SF OLSE). 2012. Administrative data.

Summers, Lawrence H. 1989. "Some Simple Economics of Mandated Benefits." *American Economic Review* 79, 2: 177–83.

U.S. Census Bureau. 2008. "County Business Patterns." www.census.gov/econ /cbp/index.html.

SIX Requiring Equal Benefits for Domestic Partners

Christy Mallory and Brad Sears

1. INTRODUCTION

In 1996, San Francisco enacted the first equal benefits ordinance (EBO) in the nation.[1] An EBO requires local government contractors to provide benefits to unmarried partners of employees on the same terms that they are provided to spouses. Since 1996, nineteen other localities and one state, California, have passed similar laws.

---

*Portions of this chapter are based on or appeared in Christy Mallory and Brad Sears, "An Evaluation of Local Laws Requiring Government Contractors to Offer Equal Benefits to Domestic Partners," Williams Institute, Los Angeles, 2012, http://williamsinstitute.law.ucla.edu.

[1] Although state-level laws are not called ordinances, the abbreviation "EBO" as used in this report refers also to California's equal benefits law. The abbreviation is used for simplicity.

San Francisco's pioneering ordinance passed unanimously. The mayor predicted that other jurisdictions would follow San Francisco's lead, and the City stated that both employees and employers would benefit because of it. However, the ordinance also generated some criticism, which focused mainly on the potential administrative costs and burden associated with enforcing the EBO. Similar arguments for and against EBOs have been raised since in other jurisdictions.

This chapter evaluates the implementation and enforcement of San Francisco's EBO and those that followed in order to determine the positive effects of these laws and the validity of arguments made against them. It is based on an original survey of the twenty-one jurisdictions that have passed EBOs, as well as ten other studies conducted by four of these jurisdictions. Our analysis also considers how San Francisco's early experience may differ from that of jurisdictions that adopted EBOs more recently and jurisdictions that adopt EBOs in the future. In addition, we discuss the implications of the findings for a federal EBO policy.

2.   SAN FRANCISCO'S EQUAL BENEFITS ORDINANCE

In 1996, the San Francisco Board of Supervisors unanimously passed the first "equal benefits ordinance."[2] When San Francisco conceptualized the EBO, it was focused on the benefits that would accrue to employees. The City stated that it enacted the ordinance as an "attempt[ ] to address one aspect of discrimination" faced by LGBT people in the workplace. Specifically, same-sex couples and unmarried heterosexual partners generally did not have access to employment benefits that, at the time, were tied to marital status.[3]

---

[2] "San Francisco to Expand Its Domestic Partners Law; Pressure from Hill Doesn't Affect Board," *Washington Post*, Aug. 11, 1998, A11. See generally S.F., CAL. ADMIN. CODE § 12B.2 (2009).

[3] San Francisco Human Rights Commission, Overview of the Equal Benefits Ordinance, available at www.sf-hrc.org/ftp/uploadedfiles/sfhumanrights/docs/over12b.pdf. Last accessed July 9, 2012.

After the EBO passed, opponents argued that it would create problems for the local government and for its private sector contractors. For example, some argued that the city would lose contractors or would not have the best contractors if they were required to comply with a policy that reached beyond federal and state laws.[4] Others criticized the ordinance as "extreme" and "unworkable," arguing that it would be costly to enforce and administratively burdensome for the local government.[5] One opponent, citing vendor markups that result in higher costs of contracting for the City, called the EBO "the expensive white elephant standing in the middle of the room that no one wants to mention."[6] A member of Congress led an effort to restrict federal funding to San Francisco because its EBO required private businesses "to adopt a policy they find morally objectionable."[7]

Over the past fifteen years, San Francisco has conducted several evaluations of its EBO. The evaluations show that the ordinance has positive effects on both employees and employers.[8] First, through the EBO San Francisco accomplished its goal of increasing the number of employees who are offered employer-sponsored benefits for their domestic part-

---

[4] See, e.g., Chris Roberts, "More LGBT Woes for Target: Chain Could Lose SF City Contract over Same-Sex Benefits," *San Francisco Appeal*, Sept. 8, 2010, http://sfappeal.com /news/2010/09/more-lgbt-woes-for-target-chain-could-lose-city-contract-over-same-sex-benefits.php.

[5] See "Starting a Revolution," *San Francisco Chronicle*, Nov. 7, 2001.

[6] John Cote, "High Cost of 'Social Justice' Contracts; S.F. Government; Vendors Overcharge Millions, Workers Say," *San Francisco Chronicle*, May 8, 2011, A1.

[7] Carolyn Lochhead, "Vote Delayed on GOP Move to Punish S.F. Partners Law; Riggs Amendment Would Cut Federal Housing Money," *San Francisco Chronicle*, July 25, 1998.

[8] See generally by the San Francisco Human Rights Commission: *The San Francisco Equal Benefits Ordinance: A Six Month Report* (1998), available at www.sf-hrc.org/modules /ShowDocument.aspx?documentid=141 (hereafter *Six-Month Report*); *Two Year Report on the San Francisco Equal Benefits Ordinance* (1999), available at www.sf-hrc.org/Modules /ShowDocument.aspx?documentid=145 (hereafter *Two Year Report*); *Three Year Report on the San Francisco Equal Benefits Ordinance* (2000), available at www.sf-hrc.org/Modules /ShowDocument.aspx?documentid=143 (hereafter *Three Year Report*); *Four Year Report on the San Francisco Equal Benefits Ordinance* (2001), available at www.sf-hrc.org/Modules /ShowDocument.aspx?documentid=144 (hereafter *Four Year Report*); *Five Year Report on the San Francisco Equal Benefits Ordinance* (2002), available at www.sf-hrc.org/Modules /ShowDocument.aspx?documentid=142 (hereafter *Five Year Report*); *Seven Year Update on the San Francisco Equal Benefits Ordinance* (2004), available at www.sf-hrc.org/Modules /ShowDocument.aspx?documentid=140 (hereafter *Seven Year Update*).

ners. At the time San Francisco's EBO was adopted, only 500 employers in the United States offered domestic partner benefits; 4,500 did so in 2002. Seventy-five percent of those 4,500 employers offered the benefits because they held contracts with the City of San Francisco or wished to bid on contracts.[9] Seven years after the ordinance passed, San Francisco estimated that its contractors provided domestic partner benefits to over 66,000 employees.[10] Today, thousands more employers offer domestic partner benefits.[11] San Francisco's early EBO has been credited as a "catalyst" in this "explosion of domestic partner benefits" offered by companies in the United States.[12]

Second, San Francisco has noted that its EBO has had "a noticeable impact on the insurance industry," including increasing the number of insurance companies willing to offer domestic partnership benefits, especially for employers with few employees, and all but eliminating the practice of levying surcharges for domestic partnership benefits as a result of "clear actuarial statistics indicating that the claims for domestic partners are no more expensive than those for spouses."[13]

Third, the EBO can benefit San Francisco's private sector contractors in ways that may not have been anticipated in 1996. San Francisco has noted in its evaluations that offering domestic partner benefits is economically good for corporate employers. More specifically, companies increase their ability to recruit and retain the best talent when they offer generous benefits and signal that they are committed to diversity.[14] Several localities that have enacted EBOs since San Francisco have also recognized that EBOs are good for employers and for the government.[15]

[9] *Five Year Report*, 1.

[10] *Seven Year Update*, 4.

[11] *See* Employee Benefit Research Institute, *Domestic Partner Benefits: Facts and Background* 1 (2009), available at www.ebri.org/pdf/publications/facts/0209fact.pdf (according to the Human Rights Campaign, over 9,300 employers offered domestic partner benefits as of May 16, 2008).

[12] Christopher Snowbeck, "At What Price Benefits? Higher Costs of Domestic Partner Coverage Feared by Pitt, not Seen in Other Plans," *Pittsburgh Post-Gazette*, Sept. 29, 1999, A1; *Five Year Report*, 1.

[13] *Five Year Report*, 9–10.

[14] San Francisco Human Rights Commission, *Overview of the Equal Benefits Ordinance*.

[15] See notes 139–44 below and accompanying text.

Fourth, San Francisco has found that the concerns expressed at the time of the EBO's passage have not been borne out. The City's evaluations have documented the impact of the ordinance on the contracting process. They indicate that administration of the ordinance has been smooth. As we discuss further below, even in the early stages of enforcement, the vast majority of contractors (91 percent) were in compliance with the EBO.[16] After seven years, the compliance rate was up to 94.6 percent.[17]

In the early days of San Francisco's ordinance, Mayor Willie Brown, who signed the EBO into law, predicted that other jurisdictions would follow San Francisco's lead and enact their own EBOs.[18] Today, nineteen other localities[19] and one state, California,[20] have passed EBOs using San Francisco's ordinance as a model.[21] These nineteen localities are located in seven states across the country, with the highest concentration (nine) in California. When passing EBOs, these jurisdictions, like San Francisco, have pointed to the benefits they will have for employees, employers,

[16] *Six Month Report*, 2.

[17] *Seven Year Update*, 2.

[18] Jason B. Johnson, "S.F. Pushing to Spread Law for Gay Benefits," *San Francisco Chronicle*, June 2, 1998, A16.

[19] Berkeley, CA (BERKELEY, CAL., CODE § 13.29.010–13.29.100 (2009)); Broward County, FL (BROWARD COUNTY, FLA., CODE § 16½-157 (2012)); Dane County, WI (DANE COUNTY, WIS., CODE § 25.016 (2010)); Key West, FL (KEY WEST, FLA., CODE § 2–799 (2012)); King County, WA (KING COUNTY, WASH., CODE § 12.19.002–12.19.100 (2009)); Long Beach, CA (LONG BEACH, CAL., CODE § 2.73.010–2.73.090 (2009)); City of Los Angeles, CA (LOS ANGELES, CAL. ADMIN. CODE § 10.8.2.1 (2009)); Miami Beach, FL (MIAMI BEACH, FLA., CODE § 2–373 (2009)); Minneapolis, MN (MINNEAPOLIS, MINN., CODE § 18.200 (2009)); Oakland, CA (OAKLAND, CAL., CODE § 2.32.010–2.32.110 (2010)); Olympia, WA (OLYMPIA, WASH., CODE § 3.18.020 (2009)); Philadelphia, PA (PHILADELPHIA, PA., CODE § 17–1900 (2012)); Portland, OR (PORTLAND, OR., CHARTER § 3.100.053–3.100.056 (2009)); Sacramento, CA (SACRAMENTO, CAL., CODE § 3.54.010–3.54.120 (2009)); San Diego, CA (SAN DIEGO, CAL., CODE § 22.4301–22.4308 (2011)); Santa Monica, CA (Santa Monica, Cal., Code § 4.65.025 (2011)); San Mateo County, CA (SAN MATEO COUNTY, CAL., CODE § 2.84.010–2.84.050 (2009)); Seattle, WA (SEATTLE, WASH., CODE § 20.45.010–.050 (2009)); Tumwater, WA (TUMWATER, WASH., CODE § 3.46.010–3.46.060 (2009)).

[20] CAL. PUB. CONTRACT CODE § 10295.3 (2012).

[21] *Five Year Report*, 1. San Francisco has also noted that its EBO played a role in encouraging states and localities to establish domestic partner registries that provide for a number of rights and obligations beyond workplace benefits (1). Only 33 jurisdictions offered these broader domestic partner registries when San Francisco's EBO was adopted, while 63 had such registries after five years of enforcement (11).

and the government.[22] In many cases, however, they continue to be met with criticism based on the same concerns that were raised in opposition to San Francisco's EBO.[23] The next two sections summarize the requirements of these EBOs and present the results of a survey evaluating their effectiveness.

3. OVERVIEW OF EQUAL BENEFITS ORDINANCES

EBOs require contractors to provide benefits to unmarried partners on the same terms that they are provided to spouses. Contractors may comply with this requirement in three ways: (1) by offering the same benefits to spouses and domestic partners (or by paying employees with domestic partners a cash equivalent);[24] (2) by offering no benefits to either spouses or domestic partners;[25] or (3) by offering no employee benefits because the contractor has no employees.[26]

In some jurisdictions, contractors may also comply by allowing employees to choose any member of the household to receive spousal

---

[22] E.g., LOS ANGELES, CAL. ADMIN. CODE § 10.8.2.1(a) (2009) (stating that the purpose of the ordinance is "to ensure that the City's contractors will maintain a competitive edge in recruiting and retaining capable employees, thereby improving the quality of the goods and services the City and its people receive, and ensuring protection of the City's property"); DANE COUNTY, WIS., CODE § 25.01 (2010) (stating in the county code chapter that includes EBO that the general purpose of the chapter is "to achieve greater efficiency and economy in the operation of Dane County government"); OAKLAND, CAL., CODE § 2.32.010 (2010) (citing that the EBO furthers "convenience" of the city government); SACRAMENTO, CAL., CODE § 3.54.010 (2009) (same).

[23] E.g., Memorandum from Joseph F. Beach, Director, Montgomery County Office of Management and Budget, to Nancy Floreen, President, Montgomery County City Council (Jan. 19, 2010), available at www.montgomerycountymd.gov/content/council/pdf/agenda/col/2010/100202/20100202_8.pdf; Matthew Leising, "Council Passes Benefits for Domestic Partners," *Contra Costa Times*, Nov. 30, 2001; Perkins Coie, "Contractors Must Provide Equal Benefits to Employees with Domestic Partners," *Washington Employment Law Letter*, Jan. 2000.

[24] See, e.g., BERKELEY, CAL., CODE § 13.29.040(A)(2) (2009).

[25] See, e.g., TUMWATER, WASH., CODE § 3.46.020(B)(3) (2009).

[26] See, e.g., Administration Dept., City of San Diego, CA, *Report to the City Council No. 11–130: Equal Benefits Ordinance Fiscal Year 2011 Annual (6-month) Report* 5 (2011), available at www.sandiego.gov/administration/pdf/eborules101213.pdf.

King County, WA
Seattle, WA
Olympia, WA
Tumwater, WA
Portland, OR
State of California
San Mateo County, CA
San Francisco, CA
Berkeley, CA
Oakland, CA
Sacramento, CA
Santa Monica, CA
Los Angeles, CA
Long Beach, CA
San Diego, CA
Minneapolis, MN
Dane County, WI
Philadelphia, PA
Key West, FL
Miami Beach, FL
Broward County, FL

Figure 6.1   Geographic distribution of equal benefits ordinances.

equivalent benefits.[27] Only one of the EBOs is explicitly limited to same-sex partners;[28] the other twenty require that any couple who meets the definition of "domestic partner" in the ordinance, whether same-sex or different-sex, be provided benefits on the same terms as spouses.[29]

The benefits required by seventeen of these EBOs include health insurance benefits and a range of other fringe benefits that make up an employee's total compensation package.[30] For example, San Diego,

[27] See, e.g., OLYMPIA, WASH., CODE § 3.18.020 (2009).

[28] Philadelphia, PA (PHILADELPHIA, PA., CODE §§ 17–1902; 9–1102(1)(r) (2012)).

[29] All EBOs cover couples who are registered as domestic partners with a state or local government registry. Many also cover couples who are registered as domestic partners with an employer's internal registry and/or meet the criteria for domestic partnership included in the EBO.

[30] Berkeley, CA (BERKELEY, CAL., CODE § 13.29.030 (2009)); Broward County, FL (BROWARD COUNTY, FLA., CODE §§ 16½-156, -157 (2012)); Dane County, WI (DANE COUNTY, WIS., CODE § 25.016(3) (2010); Key West, FL (KEY WEST, FLA., CODE § 2–799 (2012)); KING COUNTY, WASH., CODE § 12.19.020(E)); Long Beach, CA (LONG BEACH, CAL., CODE § 2.73.040 (2009)); City of Los Angeles, CA (LOS ANGELES, CAL. ADMIN. CODE § 10.8.2.1(b)(2) (2009)); Miami Beach, FL (MIAMI BEACH, FLA., CODE § 2–373(a)(1) (2009)); Minneapolis, MN (MINNEAPOLIS, MINN., CODE § 18.200(c) (2009)); Oakland, CA (OAKLAND, CAL., CODE § 2.32.040 (2010)); Philadelphia, PA (PHILADELPHIA, PA., CODE § 17–1901(1) (2012));

California's EBO defines "employee benefits" as "All remuneration other than wages, salary, bonuses, commissions, and stock options offered to an employee as part of the employee's total compensation package, including bereavement leave, family leave, no-additional-cost services, health and medical benefits, employee discounts, memberships or membership discounts, moving expenses, pension and retirement benefits, transportation and travel benefits, and any other employment or fringe benefits."[31] Olympia, Washington's EBO is limited to equal health insurance benefits (medical, dental, and vision), and San Mateo, California's EBO explicitly exempts pension and retirement benefits.[32] The State of California and Santa Monica, California's EBOs do not specify which benefits are covered.[33]

Fifteen EBOs state the geographic reach of the ordinance. All of these EBOs state that they apply to the contractor's operations that occur within the jurisdiction and elsewhere in the United States where work related to the contract is being performed.[34] Fourteen EBOs also apply to work performed on real property outside of the jurisdiction if the property is

---

PORTLAND, OR., CHARTER § 3.100.052(E) (2009)); Sacramento, CA (SACRAMENTO, CAL., CODE § 3.54.030(D) (2009)); San Diego, CA (SAN DIEGO, CAL., CODE § 22.4302 (2011)); San Francisco, CA (SAN FRANCISCO, CAL., ADMIN. CODE § 12B.1(b) (2009)); Seattle, WA (SEATTLE, WASH., CODE § 20.45.010(F) (2009)); Tumwater, WA (TUMWATER, WASH., CODE § 3.46.010(D) (2009)).

[31] SAN DIEGO, CAL., CODE § 22.4302 (2011).

[32] OLYMPIA, WASH., CODE § 3.18.010 (2009); SAN MATEO COUNTY, CAL., CODE § 2.84.010(e) (2009).

[33] CAL. PUB. CONTRACT CODE § 10295.3 (2012); SANTA MONICA, CAL., CODE § 4.65.025 (2011).

[34] Berkeley, CA (BERKELEY, CAL., CODE § 13.29.030 (2009)); State of California (CAL. PUB. CONTRACT CODE § 10295.3(a)(5) (2012)); Dane County, WI (DANE COUNTY, WIS., CODE § 25.016(3) (2010)); Long Beach, CA (LONG BEACH, CAL., CODE § 2.73.030(B) (2009)); City of Los Angeles, CA (LOS ANGELES, CAL. ADMIN. CODE § 10.8.2.1(e)(2) (2009)); Miami Beach, CA (MIAMI BEACH, FLA., CODE § 2–373(d)(2) (2009)); Minneapolis, MN (MINNEAPOLIS, MINN., CODE § 18.200(i) (2009)); Olympia, WA (OLYMPIA, WASH., CODE § 3.18.030 (2009)); Portland, OR (PORTLAND, OR., CHARTER § 3.100.054 (2009)); Sacramento, CA (SACRAMENTO, CAL., CODE § 3.54.040(B) (2009) (extends to work performed on property outside of the city but owned or occupied by the city, regardless of whether the contractor's presence on the property is related to the contract)); San Diego, CA (SAN DIEGO, CAL., CODE § 22.4303 (2011)); San Francisco, CA (SAN FRANCISCO, CAL., ADMIN. CODE § 12B.1(d) (2009)); San Mateo County, CA (SAN MATEO COUNTY, CAL., CODE § 2.84.030 (2009)); Seattle, WA (SEATTLE, WASH., CODE § 20.45.030 (2009)); Tumwater, WA (TUMWATER, WASH., CODE § 3.46.030 (2009)).

owned or occupied by the jurisdiction and the contractor's presence on the property is related to the contract.[35] In addition to these requirements, San Francisco, California's EBO states that it applies to any of a contractor's operations in the United States,[36] but a district court in California has held that the dormant commerce clause prohibits this application.[37]

All jurisdictions exempt some contracts from the EBO requirements or allow waivers in certain circumstances. Seventeen jurisdictions exempt contracts that are below a certain dollar amount.[38] The dollar thresholds in these ordinances range from $5,000 to $250,000. Three localities exempt contractors that have fewer than a specified number of employees.[39]

---

[35] All of the above, except Miami Beach.

[36] SAN FRANCISCO, CAL., ADMIN. CODE § 12B.1(d) (2009).

[37] Air Transport Ass'n v. City and County of San Francisco, 992 F. Supp. 1149 (N.D. Cal. 1998).

[38] EBO requirements apply to contracts above the following thresholds: Berkeley, CA (BERKELEY, CAL., CODE § 13.29.030 (2009)) ($25,000 or more (for-profit entities), $100,000 or more (nonprofit entities); all contracts with entities that generate $350,000 or more in annual gross receipts and which occupy City property pursuant to a written agreement for the exclusive use or occupancy of said property for a term exceeding 29 days in any calendar year)); Broward County, FL (BROWARD COUNTY, FLA., CODE § 16½-152(c) (2012)) (more than $100,000); State of California (CAL. PUB. CONTRACT CODE § 10295.3 (2012)) ($100,000 or more); Key West, FL (KEY WEST, FLA., CODE § 2–799(a)(6) (2012)) (more than $20,000); King County, WA (KING COUNTY, WASH., CODE § 12.19.020(A) (2009)) ($25,000 or more); Long Beach, CA (LONG BEACH, CAL., CODE § 2.73.030(A) (2009)) ($100,000 or more [for-profit entities]; and all contracts that generate $350,000 or more in annual gross receipts and that occupy city property pursuant to a written agreement for the exclusive use or occupancy of said property for a term exceeding 29 days in any calendar year); City of Los Angeles, CA (LOS ANGELES, CAL. ADMIN. CODE § 10.8.2.1(b)(5) (2009)) (more than $5,000); Miami Beach, CA (MIAMI BEACH, FLA., CODE § 2–373(a)(6) (2009)) (more than $100,000); Minneapolis, MN (MINNEAPOLIS, MINN., CODE § 18.200(c) (2009) (more than $100,000)); Oakland, CA (OAKLAND, CAL., CODE § 2.32.020 (2010)) ($25,000 or more); Olympia, WA (OLYMPIA, WASH., CODE § 3.18.010 (2009)) ($50,000 or more); Philadelphia, PA (PHILADELPHIA, PA., CODE § 17–1900 (2012)) ($250,000 or more); Sacramento, CA (SACRAMENTO, CAL., CODE § 3.54.040(A) (2009)) (more than $25,000); San Francisco, CA (SAN FRANCISCO, CAL., ADMIN. CODE § 12B.1(c) (2009)) (more than $5,000); San Mateo County, CA (SAN MATEO COUNTY, CAL., CODE § 2.84.010(a) (2009)) (more than $5,000); Seattle, WA (SEATTLE, WASH., CODE § 20.45.010(A) (2009)) ($44,000 in 2010 and adjusted for inflation thereafter); Tumwater, WA (TUMWATER, WASH., CODE § 3.46.010(A) (2009)) ($50,000 or more).

[39] EBO requirements apply to employers with the following numbers of employees: Broward County, FL (BROWARD COUNTY, FLA., CODE § 16½-152(d) (2012) (5 or more full-time employees); Key West, FL (KEY WEST, FLA., CODE § 2–799(a)(5) (2012)) (5 or more full-time employees); Miami Beach, FL (MIAMI BEACH, FLA., CODE § 2–373(a)(5) (2009)) (50 or more full-time employees).

These jurisdictions also offer waivers or exempt contracts in a number of different circumstances that fall into five general categories:

1. when the locality's ability to secure a good or service would be jeopardized;[40]

2. for certain types of contractors, such as other public entities, non-profit organizations, and religious organizations;[41]

3. for certain types of contracts, such as a contract for banking services or the rent or purchase of land;[42]

4. where the EBO requirements would potentially contradict other legal obligations such as an agreement with another government entity or a collective bargaining agreement;[43]

5. where compliance would result in financial loss to the contractor.[44]

Not all localities offer waivers and exemptions in all of these circumstances, but the waiver and exemption provisions in EBOs are fairly consistent across jurisdictions. All or most of the EBOs provide exemptions in the following circumstances: when the jurisdiction is responding to an

---

[40] E.g., DANE COUNTY, WIS., CODE § 25.016(3)(b) (2010) (when only one contractor has bid); MIAMI BEACH, FLA., CODE § 2–373(g)(3)(a) (2009) (when contract is necessary to respond to an emergency); OAKLAND, CAL., CODE § 2.32.090(C) (2010) (when no compliant contractor can provide the goods or services); PHILADELPHIA, PA., CODE § 17–1904(4) (2012) (when waiving the requirement would be in the best interests of the jurisdiction); SACRAMENTO, CAL., CODE § 3.54.070(A)(1) (2009) (when contractor is a sole source provider).

[41] E.g., LONG BEACH, CAL., CODE § 2.73.060(A)(3) (2009) (for contracts with a nonprofit entity); MINNEAPOLIS, MINN., CODE § 18.200(f)(6), (7) (2009) (for contracts with religious organizations); OLYMPIA, WASH., CODE § 3.18.020(C)(6) (2009) (for joint purchasing agreements with another government); PORTLAND, OR., CHARTER § 3.100.053(C)(3) (2009) (for contracts with a public entity).

[42] E.g., DANE COUNTY, WIS., CODE § 25.016(2)(d) (2010) (for purchase of goods contracts); KING COUNTY, WASH., CODE § 12.19.020(A) (2009) (for property rent or purchase contracts); LONG BEACH, CAL., CODE § 2.73.060(A)(9) (2009) (for agreements involving trusts, bonds, or securities); SAN FRANCISCO, CAL., ADMIN. CODE § 12B.5–1(d)(2) (2009) (for bulk purchasing contracts); SANTA MONICA, CAL., CODE § 4.65.030 (2011) (for contracts with corporations providing banking services).

[43] E.g., BERKELEY, CAL., CODE § 13.29.060(A)(7) (2009) (for contracts that would require specialized litigation); LOS ANGELES, CAL. ADMIN. CODE § 10.8.2.1 (i)(1)(f) (2009) (when requiring the benefits would be inconsistent with the terms of a grant from, or other agreement with, a public entity); SAN DIEGO, CAL., CODE § 22.4308(c) (2011) (when the contractor is subject to a collective bargaining agreement that was in effect before the ordinance passed).

[44] E.g., LONG BEACH, CAL., CODE § 2.73.060(A)(9) (2009).

emergency; when no compliant contractor can provide goods or services; when the contractor is a sole-source provider; when the requirements would be inconsistent with a grant or agreement with a public agency; and when the contract is with a public entity.

The procedures for establishing that a contractor is in compliance with the EBO vary by jurisdiction. Some EBOs have more stringent procedures for verifying that contractors or bidders are in compliance. For example, San Francisco requires that prospective contractors undergo an EBO compliance certification process before bidding on government contracts,[45] and several other localities require contractors to provide a copy of their domestic partner benefits plan at the time they enter into the contract.[46] Most jurisdictions require that the contractor attest to compliance in writing but do not require that they submit supporting documentation.[47] One locality, Santa Monica, California, does not explicitly require contractors to certify compliance in writing.[48]

The EBOs also vary in the remedies they provide if a contractor violates the law. Thirteen EBOs allow the government and/or an aggrieved

---

[45] San Francisco, Cal., Admin. Code § 12B.4 (2009); Dane County, Wis., Code § 25.016(8) (2010). For details on San Francisco's compliance procedure, see San Francisco Human Rights Commission, *How to Comply with the Equal Benefits Ordinance*, available at http://sf-hrc.org/index.aspx?page = 96#How%20do%20I%20Comply (last visited Sept. 14, 2011); Broward County, Fla., Code § 16½-157(b) (2012); Key West, Fla., Code § 2–799(b)(4), (5) (2012); Philadelphia, Pa., Code § 17–1905(2) (2012).

[46] Key West, Fla., Code § 2–799(b)(4) (2012); Miami Beach, FL (Miami Beach, Fla., Code § 2–373(b)(3) (2009).

[47] Berkeley, CA (Berkeley, Cal., Code § 13.29.050 (2009)); Broward County, FL (Broward County, Fla., Code § 16½-157(b) (2012)); State of California (Cal. Pub. Contract Code § 10295.3(f) (2012)); Dane County, WI (Dane County, Wis., Code § 25.016(8)(a) (2010)); King County, WA (King County, Wash., Code § 12.19.030(E) (2009)); Long Beach, CA (Long Beach, Cal., Code § 2.73.050; City of Los Angeles, CA (Los Angeles, Cal. Admin. Code § 10.8.2.1(f) (2009)); Minneapolis, MN (Minneapolis, Minn., Code § 18.200(b)(2) (2009)); Oakland, Cal., Code § 2.32.050 (2010); Olympia, WA (Olympia, Wash., Code § 3.18.020(E) (2009)); Philadelphia, PA (Philadelphia, Pa., Code § 17–1903 (2012)); Portland, OR (Portland, Or., Charter § 3.100.053(G) (2009)); Sacramento, CA (Sacramento, Cal., Code § 3.54.060 (2009)); San Diego, CA (San Diego, Cal., Code § 22.4304(e), (f) (2011)); San Mateo County, CA (San Mateo County, Cal., Code § 2.84.020 (2009)); Seattle, WA (Seattle, Wash., Code § 20.45.010–.050 (2009)); Tumwater, WA (Tumwater, Wash., Code § 3.46.020(G) (2009)).

[48] Santa Monica, Cal., Code § 4.65.025 (2011).

employee to seek civil remedies for a violation of the ordinance,[49] and four EBOs explicitly provide for individual remedies for an aggrieved employee.[50] Rules implementing San Diego, California's EBO also provide for individual remedies for an aggrieved employee.[51] Nineteen EBOs provide contract remedies, including termination of contract and debarment from future bidding, if an employer fails to provide equal benefits.[52]

4. METHODOLOGY

All of the twenty localities and one state with EBOs were contacted for purposes of this study.[53] When the jurisdictions were contacted, they were

[49] Berkeley, CA (BERKELEY, CAL., CODE § 13.29.090 (2009)); State of California (CAL. PUB. CONTRACT CODE §§ 10295.3(f)(3), 10421 (2012)); Dane County, WI (DANE COUNTY, WIS., CODE § 25.016(12) (2010)); Key West, FL (KEY WEST, FLA., CODE § 2–799(d)(4) (2012); King County, WA (KING COUNTY, WASH., CODE § 12.19.070-.080 (2009)); Long Beach, CA (LONG BEACH, CAL., CODE § 2.73. 090 (2009)); Minneapolis, MN (MINNEAPOLIS, MINN., CODE §§ 18.200(m); 141.60 (2009)); Oakland, CA (OAKLAND, CAL., CODE § 2.32.090(2010)); Portland, OR (PORTLAND, OR., CHARTER § 3.100.055 (2009)); Sacramento, CA (SACRAMENTO, CAL., CODE § 3.54.100 (2009)); San Mateo County, CA (SAN MATEO COUNTY, CAL., CODE § 2.84.040 (2009)); Seattle, WA (SEATTLE, WASH., CODE § 20.45.040 (2009)); Tumwater, WA (TUMWATER, WASH., CODE § 3.46.040 (2009)).

[50] Berkeley, CA (BERKELEY, CAL., CODE § 13.29.090(B) (2009)); Dane County, WI (DANE COUNTY, WIS., CODE § 25.016(12)(e) (2010)); Oakland, CA (OAKLAND, CAL., CODE § 2.32.060(D)(1) (2010)); and Sacramento, CA (SACRAMENTO, CAL., CODE § 3.54.100(D) (2009)).

[51] Administration Dept., San Diego, CA, *Rules Implementing the Equal Benefits Ordinance*, Feb. 15, 2011, available at www.sandiego.gov/administration/pdf/eborules101213.pdf.

[52] Berkeley, CA (BERKELEY, CAL., CODE § 13.29.090 (2009)); Broward County, FL (BROWARD COUNTY, FLA., CODE § 16½-157(d) (2012)); State of California (CAL. PUB. CONTRACT CODE §§ 10295.3(f)(3), 10421 (2012)); Dane County, WI (DANE COUNTY, WIS., CODE § 25.016(8) (2010)); Key West, FL (KEY WEST, FLA., CODE § 2–799(d) (2012)); King County, WA (KING COUNTY, WASH., CODE § 12.19.070-.080 (2009)); Long Beach, CA (LONG BEACH, CAL., CODE § 2.73. 090 (2009)); City of Los Angeles, CA (LOS ANGELES, CAL., ADMIN. CODE § 10.8.2.1(h) (2009)); Miami Beach, FL (MIAMI BEACH, FLA., CODE § 2–373(f) (2009)); Oakland, CA (OAKLAND, CAL., CODE § 2.32.090 (2010)); Olympia, WA (OLYMPIA, WASH., CODE § 3.18.020(D), (E) (2009)); Philadelphia, PA (PHILADELPHIA, PA., CODE § 17–1905 (2012)); Portland, OR (PORTLAND, OR., CHARTER § 3.100.055 (2009)); Sacramento, CA (SACRAMENTO, CAL., CODE § 3.54.100 (2009)); San Diego, CA (SAN DIEGO, CAL., CODE § 22.4301–.4307 (2011)); San Francisco, CA (SAN FRANCISCO, CAL., ADMIN. CODE § 12B.1(h) (2009)); San Mateo County, CA (SAN MATEO COUNTY, CAL., CODE § 2.84.040 (2009)); Seattle, WA (SEATTLE, WASH., CODE § 20.45.040 (2009)); Tumwater, WA (TUMWATER, WASH., CODE § 3.46.040 (2009)).

[53] Seventeen jurisdictions with EBOs (all except Santa Monica, Broward County, Key West, and Philadelphia) were contacted first by email on April 4, 2011. If the jurisdiction

asked to answer a set of questions about their experiences with adopting, implementing, and enforcing their EBOs. The positive impact of the EBOs was studied by looking at what the laws have accomplished. For example, have more contractors adopted LGBT-inclusive policies as a result of the EBOs? Have they provided redress for specific violations? The arguments against the EBOs were evaluated by asking those enforcing them if the concerns surrounding their enactment have been borne out. Have the work and operations of state or local governments been disrupted because they could not find compliant contractors? Have they been costly to administer or burdened state or local administrative agencies?

Sixteen localities and the State of California provided responses to our questions. The localities are Berkeley (California), Dane County (Wisconsin), King County (Washington), the City of Los Angeles (California), Miami Beach (Florida), Minneapolis (Minnesota), Oakland (California), Olympia (Washington), Portland (Oregon), Sacramento (California), San Diego (California), San Francisco (California), San Mateo County (California), Santa Monica (California), Seattle (Washington), and Tumwater (Washington). Their responses are presented in the next section.[54]

Most (twelve) of the jurisdictions provided detailed responses, but a few jurisdictions provided limited information. The State of California provided information only about the enforcement and implementation

---

did not respond to the email, a follow-up email was sent on April 11, 2011. If no response to the second email was received, the jurisdictions were contacted by phone on April 21, 2011. If no one was available to answer the questions by phone, a voicemail was left explaining what information was sought. The jurisdictions that did not respond were contacted again on May 13, 2011.

Santa Monica passed its EBO on April 28, 2011. The city was contacted by phone on May 5, 2011, with a request for information about any training programs that have been conducted or materials that have already been developed. The City provided the limited information it had available. On December 7, 2011, just those jurisdictions that had already responded to earlier requests were sent a set of further questions to clarify statements about compliance with their ordinances. Follow-up emails with these questions were sent on December 21, 2011.

EBOs in Broward County, Key West, and Philadelphia passed in November 2011, February 2012, and December 2012, respectively. These localities were contacted by email on July 11, 2012.

[54] Records of all information gathered from the local government agencies are on file with the authors.

of the EBO with respect to contracts entered into by the Department of General Services rather than about all contracts entered into by the state.[55] Three localities provided very limited information on enforcement of their EBOs: Berkeley,[56] King County,[57] and Olympia.[58] Santa Monica was only able to provide limited information about its EBO because the ordinance had so recently passed. However, the limited responses from these jurisdictions support that they have not invested any significant resources or hired new staff to implement or enforce their EBOs.

The agencies that provided detailed data and information for this study largely reported similar experiences with these laws. However, these agencies may be qualitatively different from agencies that provided limited or no responses to our requests. The limited responses and nonresponses may indicate a lack of staff and resources, which, in turn, may mean that these agencies are not able to dedicate the time and effort needed to implement and enforce the EBOs. They may not be equipped or available to answer contractors' questions, which alleviated resistance in almost every case for the agencies that provided information. Nevertheless, almost all of the jurisdictions provided information that can inform future debates in states and localities seeking to pass EBOs.

During the survey, we also identified ten studies that four of these jurisdictions had conducted in order to design and evaluate their ordinances: a report by Oakland evaluating other EBOs before it adopted its

[55] The California Department of General Services stated that all of California's several hundred agencies administer their own contracts, including the equal benefits requirements; there is no one agency that is responsible for overseeing the equal benefits law.

[56] The Human Resources Department and the City Attorney's Office responded that any complaints filed under the ordinance would be referred to the state enforcement agency rather than handled by the city and that all the office knew of enforcement was that contractors were required to sign an affidavit saying they offered equal benefits before they were permitted to submit bids.

[57] King County provided very limited information by email.

[58] The Olympia Administrative Services Department told the researcher that employees could file complaints of EBO ordinance violations online and the City would handle the complaint from there. The department was unable to provide any other information about the ordinance.

own;[59] six evaluations by San Francisco of its EBO, conducted in 1998,[60] 1999,[61] 2000,[62] 2001,[63] 2002,[64] and 2004;[65] a five-year cost estimate by Miami Beach in 2005 of its EBO;[66] a survey by Miami Beach of its contractors before it passed its EBO to measure any potential resistance;[67] and an evaluation by San Diego of its EBO six months after the ordinance went into effect.[68] Information from these reports is also summarized below.

5. COMPLIANCE WITH LGBT-INCLUSIVE CONTRACTOR REQUIREMENTS

Compliance

Administrative agencies have found that almost without exception, private businesses interested in contracting with the government are willing to adopt and comply with EBOs. In almost all jurisdictions that responded, any resistance to these laws was minimal and short-lived. In the few localities that reported some initial resistance, contractors quickly agreed to comply with the laws.

The jurisdictions reported that contractors were generally willing to offer benefits to domestic partners. These jurisdictions reported that most contractors were willing to comply when they received more information from administrative enforcement agencies on how to implement the benefits.

---

[59] CITY OF OAKLAND, CAL., COUNCIL AGENDA REPORT, RE: EQUAL BENEFITS FOR DOMESTIC PARTNERS (Nov. 13, 2001) (on file with the Williams Institute).

[60] *Six Month Report.*

[61] *Two Year Report.*

[62] *Three Year Report.*

[63] *Four Year Report.*

[64] *Five Year Report.*

[65] *Seven Year Update.*

[66] City of Miami Beach Commission Memorandum from Jorge M. Gonzalez, City Manager, to David Demer, Mayor, and Members of the Commission (Oct. 19, 2005) (on file with the Williams Institute).

[67] Ibid.

[68] Administration Dept., City of San Diego, CA, note 26 above.

Six of the twelve localities that provided detailed responses reported some resistance to their EBOs: Dane County, Miami Beach, San Francisco, San Mateo County, Seattle, and Tumwater. All of these localities reported that when resistant contractors were given information clarifying the requirements of the ordinance, the contractors were willing to comply in most cases. The other localities and California's Department of General Services reported no resistance to the EBOs.

Three localities, Miami Beach, San Francisco, and Seattle, reported that most resistance was from contractors that did not want to offer benefits to different-sex partners, even though they already did, or were willing to, offer the benefits to same-sex partners. These contractors were mainly concerned that covering different-sex partners would greatly increase costs or that they would be forced to move to another insurance carrier because their current carrier would not cover different-sex partners. Miami Beach and San Francisco both said that they explained to these contractors that they could comply by paying a cash equivalent to employees with different-sex domestic partners rather than switch carriers. San Francisco also explained that under its ordinance, if any employee of the contractor has a preexisting medical condition or if other insurers do not have the same pool of doctors, the contractor is not required to switch carriers and may use their current insurer's definition of "domestic partners."

Seattle also reported that several contractors based outside of Washington State resisted complying, claiming that offering same-sex domestic partner benefits "was barred by the state [where they were based]." San Mateo reported that no contractors resisted because of costs, but a few resisted because they found it "politically unacceptable" to offer the benefits.

Before Miami Beach passed its EBO, the city's Procurement Division surveyed contractors that were doing business with the city at that time.[69] The purpose of the survey, in part, was to gauge contractors' reactions to the requirements. More than 2,800 surveys were distributed, and 604 responses were received (22 percent). When asked if they already

[69] City of Miami Beach Commission Memorandum from Jorge M. Gonzalez, City Manager, to David Demer, Mayor, and Members of the Commission, note 66 above.

provided domestic partner benefits, 64.7 percent of contractors reported that they did. When asked whether they would continue to do business with the city if they were required to offer domestic partner benefits, 76.3 percent reported that they would, 19.2 percent reported that they would not, and 4.5 percent did not answer. Since the ordinance went into effect, Miami Beach reported that only two noncompliant contractors submitted bids, but in neither case were the companies the lowest bidders, so there was no need for the city to pursue enforcement of the EBO.

In an evaluation of its EBO, San Diego found that all of its 302 contractors were in compliance with the EBO during the first six months of enforcement. The vast majority of contractors (72 percent) complied by offering benefits to domestic partners. Twenty percent of contractors were in compliance because they offered no spousal or domestic partner benefits, and 3 percent had no employees. The remaining one percent did not offer the benefits but were deemed in compliance with San Diego's EBO under a provision that exempts firms subject to a collective bargaining agreement that existed before the EBO went into effect.[70]

In an evaluation of its EBO, San Francisco also found that the vast majority of contractors that have undergone the certification procedure have been found in compliance with the EBO and that compliance increased over time. During the first seven years of the EBO, it found that compliance increased from 91 percent in the first six months of implementation to 94.6 percent after seven years.[71] In 2011, in response to the present survey, San Francisco reported that the compliance rate was 93.6 percent.

There are three ways to comply with San Francisco's EBO, and the most recent evaluation (after seven years of enforcement) found that the majority (45 percent) of contractors complied by offering equal benefits to spouses and domestic partners, 28 percent complied by not offering any benefits based on marital or domestic partnership status, and

[70] Administration Dept., City of San Diego, CA, 3, note 26 above.
[71] The compliance rate rose steadily between 1998 and 2004, from 90.73 percent compliance in 1998, 92.73 percent in 1999, 93.1 percent in 2000, 93.5 percent in 2001, 94 percent in 2002, to 94.6 percent compliance in 2004. *Six Month Report,* 1; *Two Year Report,* 9; *Three Year Report,* 5; *Four Year Report,* 2; *Five Year Report,* 3; *Seven Year Update,* 2.

27 percent complied because they had no employees (i.e., they were sole proprietorships).

Over the first seven years of enforcement, San Francisco found that there was an 8 percent decrease in those contractors complying by offering no employee benefits to spouses or domestic partners. It concluded, "This decline refutes the assertion that Equal Benefits legislation encourages employers to take away benefits they might otherwise offer." It also found that most of the contractors that complied by not offering benefits to spouses or domestic partners had fewer than twenty employees and offered no employee benefits to any employee, single, married, or partnered.

At the end of seven years, San Francisco estimated that 66,492 employees of its contractors were taking advantage of domestic partner benefits provided by the EBO. It also found that contractors that complied by offering equal benefits could be found in forty states and the District of Columbia and in over six hundred cities nationwide, and reported compliance by large (5,000 or more employees), medium (500 to 4,999 employees) and small companies (under 500 employees), "in proportions reflective of the U.S. business community in general."[72] San Francisco's data are consistent with several media reports of companies changing their policies in order to bid on local government contracts.[73]

The results of this survey indicate that EBOs have increased workplace protections for LGBT people. The fact that even resistant contractors were willing to comply when the laws were explained suggests that the EBOs have resulted in more companies offering domestic partner benefits. The minimal resistance to these laws reported by the agencies also indicates that the EBOs have caused little, if any, disruption to the contracting process, for both the governments and the contractors.

Because agencies do not track whether contractors had the policies in place before they decided to bid on contracts, it is difficult to determine how many more contractors offer domestic partner benefits because of the EBOs. However, even if many of the businesses that were awarded

[72] *Seven Year Update*, 3–4.
[73] E.g., Rachel Gordon, "Bechtel Agrees to Extend Its Benefits Policy," *SFGate*, May 4, 2000; Eve Mitchell, "Benefits for Both," *Alameda Times-Star*, Aug. 3, 2003; Julie Forster, "Domestic Partner Benefits Solid," *Saint Paul Pioneer*, Mar. 14, 2004.

contracts already had internal equal benefits policies, the EBOs provide an external enforcement mechanism for the preexisting internal corporate policies. The EBOs establish an administrative complaint procedure and provide remedies for violations that go beyond internal remedies available for breach of corporate policies. In this way, EBOs provide greater protection for LGBT people, whether or not contractors already have an internal policy in place.

States and localities interested in passing EBOs may find more contractor support for the laws if they only require benefits for same-sex partners. The majority of contractor resistance reported by the jurisdictions in this study was to the requirement that benefits be provided to different-sex partners. However, limiting benefits to same-sex partners may be politically less popular and may open up the EBOs to equal protection challenges.[74]

The Impact of Waivers on Compliance

In evaluating compliance with these laws, it is important to consider that all jurisdictions with EBOs allow contractors to request waivers from the EBO requirements under certain circumstances. Although these contractors are offering spousal benefits but not domestic partner benefits, the locality does not consider them out of compliance with the EBO. Data collected from four of the localities with EBOs indicate that contractors primarily comply with EBOs through nondisciminatory benefits policies, as opposed to obtaining waivers.

Four localities, San Francisco, Miami Beach, Minneapolis, and Sacramento, provided specific details about their waiver programs (table 6.1). During the third year of the EBO, San Francisco entered into 187,575 transactions covered by the ordinance, 0.7 percent of which were entered into pursuant to a waiver. During each of the years that San Francisco evaluated its EBO, between 1,232 and 1,604 waivers were requested.[75] In

---

[74] Irizarry v. Chicago B'd of Educ., 251 F.3d 604 (7th Cir. 2001).
[75] *Two Year Report; Three Year Report*, 5; *Four Year Report*, 2; *Five Year Report*, 3; *Seven Year Update*, 2.

Table 6.1   Waivers Granted to San Francisco Contractors, 1998–2002 and 2004

Type of Waiver	*Percentage* of Waivers Granted, by Year*					
	1998	1999	2000	2001	2002	2004
Sole source or blanket sole source**	93.1	93.1	90.2	93.2	91.4	92.5
Public entity	3.0	2.4	2.9	2.1	2.5	3.3
Company was a shell company for a noncompliant company	0	0	0	0	0	0
No compliant company bid	3.1	4.8	6.6	<0.1	0	0.3
Bulk purchasing	0.5	0	<0.1	4.4	5.7	4.0
Emergency	0	0.4	0.1	0.2	0.5	0
Total requested	1,474	1,393	1,389	1,232	1,287	1,604
Total granted	1,398 (94.8%)	1,383 (99.3%)	1,371 (98.7%)	1,216 (98.7%)	1,263 (98.1%)	1,527 (95.2%)

* May not add up to 100 percent due to rounding.

** Blanket sole source is a designation for those contractors who would be approved as a sole source for every contract they were to enter into with the city, and as such do not have to be approved as a sole source on each individual contract submitted.

these years, it granted most of these waivers, between 94.8 percent and 99.3 percent of all requests for waivers.[76] The vast majority of these waivers were granted because the noncompliant contractor was a sole source for the goods or services needed.

San Francisco's evaluations point out that just because a contractor obtains a waiver does not mean that it is not providing at least some form of domestic partner benefits to employees. For example, companies that extended domestic partner benefits only to same-sex domestic partners have to obtain a waiver because the EBO requires that same-sex and

[76] Data on the total number of covered transactions are only available for the third year.

different-sex domestic partners be covered. In addition, if companies just extend medical benefits to domestic partners, but not retirement or leave benefits, they also must seek a waiver because the EBO requires equal medical, retirement, and leave benefits. For example, San Francisco found that out of the ten largest contractors (in terms of dollars awarded) that received waivers in the first five years of enforcement, one had since become compliant by offering domestic partner benefits, and five offered domestic partner benefits but did not fully comply with the EBO. Three of the remaining four that did not offer benefits were public entities that San Francisco was required to work with to satisfy a federal or state mandate.[77]

In 2005, Miami Beach determined that waivers would have been granted to twenty-eight contractors if the EBO had been in effect for the previous five years.[78] This represented 16 percent of the 174 contracts awarded in those five years.

Minneapolis reported that of the 143 contracts entered into in 2010, totaling approximately $65 million, 102 contracts (amounting to $28 million) were covered by the EBO. The city reported that 41 contracts were not covered either because the contractor received a waiver or because the contracts did not fall within the ordinance. Under the Minneapolis ordinance any contract for less than $100,000 and all construction contracts are not required to comply with the EBO.

Sacramento reported that it most commonly grants waivers for companies that have "world-wide operations," where the relationship between the city and the company is such that there is a possibility that the city will interact with an employee of another country at any time. These companies requested waivers based on the difficulty of offering domestic partner benefits to employees all over the world, where cultures and laws differ.[79] However, Sacramento was unable to provide data

[77] *Five Year Report*, 9.

[78] City of Miami Beach Commission Memorandum from Jorge M. Gonzalez, City Manager, to David Demer, Mayor, and Members of the Commission, note 66 above.

[79] The specific example the City gave was a company that contracts to provide IT support to the City. The City said that in this case, when Sacramento employees call for IT support, they are often routed to technicians outside the United States. The IT provider was concerned that all of these employees were working on the contract and therefore would have to be offered domestic partner benefits under the EBO.

on the number of contracts covered by the EBO and the number of contractors that received a waiver.

The data indicate that most contractors comply with EBOs, as opposed to receiving waivers. The only two jurisdictions that provided enough data to determine the impact of the waiver programs on compliance were San Francisco, with 0.7 percent of EBO-covered contracts entered into pursuant to a waiver, and Miami Beach, reporting 16 percent of EBO-covered contracts entered into pursuant to a waiver. And as noted above, the San Francisco data indicate that some of the contractors that received waivers provided some form of domestic partnership benefits but not enough to fully comply with San Francisco's EBO.

Investigation and Enforcement of Individual Violations

All of the state and local administrative agencies reported having established complaint procedures as required by the EBOs. However, very few individual complaints have been made under the laws.

The ten localities[80] that provided detailed information about their EBOs all reported that they monitored compliance by requiring contractors to submit an affidavit of compliance when they bid on contracts. Miami Beach said that in addition to requiring an affidavit, the city requires contractors to verify that they offer the benefits with company-produced documentation (an employee handbook, for example).

San Francisco has a more intensive procedure to evaluate contractor compliance.[81] First, vendors are required to submit documentation to the agency verifying that they have an equal benefits policy. The agency then reviews the materials and determines whether the vendor is in compliance or if additional materials are needed to demonstrate compliance.

---

[80] Dane County, City of Los Angeles, Miami Beach, Minneapolis, Oakland, Portland, Sacramento, San Diego, San Mateo County, and Seattle.

[81] San Francisco Human Rights Commission, City of San Francisco, CA, Chapter 12B Equal Benefits Ordinance File Review Flow Chart (on file with the Williams Institute); San Francisco Human Rights Commission, City of San Francisco, CA, Equal Benefits Documentation Guide (on file with the Williams Institute).

The determination is then logged in a database so that government departments may access the information when they are evaluating vendors that have bid on contracts.[82] In all of these jurisdictions, once a contractor has signed an affidavit and submitted any other required documentation, it is no longer monitored, and enforcement becomes a complaint-driven process.

Eleven localities[83] and California's Department of General Services reported that no complaints had been filed under their EBOs since they went into effect. Nine localities[84] further reported that although no complaints had been filed under their EBOs, if they were to receive complaints, the handling procedures set out in the ordinances would be strictly followed. In addition, King County noted that if a complaint were filed against a King County contractor for a violation of another locality's EBO or a state or local nondiscrimination law and a finding of reasonable cause was made, King County would consider debarment based on that evidence.

Los Angeles reported that one complaint had been filed under its EBO. The complaint alleged that the employer's health benefits were not made available to the employee's domestic partner. The city conducted a compliance investigation and determined that the benefits were governed by ERISA, and as such, the employer did not have to provide them.

All of the twelve localities[85] that provided information about their EBOs and California's Department of General Services reported that none of their contractors had been debarred from contracting under the

[82] San Francisco Human Rights Commission, City of San Francisco, CA, Chapter 12B Equal Benefits Ordinance File Review Flow Chart (on file with the Williams Institute). Documentation may be letters from insurance carriers, employee handbooks, and portions of insurance plans purchased by the employer. San Francisco Human Rights Commission, City of San Francisco, CA, Equal Benefits Documentation Guide (on file with the Williams Institute).

[83] Dane County, King County, Miami Beach, Minneapolis, Oakland, Portland, Sacramento, San Diego, San Mateo County, Seattle, and Tumwater.

[84] Dane County, Miami Beach, Oakland, Portland, Sacramento, San Diego, San Francisco, San Mateo County, and Seattle. Tumwater did not respond to this question.

[85] Dane County, City of Los Angeles, Miami Beach, Minneapolis, Oakland, Portland, Sacramento, San Diego, San Francisco, San Mateo County, Seattle, and Tumwater.

EBO. One locality, Oakland, had terminated an office supply contract because the contractor was found out of compliance, however.[86]

In this survey, the jurisdictions were not asked to explain why they had so few individual complaints. However, at least two reasons seem likely to contribute to the scarcity of enforcement actions. First, the lack of individual complaints may reflect a lack of investment in the enforcement agencies. Second, the lack of individual complaints may be the result of widespread compliance.

Lack of Investment in Enforcement

Administrative agency limitations, particularly at the local level, may account for the lack of complaints filed under EBOs. Studies of complaints filed on the basis of sexual orientation and gender identity under local nondiscrimination ordinances have concluded that local enforcement agencies often lack the staff and resources needed to fully enforce the ordinances.[87] Similar limitations were documented in academic literature describing the role of agencies enforcing state and local civil rights laws prior to the enactment of the Civil Rights Act of 1964.[88]

Nine of the twelve localities with EBOs that responded and California's Department of General Services did not indicate that they hired additional staff to implement or enforce the EBOs.[89] Of the other three, only

[86] Memorandum from David E. Dise, Director, Montgomery County Dep't of General Svcs., to Jack Gibala, Program Manager, Office of Business Relations and Compliance, Montgomery County Dept. of General Svcs (Dec. 21, 2009), available at http://www6.montgomerycountymd.gov/content/council/pdf/agenda/col/2010/100202/20100202_8.pdf.

[87] Roddrick A. Colvin, "Improving State Policies Prohibiting Public Employment Discrimination Based on Sexual Orientation," *Review of Public Personnel Administration* 20, 5 (2000); Norma M. Riccucci and Charles W. Gossett, "Employment Discrimination in State and Local Government: The Lesbian and Gay Male Experience," *American Review of Public Administration* 26, 175 (1996); Brad Sears, Nan D. Hunter, and Christy Mallory, "Administrative Complaints on the Basis of Sexual Orientation and Gender Identity," in *Documenting Discrimination on the Basis of Sexual Orientation and Gender Identity in State Employment* (2009), available at http://wiwp.law.ucla.edu/wp-content/uploads/11_AdministrativeComplaints.pdf.

[88] Alfred W. Blumrosen, *Black Employment and the Law* (New Brunswick, NJ: Rutgers University Press, 1971), 14.

[89] Dane County, City of Los Angeles, Minneapolis, Oakland, Portland, Sacramento, San Diego, Seattle, and Tumwater.

one, San Francisco, hired additional permanent, full-time staff. San Francisco hired six full-time staff members to start up its EBO program and now retains the equivalent of 4.5 full-time staff members to enforce the EBO.[90] San Mateo hired one temporary staff person to start up its EBO program; then existing Procurement Department staff became responsible for enforcing the program after it was developed. Miami Beach hired one additional staff member to implement and enforce both its EBO and its living wage ordinance.

The fact that few staff were hired as the result of these laws can be looked at in two ways. First, the lack of staff may indicate a lack investment in enforcement of the EBOs—contributing to the low number of individual complaints. Alternatively, these jurisdictions could have been making reasonable resource allocations by not investing further in enforcement. They may have determined that given the small size of the LGBT population and the existing capacity of their enforcement staff, no additional staff were necessary to enforce the LGBT-specific contractor provisions. Research by the Williams Institute has shown that only 3.8 percent of the population identifies as LGBT[91] and that the take-up rate for same-sex and different-sex domestic partner benefits would be 0.3 percent to 2.3 percent of a contractor's employees.[92]

[90] According to a 2001 report by the Oakland Contract Compliance & Employment Services Division before it adopted its EBO, staffing for the EBO in San Francisco was equivalent to five full-time employees; thirteen existing full-time staff members responsible for contract enforcement handled EBO implementation and enforcement in Los Angeles; and Seattle and Berkeley each dedicated one full-time position to EBO enforcement. As noted above, the Oakland report contradicts what Seattle and Berkeley indicated in the current survey and Los Angeles confirmed it hired no new employees. City of Oakland, CA, Council Agenda Report, note 59 above.

[91] Gary J. Gates, "How Many People Are Lesbian, Gay, Bisexual, and Transgender?" (2011), 1, available at http://williamsinstitute.law.ucla.edu/wp-content/uploads/Gates-How-Many-People-LGBT-Apr-2011.pdf.

[92] Michael A. Ash and M. V. Lee Badgett, "Separate and Unequal: The Effect of Unequal Access to Employment-Based Health Insurance on Same-Sex and Unmarried Different-Sex Couples," *Journal of Contemporary Economic Policy* 24, 582 (2006): 582–99.

Widespread Compliance

The lack of individual enforcement action may indicate widespread compliance. All of the responding localities at least require contractors to submit an affidavit of compliance when they bid on contracts, if not more extensive preclearance information. Thus, for there to be a violation by these contractors, they would have to lie about a policy that is easy to verify or change their entire benefits plan after receiving a contract.

In addition, the education efforts by the jurisdictions may have contributed to widespread compliance and the lack of complaints. All of the localities that responded,[93] except Tumwater and Minneapolis,[94] provided materials on their EBOs that they created for staff, contractors, and employees of contractors or make these documents available online. California's Department of General Services also indicated that it provides such materials. One city that did not respond, Long Beach, makes these documents available online. The materials provided by these jurisdictions include the following:

- Detailed web pages directed to contractors with information on compliance and access to the necessary forms.[95]

---

[93] Berkeley, King County, City of Los Angeles, Dane County, Long Beach, Miami Beach, Oakland, Olympia, Portland, Sacramento, San Diego, San Mateo County, San Francisco, and Seattle.

[94] Minneapolis provides a link to its EBO on the city website but no more detailed information regarding implementation or enforcement. Procurement Division, Minneapolis, MN, Purchasing Division, www.ci.minneapolis.mn.us/procurement/.

[95] Purchasing Division, Dane County, WI, Summary of Domestic Partner Equal Benefit Requirement, www.danepurchasing.com/partner_benefit.aspx; Procurement, King County, WA, Equal Benefits to Employees with Domestic Partners, www.kingcounty.gov/operations/procurement/Services/Equal_Benefits.aspx; Long Beach, CA, Equal Benefits Ordinance, http://www.longbeach.gov/news/displaynews.asp?NewsID=4413&targetid=41; Administrative Services, City of Olympia, WA, Equal Benefits, http://olympiawa.gov/city-government/departments/administrative-services/equal-benefits.aspx; Management & Finance, City of Portland, OR, Equal Benefits, www.portlandonline.com/omf/index.cfm?c=43774; San Francisco Human Rights Commission, City of San Francisco, CA., How to Comply with the Equal Benefits Ordinance, http://sf-hrc.org/index.aspx?page=96. The City of Los Angeles's EBO web page includes compliance information directed to contractors and to city departments. Bureau of Contract Administration, City of Los Angeles, CA, Equal Benefits Ordinance, http://bca.lacity.org/index.cfm?nxt=ee&nxt_body=content_ebo.cfm.

- Detailed rulebooks, handouts, and compliance guides.[96]
- Short fact sheets, FAQs, and brochures on the ordinances.[97]
- Compliance posters for employers.[98]

6. ARGUMENTS AGAINST EBOS

The survey also asked the jurisdictions to respond to the concerns raised prior to the passage of the EBOs, including the concern that they would be unable to secure contractors to effectively carry out their work and that the laws would be administratively burdensome, would be costly to implement, and would result in litigation.

Disruption of Work and Operations of Government

As indicated by the discussion of widespread compliance with EBOs above, none of the jurisdictions that responded to the survey reported

---

[96] City of San Diego, CA, Rules Implementing the Equal Benefits Ordinance, above note 52; City of San Diego, CA, Equal Benefits Ordinance Certification of Compliance, February 15, 2011 (on file with the Williams Institute); City of Oakland, CA, EBO How-To Guide, November 2004 (on file with the Williams Institute); City of Miami Beach, FL, Quick Reference Guide to Equal Benefits Compliance (on file with the Williams Institute); City of Sacramento, CA, Requirements of the Non-Discrimination in Employee Benefits Code, available at www.cityofsacramento.org/generalservices/procurement/ordinances/documents/EBO-Packet.pdf.

[97] City of Berkeley, CA, Equal Benefits Ordinance Fact Sheet, available at www.ci.berkeley.ca.us/uploadedFiles/Online_Service_Center/Level_3_-_General/EBOFactsheet%5B1%5D.pdf; City of San Diego, CA, EBO [brochure], February 15, 2011 (on file with the Williams Institute); City of San Diego, CA, Overview of Equal Benefits Ordinance, February 15, 2011 (on file with the Williams Institute); City of San Diego, CA, Equal Benefits Ordinance Frequently Asked Questions, Feb. 15, 2011 (on file with the Williams Institute); City of Oakland, CA, Equal Benefits, Non-Discrimination, Equal Access: FYI, July 2002 (on file with the Williams Institute); San Mateo County, Cal., Frequently Asked Questions: Equal Benefits Ordinance, available at www.cityofsacramento.org/generalservices/procurement/ordinances/documents/EBO-Packet.pdf; Department of Executive Administration, City of Seattle, WA, Equal Benefits Ordinance: Frequently Asked Questions, Feb. 13, 2009, available at www2.ci.seattle.wa.us/EqualBenefits/Faq.pdf.

[98] Purchasing Division, Dane County, WI, Notification of Domestic Partner Equal Benefits Requirement, available at http://danedocs.countyofdane.com/webdocs/pdf/purch/partner_poster.pdf. Last accessed Sept. 20, 2011.

that the EBOs in any way hampered their ability to carry out their work. None of the jurisdictions reported that because of the EBOs they were unable to hire the contractors that they needed.

Administrative Burden

Almost every jurisdiction in this study said that their EBOs did not create an administrative burden. When specifically asked whether EBOs were burdensome administratively, eleven localities said that they were not.[99] These localities reported that the ordinances were fairly easy and quick to implement, and enforcement duties were assumed by the local governments without any major problems. Portland added that the program has been particularly easy to implement since the city switched to an online system for compliance verification that allows contractors to submit affidavits electronically. King County said that the EBO does present an administrative burden on the Procurement Department but did not respond to a request for more details. San Francisco reported that the administrative burden of the EBO has not been measured. California's Department of General Services also said that it did not have enough information to answer the question.

Costs

The survey asked localities about two types of costs: costs associated with implementing and enforcing the ordinances and whether the ordinances resulted in an increase in contract prices for the localities.

ADMINISTRATIVE COSTS

Consistent with the discussion above on the jurisdictions reporting little administrative burden resulting from EBOs and that only one, San Francisco's, resulted in the hiring of new, full-time, permanent staff, the

---

[99] Dane County, City of Los Angeles, Miami Beach, Minneapolis, Oakland, Portland, Sacramento, San Diego, San Mateo County, Seattle, and Tumwater.

jurisdictions reported very little administrative costs associated with these ordinances.

However, San Diego assessed the costs associated with its EBO in its evaluation, and one study quantified administrative costs for three of the larger localities with EBOs: Berkeley, Seattle, and San Francisco. In the first six months of enforcement, San Diego found that "there is no additional cost for the City of San Diego associated with the EBO."[100] According to a 2001 report by the Oakland Contract Compliance & Employment Services Division, yearly EBO administration costs for Berkeley, Seattle, and San Francisco were $95,000, $100,000, and $450,000, respectively, as reported by these localities.[101] There was no dollar estimate provided for the administration of the Los Angeles EBO, but the Oakland report states that it costs more than that of San Francisco. In response to this survey, San Francisco reported that it has not recently ascertained the administrative cost associated with its EBO.

The costs associated with EBOs are likely due to administration of the waiver provisions and, in some cases, compliance checks that go beyond getting an affidavit from the contractor. However, as noted above, despite the additional work these ordinances may create, only San Francisco reported hiring any new, permanent, full-time staff to implement its EBO.

CONTRACTING COSTS

Data were collected on increased contract costs for three localities with EBOs. In a 2005 recommendation for its EBO, the Miami Beach City Commission estimated that it would cost the city approximately $73,224 per year.[102]

---

[100] Administration Dept., City of San Diego, CA, 5, note 26 above.

[101] City of Oakland, CA, Council Agenda Report, note 59 above.

[102] City of Miami Beach Commission Memorandum from Jorge M. Gonzalez, City Manager, to David Demer, Mayor, and Members of the Commission, above note 66. This figure was calculated by comparing the lowest and best bids that did not meet the requirement of the EBO and the next lowest and best bids that did meet the requirements of the EBO for all contracts in the five years before the report was produced. If the lowest and best bidder did not meet the requirements of the EBO but would qualify for a waiver (16 percent of contractors), that bid was used in the calculation rather than the lowest and best bidder that offered equal benefits.

The 2001 Oakland report, discussed above, estimated that the financial impact of an EBO on Oakland contractors was an increase of 0.5 percent to 2 percent over the normal cost of doing business.[103] It also stated that San Francisco reported an average increase in costs of approximately 2 percent (ranging from 1.5 percent to 3 percent) for its contractors to comply with its EBO. It should be noted that the Oakland and San Francisco EBOs under consideration extended benefits to same-sex and different-sex partners.

Only San Francisco's EBO, which has a more robust preclearance procedure and applies to same-sex and different-sex domestic partners, had administrative costs estimated at over $100,000 per year. Estimates for Miami Beach City, San Francisco, and Oakland indicate that contractor costs increased from 0.5 percent to 3 percent per year. However, none of these studies considers the economic benefits from the EBO, such as contractors attracting and retaining a more highly skilled and productive workforce.

Litigation

EBOs in three jurisdictions, San Francisco, New York, and Minneapolis, have been challenged in court six times. Four of these challenges were to San Francisco's EBO, the first EBO enacted. The last of these cases, a challenge to Minneapolis's EBO, was brought in 2004. We have found no litigation involving EBOs since 2004.

In two of these six cases, courts found that the EBOs were partially preempted by the Employee Retirement Income Security Act (ERISA)—in particular, to the extent that they require self-insured employers to offer health care coverage to domestic partners.[104] In the challenge to New York City's EBO, the court found not only that the health care component was preempted by ERISA but also that the entire EBO was preempted by a New York State procurement statute.[105] The three other cases

---

[103] City of Oakland, CA, Council Agenda Report, note 59 above.

[104] Air Transport Ass'n, 992 F. Supp. 1149; Council of New York v. Bloomberg, 846 N.E.2d 433 (N.Y. 2006).

[105] Council of New York, 846 N.E.2d 433.

either upheld the EBO or were dismissed for lack of standing before substantive issues were reached.[106]

ERISA PREEMPTION

Both times ERISA preemption was litigated EBOs have been limited, in part, as a result.[107] The biggest difference between these challenges was how the courts applied the availability of a "marketplace participant" exception to ERISA preemption.[108] The "marketplace participant" exception has been borrowed by courts from preemption cases involving the National Labor Relations Act (NLRA).[109] In effect, this exception allows a locality to regulate in ways that would otherwise be preempted by federal laws that seek to standardize an industry (like the NLRA and ERISA) so long as the city "wields no more power than an ordinary consumer" would in the transaction.

New York's highest court held that the city could not rely on the exemption any time it required ERISA-regulated benefits under the EBO because the city was "setting policy" rather than engaging in the buying process like a normal consumer.[110] However, a district court in California left open the possibility of a "marketplace participant" exception to ERISA preemption of EBOs when the city "wields no more power than an ordinary consumer."[111] In that case, *Air Transport v. San Francisco*, the

---

[106] S.D. Meyers v. San Francisco, 253 F.3d 461 (9th Cir. 2001) (S.D. Meyers I); S.D. Meyers v. San Francisco, 336 F.3d 1174 (9th Cir. 2003) (S.D. Myers II); Titus Construction v. City of Minneapolis, No. 04–1487 (D. Minn. Sept. 21, 2004). The fourth case was a challenge to San Francisco's EBO brought by an electrical contracting company that had religious objections to the EBO. *Five Year Report*, 13.

[107] A third case also limited a Portland, ME, ordinance that was similar to an EBO based on ERISA preemption. The ordinance required that equal benefits be provided to the domestic partners of employees of the city, the Portland School Committee, and any organization accepting Housing and Community Development funds from the City. An organization that accepted housing funds argued that the ordinance was preempted by ERISA. The court agreed, limiting the ordinance to non-ERISA fringe benefits, such as bereavement leave and leaves of absence. Catholic Charities of Maine, Inc. v. City of Portland, 304 F. Supp. 2d 77 (D. Me. 2004).

[108] Air Transport Ass'n, 992 F. Supp. 1149; Council of New York, 846 N.E.2d 433.

[109] Air Transport Ass'n, 992 F. Supp. at 1178–80.

[110] Council of New York, 846 N.E.2d at 442.

[111] Air Transport Ass'n, 992 F. Supp. at 1179–80.

court determined that the city had more "economic power" over an airport than a normal consumer would, so it could not require the airport to provide the benefits.

As a result of the *Air Transport* ruling, San Francisco has only allowed companies to limit their compliance with its EBO in "rare instances" where the city determines that it "wields more power than an ordinary consumer." In 2005, only thirty-three companies chose to limit their benefits on this basis.[112] To put that number in perspective, San Francisco entered into 187,575 transactions in 2003.[113] The city still relies on the "marketplace participant" exception in all other situations ("most often," according to the City), requiring contractors to offer ERISA-regulated benefits. King County, Washington, and Los Angeles, California, have also issued rules implementing their EBOs that apply the *Air Transport* holding. The rules, issued in 2011, state that employers are required to offer ERISA-regulated benefits in a nondiscriminatory manner, unless the contractor demonstrates that the county cannot meet the "marketplace participant" exception with respect to a particular contract.[114] San Francisco's ordinance and Los Angeles's and King County's practices adopted in light of *Air Transport* have not generated any further ERISA-related litigation.

Whenever a state or locality requires contractors to provide health care benefits in its EBO, there is a possibility that the law will be challenged on ERISA preemption grounds. However, even in cases that find that ERISA preemption applies, the scope of preemption is limited. ERISA only regulates some benefits, most significantly health care benefits, and only regulates self-insured employers.[115] Therefore, even if ERISA preemption is

---

[112] *Five Year Report*, 13.

[113] *Three Year Report*, 8.

[114] Office of Contract Compliance, Dept. of Public Works, Los Angeles, CA, Rules and Regulations Implementing the Equal Benefits Ordinance 10–11 (Aug. 15, 2011), available at http://bca.lacity.org/site/pdf/ebo%5CRules%20&%20regulations%20for%20the%20implementation%20of%20EBO.pdf; Exec. Svcs, King County, WA, Rules Implementing Equal Benefits Ordinance 14823 and Ordinance 16856 5 (Jan. 30, 2011), available at www.kingcounty.gov/operations/policies/rules/contracting/con7151pr.aspx.

[115] Employee Retirement Income Security Act of 1974 (ERISA), P.L. No. 93–406, 88 Stat. 829 (codified as amended in scattered sections of 5 U.S.C., 18 U.S.C., 26 U.S.C., 29 U.S.C., and 42 U.S.C.); Hinda Ripps Chaikind, CRS Report for Congress, ERISA Regulation of Health Plans: Fact Sheet (2003), www.allhealth.org/briefingmaterials/erisaregulationofhealthplans-114.pdf.

found to apply, localities may still require all contractors to offer benefits that ERISA does not regulate and may require contractors that are not self-insured to offer all benefits on equal terms. Further, San Francisco's experience following the *Air Transport* ruling strongly suggests that in some jurisdictions the "marketplace participant" exception will shield the EBO from ERISA preemption in the vast majority of cases. Moreover, we have not been able to find a challenge brought against an EBO since 2004, and, according to agencies, contractors are complying with all EBO requirements. Finally, despite ERISA litigation, health benefits are included in all EBOs passed since 2004 that specify which benefits must be offered.[116]

Other Arguments

LIMITS ON GEOGRAPHIC SCOPE

The *Air Transport* case also limited the geographic scope of San Francisco's EBO. The court found that the dormant commerce clause of the U.S. Constitution prohibits application of the EBO to "out-of-state conduct that is not related to the purposes of the City contract." The result of this ruling is that EBOs may reach contractors' operations in the jurisdiction; contractors' operations that occur elsewhere in the United States where work related to the contract is being performed; and work performed on real property outside of the locality if the property is owned or occupied by the jurisdiction and the contractor's presence is related to the contract.[117] All of the EBOs passed since this decision that specifically state their geographic reach are structured to apply to only this conduct.[118]

---

[116] Three localities that define "employee benefits" to include health benefits have passed EBOs since 2004: Dane County, WI (2008), Long Beach, CA (2009); San Diego, CA (2010); and Portland, OR (2006). DANE COUNTY, WIS., CODE § 25.016(b) (2010); LONG BEACH, CAL., CODE § 2.73.040(A) (2009); SAN DIEGO, CAL., CODE § 22.4302 (2011); PORTLAND, OR., CHARTER § 3.100.052(E) (2009). However Portland's ordinance does state that "employee benefits" do not include benefits that are preempted by state and federal law. PORTLAND, OR., CHARTER § 3.100.053–3.100.052(E) (2009).

[117] Air Transport Ass'n, 992 F. Supp. at 1161–66.

[118] See notes 34–37 above and accompanying text.

In another case against San Francisco's EBO, the Ninth Circuit affirmed the extraterritorial applications of the EBO that were upheld in the *Air Transport* case.[119] In the case, brought under the California Constitution, the court noted that while the state constitution forbids a municipal corporation from "'exercis[ing] its *governmental* functions beyond its corporate boundaries,'" it "may exercise its *proprietary* powers,'" including the power to control commercial relationships, outside of the city's corporate boundaries.[120]

PREEMPTION BY STATE AND FEDERAL LAWS OTHER THAN ERISA

In one case brought against San Francisco's EBO, the contractor argued that the ordinance was preempted by California's broad domestic partnership law. This case reached the Ninth Circuit, and the court upheld the EBO finding that the domestic partnership law did not explicitly preclude San Francisco from enacting the EBO or "occupy the field" of domestic partnership regulation in the state.[121]

The *Air Transport* case also upheld San Francisco's EBO to preemption challenges based on the Railroad Labor Act and the Airline Deregulation Act, except "when it is applied in a manner that creates coercive economic incentives for air carriers to alter their routes." The court explained that coercion would only occur "if the burden of compliance is so great that carriers will reject City contracts that are essential to operating out of the Airport."[122] It is not clear from the information provided by San Francisco whether any air carriers are exempt from the EBO as a result of this decision.

The New York case that resulted in an ERISA preemption decision also held that the EBO was preempted by a state procurement statute that required that a contract be awarded to the "lowest responsible bidder."[123]

---

[119] S.D. Meyers I, 253 F.3d 461.
[120] Ibid., 473 (citing City of Oakland v. Brock, 67 P.2d 344, 345 (Cal. 1937)).
[121] S.D. Meyers II, 336 F.3d 1174.
[122] Air Transport Ass'n, 992 F. Supp. at 1187–88, 1191.
[123] Council of New York, 846 N.E.2d at 438–40.

7. SAN FRANCISCO'S EXPERIENCE COMPARED TO OTHER JURISDICTIONS

Because San Francisco's EBO was the first in the country, its early experiences with implementation and enforcement may be different from the experiences of jurisdictions that have more recently enacted EBOs. These differences may be important to jurisdictions that consider enacting EBOs in the future.

First, potential contractors are more likely to offer domestic partner benefits regardless of the existence of an EBO now than they were in 1996. In 1996, only 500 employers offered domestic partner benefits. As of May 2008, over 9,300 employers offered such benefits.[124] That number is likely even higher today. These data suggest that many employers that bid on contracts will not have to change their policies in order to bid and that future EBOs will likely face even less resistance by contractors than did San Francisco's. Further, if more contractors already have the policies in place, state and local agencies should not have to spend as much time providing compliance assistance to contractors. Less time spent enforcing EBOs should result in savings to the government agencies.

Second, localities that enacted EBOs after San Francisco have decided not to include the same intensive prebid compliance review procedure. Instead, these localities generally require only that contractors attest to compliance in writing.[125] San Francisco's prebid procedure has generated some criticism from contractors that think the process takes too long. The latter approach likely makes EBOs less burdensome for agencies to enforce.

Third, localities that enacted EBOs after San Francisco have not hired new, full-time, permanent staff to administer the EBO. From the available data, it is difficult to say why this is the case. It may be because San Francisco has more resources available to dedicate to implementation and enforcement of the EBO than other jurisdictions. It may be because San Francisco's prebid compliance review procedure is more demanding of staff. In any case, that jurisdictions are able to successfully implement

[124] Employee Benefit Research Institute, Domestic Partner Benefits: Facts and Background, 1, note 11 above.

[125] See notes 80–82 above and accompanying text.

and enforce their EBOs without hiring new, full-time, permanent staff suggests that localities that enact EBOs in the future may also be able to use existing staff to handle EBO enforcement.

Fourth, the more recently enacted ordinances have faced less litigation than San Francisco's ordinance. San Francisco's ordinance was challenged in court four times. Only two challenges have been brought to EBOs enacted after San Francisco's. The most recent challenges were brought in 2004.[126] The absence of recent EBO litigation may indicate that future EBOs are unlikely to be challenged in court. Moreover, jurisdictions that design EBOs in the future can benefit from the legal precedent that has been established in earlier cases. Finally, the only two cases that limited or invalidated EBOs did so, at least in part, because the courts found that health care benefits required by the ordinances were preempted by ERISA.[127] While the legal issue is complex, practically speaking, local government experience shows that contractors agree to offer certain benefits under the EBOs even though a court may find that they are preempted by ERISA.[128] This suggests that, for employers, offering even ERISA-regulated benefits is not controversial and may be easier and less costly than going to court. In short, state and local governments that enact EBOs in the future will probably not face the same legal challenges as San Francisco.[129]

8.   IMPLICATIONS FOR A FEDERAL EBO POLICY

Executive Order 11246 currently prohibits federal contractors from discriminating based on race, religion, sex, and national origin.[130] A new executive

---

[126] Although *Council of New York v. Bloomberg* was decided in 2006, the challenge was filed in 2004. Council of New York, 846 N.E.2d at 435. A challenge to Minneapolis's EBO was also brought in 2004. Titus Construction v. City of Minneapolis, No. 04–1487 (D. Minn. Sept. 21, 2004).

[127] See notes 104–23 above and accompanying text.

[128] For example, only one locality, Los Angeles, reported that a contractor was unwilling to offer ERISA-regulated benefits. San Francisco reported that only thirty-three contractors chose to not offer ERISA-regulated benefits in 2005 in response to the *Air Transport* ruling.

[129] Note also that state laws cannot be subject to challenges based on the scope of local power, like New York's ordinance.

[130] E.O. No. 11,246, § 202, 3 C.F.R. 339 (1964–65).

order could prohibit contractors from discriminating against their employees based on sexual orientation and gender identity. Like current state and local EBOs, the order could also require that federal contractors offer domestic partner benefits to their employees (EBO executive order).

An EBO executive order may have several advantages over state and local EBOs. First, it would have broader reach than state and local laws. Executive Order 11246 currently applies to almost 200,000 contractors, offering protection to 26 million employees (22 percent of the civilian workforce).[131] While many of these employers likely already provide domestic partner benefits, the Williams Institute has estimated that an additional 14.3 to 15.3 million employees would have access to coverage for a domestic partner if an EBO executive order were issued. However, given the low take-up rates for domestic partner benefits, a much smaller number would sign up a partner for coverage.[132]

Second, an EBO executive order would not be vulnerable to ERISA preemption like state and local laws are. ERISA broadly and explicitly preempts "any and all State laws insofar as they . . . relate to any employee benefit plan covered by ERISA." This preemption clause also applies to local ordinances.[133] However, ERISA explicitly states that it does not preempt other federal laws.[134] Courts have applied this "federal savings" clause to hold that ERISA does not preempt federal laws, including the Age Discrimination in Employment Act (ADEA), the Railway Labor Act (RLA), the NLRA, and federal common law on labor relations.[135] Thus an

[131] U.S. Dept. of Labor, Office of Federal Contract Compliance, Facts on Executive Order 11246—Affirmative Action (Jan. 4, 2002), www.dol.gov/ofccp/regs/compliance/aa.htm.

[132] M. V. Lee Badgett, the Williams Institute, "The Impact of Extending Sexual Orientation and Gender Identity Non-Discrimination Requirements to Federal Contractors" (2012), available at http://williamsinstitute.law.ucla.edu/wp-content/uploads/Badgett-EOImpact-Feb-201211.pdf.

[133] E.g., Council of New York, 846 N.E.2d at 440–41; Catholic Charities of Me., Inc. v. City of Portland, 304 F.Supp 2d at 84–93; Air Transport Ass'n, 992 F. Supp. at 1149.

[134] 29 U.S.C. § §1444(d) (2012).

[135] See, e.g., Murphy v. Heppenstall Co., 635 F.2d 233 (3d Cir. 1980), cert. denied, 454 U.S. 1142 (1982) (NLRA and federal common law of labor relations not preempted); Airline Pilots Ass'n Int'l v. Northwest Airlines, 627 F.2d 272 (D.C. Cir. 1980) (mandatory arbitration provision of the RLA not preempted); Nemeth v. Clark, 677 F.Supp. 899 (W.D. Mich. 1987) (ADEA not preempted).

EBO executive order should not be vulnerable to challenges based on ERISA preemption.

The president has the power to issue an executive order so long as it advances the economy and efficiency of the federal government.[136] Courts have found that Executive Order 11246 meets this standard.[137] The current study would support a finding that an EBO executive order would also advance the economy and efficiency of the federal government.

The responses from state and local agencies show that these requirements do not disrupt the contracting process for either contractors or government agencies. In nearly every case, contractors were willing to comply with the EBOs in order to contract with the government. There is evidence that more contractors are providing equal benefits as a direct result of the contracting laws. And high compliance rates show that contractors are willing to accept the possibility of external enforcement in order to contract.

No jurisdiction reported that the EBO inhibited its ability to carry out the operations and work of its government. Almost every jurisdiction that provided information reported that these ordinances were not administratively burdensome to enforce. For almost all jurisdictions, any demands created by these laws were handled by existing staff, and training was developed to ensure smooth integration of the new responsibilities. Several of the larger localities with EBOs estimated the administrative or contractor costs associated with their EBOs. These estimates showed a minimal increase in contractor costs but did not consider any of the economic benefits resulting from the EBOs, such as having contractors with more highly skilled and productive employees.[138]

Moreover, many of the jurisdictions have stated that they enacted their EBOs because it was economically good for businesses and the

---

[136] 40 U.S.C. § 471 (2012). See Contractors Ass'n of E. Penn. v. Schultz, 442 F.2d 159, 169–71 (3d Cir. 1971).

[137] See, e.g., Contractors Ass'n of E. Penn. 442 F.2d 159; Farmer v. Philadelphia Elec. Co., 326 F.2d 3 (3d Cir. 1964); Farkas v. Tex. Instrument, Inc., 375 F.2d 629, 632 n.1 (5th Cir. 1967).

[138] See Brad Sears and Christy Mallory, "Economic Motives for Adopting LGBT-Related Workplace Policies" (2011), available at http://williamsinstitute.law.ucla.edu/wp-content/uploads/Mallory-Sears-Corporate-Statements-Oct-20111.pdf.

government. For example, the preamble to Minneapolis, Minnesota's EBO states:

> Requiring contractors to provide to employees with domestic partners benefits equal to those provided to employees who are married will require contractors to maintain a competitive advantage in recruiting and retaining the highest quality work force, thereby improving the quality of goods and services that the city receives. The City of Minneapolis has a fiscal responsibility to ensure that it purchases the best quality goods and services possible within its budgetary constraints. To ensure that the City of Minneapolis receives improved quality of goods and services, the functions of the purchasing agent are expanded as provided in this section.[139]

Similarly, San Francisco has said that companies increase their ability to recruit and retain the best talent when they offer generous benefits and signal that they are committed to diversity,[140] and Los Angeles's EBO states that its purpose is "to ensure that the City's contractors will maintain a competitive edge in recruiting and retaining capable employees, thereby improving the quality of the goods and services the City and its people receive, and ensuring protection of the City's property."[141] Oakland's[142] and Sacramento's[143] EBOs also cite furthering "convenience" as a benefit to the city governments.[144]

Academic research and corporate experience support that offering domestic partner benefits to employees makes good business sense. In a recent study, the Williams Institute found that 53 percent of the top U.S. companies have linked LGBT nondiscrimination policies or domestic partner benefits policies to a positive business impact. For example, a top federal contractor, Lockheed Martin, has said of these policies, "Ensuring a positive and respectful workplace and a robust set of benefits for every-

---

[139] MINNEAPOLIS, MINN., CODE § 18.200 (2010).

[140] San Francisco. Human Rights Commission, Overview of the Equal Benefits Ordinance, note 3 above.

[141] LOS ANGELES, CAL. ADMIN. CODE § 10.8.2.1(a) (2009).

[142] OAKLAND, CAL., CODE § 2.32.010 (2010).

[143] SACRAMENTO, CAL., CODE § 3.54.010 (2009).

[144] In addition, Dane County, WI, states in the county code chapter that includes its EBO that the general purpose of the chapter is "to achieve greater efficiency and economy in the operation of Dane County government." DANE COUNTY, WIS., CODE § 25.01 (2010).

one is critical to retaining employees." Other commonly mentioned economic benefits resulting from these policies include more effective customer service, increased employee productivity, a wider range of ideas and innovations, and a boost in employee relations and morale.[145] Several surveys and academic studies also show that LGBT workers are happier and healthier when their company offers domestic partner benefits.[146]

All of these data and this information supports that an EBO executive order would advance the economy and efficiency of the federal government.

9.   CONCLUSION

The legal landscape for same-sex couples has changed a great deal since San Francisco passed its pioneering EBO in 1996. Many more employers now offer domestic partner benefits, and offering domestic partner coverage has become common in the insurance industry. Since 1996, state and local domestic partner registries have been established in jurisdictions around the country, and same-sex couples can legally marry in thirteen states and Washington DC.[147] Nineteen other localities and one

[145] The study looked at statements issued by the top fifty federal contractors and the top fifty Fortune 500 companies. Sears and Mallory, "Economic Motives for Adopting LGBT-Related Workplace Policies."

[146] E.g., Belle Rose Ragins and John M. Cornwell, "The Influence of Gay Family-Friendly Policies on Gay, Lesbian and Bisexual Employees," in *Sexual Orientation Discrimination: An International Perspective*, ed. M. V. Lee Badgett and Jefferson Frank (New York: Routledge, 2007), 105; Belle Rose Ragins and John M. Cornwell, "Pink Triangles: Antecedents and Consequences of Perceived Workplace Discrimination Against Gay and Lesbian Employees," *Journal of Applied Psychology* 86, 1244 (2001): 1244–61; Press Release, Out & Equal, Harris Interactive & Witeck-Combs Communications, "Majority of All Adults Agree that Companies Should Have Freedom to Decide the Benefits Offered to Employees and Their Spouses and Partners—not Federal or State Policy Designed to Ban Gay Marriage" (May 22, 2006), available at http://outandequal.org/documents/2006_Workplace_Survey052306.pdf; Derek Johnston and Mary A. Malina, "Managing Sexual Orientation Diversity: The Impact on Firm Value," *Group and Organization Management* 33, 602 (2008): 602–25.

[147] National Gay and Lesbian Task Force, "Relationship Recognition for Same Sex Couples in the U.S.," June 28, 2011, www.thetaskforce.org/downloads/reports/issue_maps/rel_recog_6_28_11_color.pdf.

state now have EBOs. San Francisco's EBO has been credited with sparking or encouraging many of these changes.

This study shows that implementation and enforcement of San Francisco's EBO and the EBOs that followed have not been disruptive to the contracting process for either contractors or governments. Also, EBOs actually benefit both contractors and governments, in addition to the employees who receive benefits under them. The study's findings indicate that jurisdictions that consider EBOs in the future can expect widespread compliance, with little resistance by contractors and minimal administrative burden.

Finally, the study supports the finding that a presidential executive order requiring federal contractors to offer domestic partner benefits would advance the economy and efficiency of the federal government.

SEVEN Universal Paid Sick Leave

Vicky Lovell

1. INTRODUCTION

Of the twenty-two countries with the most highly developed economies, only the United States fails to ensure that workers are provided with pay and job protection when they miss work due to illness (Heymann et al. 2009). Australians are guaranteed ten days of paid sick leave at full pay; in Germany, workers receive full pay for up to six weeks of illness leave and may take up to seventy-eight more weeks at reduced pay. Some employers

*Portions of this chapter are based on or appeared in Robert Drago and Vicky Lovell, "San Francisco's Paid Sick Leave Ordinance: Outcomes for Employers and Employees" (Institute for Women's Policy Research, Washington DC, 2011), www.iwpr.org/publications/pubs/San-Fran-PSD.

in the United States voluntarily help fill the gap, but 42 percent of workers face a loss of pay if they are too sick to work (Williams et al. 2011). State and federal government employees, white-collar workers, those on full-time work schedules, higher-paid workers, and employees of larger firms are among the groups most likely to have paid sick leave. The typical private sector worker covered by paid sick leave (PSL) in the United States can take up to eight days of leave per year (U.S. Bureau of Labor Statistics 2010).

In November 2006, San Francisco voters approved an ordinance requiring all San Francisco employers to provide PSL to all their workers—the first such mandate in the United States. Under Proposition F, the Paid Sick Leave Ordinance (PSLO), workers earn PSL in proportion to their paid work hours. PSL may be used for workers' own health needs, including preventive care, and to care for family members (table 7.1). San Francisco's Office of Labor Standards Enforcement (OLSE), which was in place prior to adoption of the PSLO, oversees its implementation.

The campaign for the PSLO focused on expected public health benefits and was largely unopposed by business interests. Both city officials and San Francisco employer groups have characterized the PSLO as having a low impact on employers and being relatively easy to implement. In 2008, the Golden Gate Restaurant Association called sick leave "an important public policy" and characterized the PSLO as "affordable [for businesses], considering the public benefit."[1]

This chapter begins with a brief look at the importance of PSL for workers' health and economic security and for public health. Section 3 reviews the campaign to pass the law in San Francisco. Section 4 presents an overview of the potential costs and benefits of universal PSL; and section 5 describes two surveys, one of employers and one of workers, conducted to measure the PSLO's impacts on each group. Sections 6 and 7 present the findings of each of these surveys on the actual impact of San Francisco's PSLO. Section 8 then assesses the overall effects of the PSLO. The final section discusses efforts to pass PSL policies elsewhere and draws lessons from San Francisco's PSLO for further policy development.

---

[1] Kevin Westley, executive director, Golden Gate Restaurant Association, quoted in Lifsher 2008.

Table 7.1   Key Provisions of the San Francisco Paid Sick Leave Ordinance

Topic	Provision
Eligibility	Workers begin to accrue leave after being on the job for 90 days.
Accruing leave	Workers earn one hour of paid leave for every 30 hours of paid work, to a maximum of 9 days in firms with 10 or more employees and 5 days in smaller firms.
Using leave	Leave may be used for workers' own illness, injury, health conditions, and medical appointments and to care for family members or a "designated person."
Rollover	Unused leave carries over from one year to the next.
Anti-retaliation	It is unlawful for employers to retaliate against workers for requesting or using leave under the PSLO.
Employer posting	Employers are required to post information about the PSLO and maintain records on hours worked and PSD used.
Enforcement	The San Francisco Office of Labor Standards Enforcement has authority to investigate worker complaints and levy penalties.

2. THE IMPORTANCE OF PAID SICK LEAVE

Before enactment of the PSLO, one-fourth of private sector workers—more than 116,000 individuals—in San Francisco did not have paid leave as now required by the PSLO.[2] Workers without PSL were primarily employed in low-wage or part-time jobs, and Latinos were the most likely workers to lack PSL.

Workers with good jobs and comprehensive benefit packages may have a hard time imagining what it means not to have PSL. Without an employer's approval to stay home or without pay while off work, many workers have to stay on the job regardless of how sick they are because missing a day's pay means they cannot pay their bills or because they will be fired if they call in sick. Many workers report this as a fact of life.

[2] City/county, state, and federal employees in San Francisco had PSL before the PSLO. See Lovell 2006, 3.

> There is no sick time, you come to work either way. If you don't come you don't get paid and if you stay off too long you get fired, that's it. (Michigan food server [Restaurant Opportunities Centers United 2010, 12])

> I would stay sick for several days, and even up to a week, and all I really needed was a full day or two to rest and recover. . . . I am always forced to come in and if I don't, I know I will be fired or my hours will be drastically reduced. . . . If it were up to me I'd stay at home to recuperate but my employers won't allow it—so in turn I jeopardize my own health and safety, that of my co-workers and that of you the consumer, and it is not fair to any of us. (Chicago food server [Restaurant Opportunities Centers United 2010, 14])

A doctor discussed the potentially extreme consequences of not being able to miss work to get preventive health care:

> I was saddened to learn this week that a patient under my care had died. A man in his 50s who worked hard on his feet all day in the food service industry, he was afraid of losing his job if he came to the doctor. He missed countless appointments.[3]

The PSLO aimed to increase job and income security by ensuring that everyone who works in San Francisco can take job-protected time off with pay to care for their health and their families' health.

3.   THE CAMPAIGN FOR VOTER SUPPORT IN SAN FRANCISCO

The PSLO was launched in the wake of the successful campaign for a citywide minimum wage, which was adopted by voters in November 2003.[4] When Young Workers United (YWU), a workers' center that was a key part of the minimum wage coalition, surveyed low-wage service sector workers across San Francisco about their workplace concerns, sick leave was identified as a top issue. YWU saw a campaign for PSL not

[3] Dr. William Jordan, quoted in Rankin 2012.
[4] The discussion of the campaign for the PSLO in this section is based largely on information provided by a cofounder of YWU (Flocks 2012).

only as a way, if successful, to provide an important worker benefit but also, like the minimum wage campaign, as an organizing tool for YWU's longer-term progressive activism.

With many of its members working part-time and in small businesses, YWU was committed to a PSL policy that would cover all workers, no matter how few hours they worked or how small their employer. That commitment was a key driver of the campaign's strategic decisions, because it meant the campaign had to avoid being in a situation that would require compromise with opponents over part-time employees and small businesses. Since framing PSL as something workers earned was also seen as an essential element in securing PSL for part-time workers, the proposal had workers accrue PSL as a share of hours worked instead of being granted a set number of leave days.

YWU conducted a poll that found that a PSL proposal would have substantial public support. That information encouraged YWU and its coalition partners to choose a ballot initiative instead of going through the city's Board of Supervisors, where PSL opponents might have the power to scale back the policy. YWU met with the San Francisco Chamber of Commerce, the Golden Gate Restaurant Association, and the City's Small Business Commission to inform them about the proposed PSLO and offer an opportunity for businesses to provide input on the final language.

After a public hearing on sick leave and two meetings with YWU, the San Francisco Chamber of Commerce remained opposed to the PSL proposal. This opposition only reinforced the decision to place the ordinance on the November ballot. The Center for Young Women's Development, the Chinese Progressive Association, Parents' Voices, SEIU's Committee of Interns and Residents, St. Peter's Housing Committee, UFCW Local 101, Unite HERE Local 2, and Young Community Developers joined YWU in the Coalition for Paid Sick Days. The coalition launched an intensive worker and voter education campaign to support the PSLO, with phone banks, canvassing, and press conferences. The restaurant association, which represents many employers that did not offer PSL, chose not to work against it, concluding that "if we fight it, we look like complete jerks" (Dornhelm 2006).

On November 7, 2006, 61 percent of voters endorsed the PSLO, and the ordinance was implemented on February 5, 2007. The San Francisco Board of Supervisors subsequently approved a 120-day transition period to allow time for OLSE to write regulations and for employers to adapt their payroll systems to the requirements of the new law. Workers were allowed to use PSL during that period, but employers were not required to pay for leave until June 5, 2007. The final policy included some accommodations for small businesses: a lower cap on leave accrual for workers in small firms, a longer probationary period before workers could use PSL, and recognition of employers' existing PSL policies. To inform San Franciscans about the requirements of the PSLO, in addition to employer education conducted as part of the rule-making process, OLSE implemented an advertising campaign, contracted with community organizations to educate workers, and produced resource materials for employers and workers translated into six languages.

4. POTENTIAL COSTS AND BENEFITS OF PSL

Early studies of the possible impacts of paid sick leave predicted a variety of costs and benefits for employers and workers, from short-term increases in payroll costs to longer-term effects such as better management of chronic diseases.

Increased Payroll Costs

Providing paid time off entails direct costs for employers, including wages paid to absent workers and record-keeping expenses, possible hiring of replacement workers or loss of productivity when workers are absent, and the administrative costs of tracking and processing payments. The Partnership for New York City estimated that a PSL proposal for that city would increase private payroll costs 0.3 percent (Partnership for New York City 2010). PSL opponents argue that these costs will cause firms—particularly small firms—to reduce jobs. The National Federation of Independent Businesses predicted that the costs of universal PSL would reduce employment in small firms by 1.4 percent, assuming full use of all available leave and full replacement of absent workers (Phillips 2008).[5] (The study did not offer evidence supporting either assumption.)

Other researchers predicted smaller costs, some of which would be offset by the benefit to firms of lower turnover and increased productivity (Lovell 2006). In addition, an early qualitative study of the PSLO indicated that employers were sometimes able to pass increased costs to workers, by reducing compensation or other paid leave, or to customers, by charging higher prices (Boots, Martinson, and Danziger 2009).[6] And an analysis of employment levels in California by county over the period 2003–9 found that the PSLO generated job growth of 0.5 percent to 2.0 percent (Van Kammen 2013), contradicting PSL critics' predictions.

Reductions in the Spread of Disease

PSL policies may reduce the spread of disease in workplaces by decreasing "presenteeism"—the practice of workers remaining on the job when they are ill. Workers report going to work while sick if they cannot afford to take unpaid time off (NPR/Kaiser Family Foundation/Harvard School of Public Health 2008, 13) or if they may lose their job or have their work hours reduced if they stay home. PSL can reduce presenteeism (Drago and Miller 2010, 8) and decrease the spread of disease (Li et al. 1996). Presenteeism is costly for employers because sick workers are paid their full salary though their performance suffers, sick workers are more likely to be injured or make costly mistakes (CCH 2007), and an illness spreading through a work site leads to additional absences (ComPsych 2004). Reducing presenteeism may improve public health by minimizing the spread of disease. A study of the H1N1 influenza virus in winter 2009–10 estimated that seven million flu cases might have been prevented had sick workers stayed home while they were contagious (Drago and Miller 2010, 7). As one human resources expert put it, "The

---

[5] In Phillips's analysis, "small employers" have fewer than 500 workers.

[6] Employers who passed costs on to clients stated they were responding to the combination of the PSLO and San Francisco's minimum wage and health care mandates as well as the declining economy, not just the PSLO.

bottom line for most organizations is that it's in everyone's best interest for sick workers to simply stay away."[7]

Better Preventive Care, Fewer Injuries, Faster Recovery, and Lower Health Care Costs

PSL may also reduce barriers to accessing health care, improving health, reducing health care costs, and benefiting employers (Lovell 2006). Workers with PSL are more likely to seek out preventive health care, including cancer screenings (Peipins et al. 2012), and are less likely to be injured on the job (Asfaw, Pana-Cryan, and Rosa 2012). And workers recover faster from health problems when they can take time to recuperate (Grinyer and Singleton 2000). Some researchers expect that PSL policies will have longer-term impacts by improving the management of chronic diseases such as diabetes. These impacts could reduce health care costs for workers and their families, employers, and the public.

Reduced Turnover, Easier Absence Management, and Better Morale, with Cost Savings for Employers

Workers who have PSL are less likely to change jobs (Cooper and Monheit 1993), sparing employers the turnover-related costs of filling vacancies such as interviewing, testing, and training new workers (Phillips 1990). Workers with PSL may be more likely to give advance notice of health-related absence, allowing firms to avoid the more expensive impact of unplanned time off (WoltersKluwer/CCH n.d.). Policies that make it easier for employees to attend to their health needs may reduce stress, increase loyalty, and improve morale (U.S. Centers for Disease Control and Prevention 2011). This may benefit employers: Fringe benefits affect job satisfaction, and better job satisfaction is associated with higher business profitability (Harter, Schmidt, and Hayes 2002; Artz 2008).

---

[7] Brett Gorovsky, cited in Miller 2008.

More Parental Care for Sick Children for Lower Spread of Disease and Reduced Sibling Absence

According to Heymann (2000), PSL is the primary factor in parents' decisions about staying home when their children are sick. Sending children to school or child care when they have a contagious illness is analogous to presenteeism for workers: It spreads disease to other children and families (Heymann, Earle, and Egleston 1996). Research suggests that PSL is more effective than vacation leave in allowing parents to stay home with sick children—perhaps because vacation leave policies may not be flexible enough to be used when children become sick (Clemans-Cope et al. 2008).

Without PSL, parents may rely on older children to stay home with sick youngsters. This can have serious impacts on the older sibling's education, as noted by the principal of a Denver school:

> I had a young gal who missed 40 days of school to care for a sick younger brother. . . . The mom was very upfront. [She said,] "I'll lose my job if I take time off work, and if I lose my job, we lose the house. So the next best thing is for my oldest daughter to stay home." (Towne et al. 2011, 1)

While these potential costs and benefits of PSL have been widely noted, they draw on observational and theoretical studies rather than evidence from the introduction of a PSL mandate. We turn next to such evidence.

5. THE EMPLOYER AND WORKER SURVEYS

To study the impact of the PSLO, researchers at the University of California and the Institute for Women's Policy Research (IWPR) added questions about the ordinance to a 2009 survey of private sector San Francisco employers and IWPR commissioned a 2010 survey of adults working in private sector San Francisco firms. The surveys were thus conducted two and a half to three years after the PLSO's implementation. The surveys were designed to measure how individuals and firms responded to the PSL ordinance, including the degree to which employers changed policies in response to the law, how they absorbed its costs, and the extent to which workers utilized the offered PSL.

The 2009 Bay Area Employer Health Benefits Survey was conducted by telephone in July through December 2009.[8] The sample was stratified by nonprofit status and firm size. Interviews targeted at benefits managers were completed with 727 San Francisco firms. Post-stratification weights benchmarked the survey against data from the U.S. Census Bureau's 2008 County Business Patterns survey.

The survey of workers was conducted by telephone in January and February 2010. The sample frame was based on zip codes inside and outside San Francisco and included land line and cell phone numbers. Survey respondents were at least eighteen years old and had worked at least ten hours per week, on average, for at least three months for a private sector San Francisco firm at some time after February 2007. Interviews were completed with 1,194 workers. Missing wage data were imputed, and post-stratification weights benchmarked the survey against data from the U.S. Census Bureau's 2008 American Community Survey.

6. EMPLOYERS' REPORTS OF THE IMPACT OF THE PSLO

More than two years after the PSLO went into effect, the vast majority— but not all—of San Francisco's firms reported offering PSL. More than one in four firms reported they had expanded eligibility, increased the number of sick days, and/or added new PSL policies in response to the law. Approximately one in eight firms providing PSL reported they found it "very difficult" to implement one or more aspects of the PSLO. However, nearly three-fourths of firms with PSL[9] were either supportive or very supportive of the PSLO.[10]

---

[8] For more information about the survey, see Dow, Dube, and Colla 2010.

[9] Firms or employers "with PSL" are those that reported offering PSL at the time of the survey.

[10] Support was high even among the employers who were most affected by the PSLO— those that significantly expanded a pre-PSLO policy or added a new policy—with two-thirds of both groups favoring the ordinance (Lovell 2013).

Changes in Employers' PSL Policies in Response to the PSLO

Two-thirds of San Francisco's employers reported that they offered PSL to at least part of their workforce before the PSLO (table 7.2). In response to the new law, one of six firms enacted a new PSL policy, bringing the share of employers with a PSL policy to 82.1 percent and expanding PSL to more than 59,000 workers.[11] In addition, nearly one of five firms increased their existing PSL accrual rate or expanded the share of their workforce covered by PSL. More than one quarter reported making one or more of these changes.

San Francisco's smallest firms—those with fewer than ten workers—reported making the fewest changes to their PSL policies following enactment of the PSLO. Although they were approximately as likely as slightly larger firms to offer PSL before the ordinance, they were significantly *less* likely to offer PSL at the time of the surveys, indicating a lower level of compliance with the law. In contrast, the share of firms adding PSL was highest in the two industries with the lowest rates of PSL before the ordinance: hospitality and construction. Low-wage firms and those with a high share of part-time workers were also more likely to implement a new PSL policy, closing some of the coverage gap with higher-wage and higher-hours firms.

Ease of Implementation

Among firms offering PSL, more than half reported that it was "not difficult" or "not too difficult" to understand the requirements of the PSLO (53.9 percent) or to administer PSL (55.6 percent). Firms in the hospitality and construction industries had the most difficulty understanding and managing the PSLO. Firms with fewer than twenty-five workers found it more difficult to understand what the PSLO required than larger firms—possibly because they may not have had specialized staff to manage PSL—but were not more likely to find it difficult to administer the PSLO. Somewhat counterintuitively, firms that had PSL before the PSLO but made changes in response to the ordinance found it harder to understand and administer the PSLO than firms that enacted new policies. It may be

[11] Assuming all employees are covered in firms with new policies.

Table 7.2 Impact of the PSLO on Paid Sick Leave Policies

Firm Characteristics (%)	Provided PSL before the PSLO	After the PSLO			
		EXPANDED ELIGIBILITY	INCREASED NUMBER OF LEAVE DAYS	ENACTED NEW	PROVIDES PSL
All	65.7	19.8	18.5	16.4	82.1
Number of workers					
1 to 9	64.1	13.4	14.6	14.3	78.4
10 to 24	66.5	34.3	31.9	25.5	92.0
25 to 49	74.3	38.8	26.2	23.2	97.5
50 or more	83.6	46.6	25.9	15.8	99.4
Industry					
Construction	40.8	29.1	52.3	28.5	69.3
Education, health care, and social services	67.7	14.4	15.2	21.5	89.2
Finance, insurance, and real estate	87.0	9.0	8.8	6.2	93.2
Hospitality	24.0	37.3	27.1	38.1	62.1
Professional, scientific, and technical services	80.1	15.5	12.3	5.2	85.3
Retail and wholesale trade	62.0	21.7	19.5	15.9	77.9
Other services	56.4	32.8	41.8	22.1	78.5
Other	79.9	17.4	9.7	11.7	91.6
Wage level					
Low-wage	52.5	22.9	26.2	17.2	69.7
Higher-wage	72.0	15.5	16.8	15.1	87.1
Work hours					
Low hours	52.6	21.6	19.8	21.1	73.7
Higher hours	79.1	16.5	15.5	9.6	88.7
Racial/ethnic workforce					
50 percent or more workers of color	73.3	14.9	18.7	11.2	84.5
Other firms	50.0	28.2	18.1	26.1	76.1

SOURCE: Author's analysis of employer survey.

NOTES: At least one worker in "low-wage" firms earns less than $10 per hour; all employees in "higher-wage" firms earn more than $15 per hour. More than 30 percent of employees in "low hours" firms work less than 10 hours per week; in "high hours" firms, all employees work at least 30 hours per week. The difference between the share of employers providing PSL before and after the PSLO is statistically significant at the $p < .01$ level for all categories of firm characteristics, based on Chi-squared tests.

that guidance on setting up new policies was more readily available than information about how to modify an existing policy to comply with the PSLO. Only one of four firms starting a new PSL policy after the PSLO was adopted had difficulty understanding what the ordinance required.

In general, firms found it more difficult to adjust workload to employees' use of PSL than to understand and administer the PSLO: more than two-fifths found it difficult to reassign or delay work. Firms in the hospitality industry and the smallest firms were particularly likely to cite this concern.

Overall, just one of eight employers starting a new PSL policy after passage of the PSLO reported that it was "very difficult" to understand or comply with one or more of the new requirements—just a slightly higher share than for employers who were not significantly impacted (12.8 percent and 11.0 percent, respectively).

Benefits and Costs for Employers

Very few firms with PSL reported that the PSLO had an impact on employee morale, customer service, or presenteeism. Somewhat larger shares felt the PSLO affected the predictability of workers' absences. However, one of six firms reported that the PSLO negatively affected profitability. Those changing an existing policy reported the greatest impact on profits, compared to firms enacting new policies and firms with no policy changes. Hospitality and construction firms, which were the most likely to add PSL policies and among the most likely to change existing policies, reported the biggest impact on profitability. Low-wage and low-hours firms also noted higher than average impacts on profits.

Passing Costs on to Workers or Customers

One quarter of firms with PSL reported passing costs along to workers and/or customers. Most firms—four of five—implemented the PSLO without reducing other employee compensation, but 8.2 percent converted vacation leave to paid time off (PTO) or PSL, 7.6 percent reduced wages or bonuses, and 3.1 percent cut vacation benefits. These changes were most common among firms starting new PSL policies, higher-wage firms, and firms with fewer workers of color. More than three of five firms in the hospitality industry and nearly one-third of those in the construction industry reported increasing prices to recoup costs of the PSLO. Overall, of firms offering PSL, one of eight reported passing part of the cost of the PSLO on to customers.

Costs of Hiring Replacement Workers

Very few firms reported hiring replacements when workers use PSL: just 1.2 percent always did, and 3.1 percent frequently did.[12] Among firms offering PSL, replacing absent workers is most common in the construction and education/health care/social services industries, in low-wage firms, and in firms with fewer workers of color.

Employer Support for the PSLO

Employer support for the PSLO is surprisingly high, even among firms that were affected the most by the new policy. More than one-third of firms are "very supportive" of the PSLO, and another third are "supportive." Small firms, those in the education/health care/social services and finance services sectors, and those with higher wages, more part-time workers, and more workers of color are the most supportive. More than three-fourths of firms that did not have to add or expand their PSL policies support the ordinance, but even among those making changes, more than two-thirds are supportive (68.3 percent of firms enacting new policies and 68.5 percent of firms changing existing policies).

7. WORKERS' REPORTS OF THE IMPACT OF THE PSLO

Three years after the PSLO went into effect, 44.1 percent of San Francisco workers reported accruing and being able to use PSL as required by the

---

[12] An additional 26.6 percent "rarely" hire replacements.

ordinance, 29.0 percent lacked at least one element required by the ordinance, and 26.9 percent did not know if they had full PSL. Workers used far fewer sick days than they earned. Workers with PSL reported that the ordinance allowed them to better care for their and their families' health, provided them with additional PSL, and enhanced their employers' support for their use of PSL. At the same time, nearly one-fourth reported that their employer violated the PSLO by penalizing workers for using PSL or requiring workers to "make up" their time off or find their own replacement.

Workers' Need for and Access to PSL

More than two-thirds of workers reported that they had wanted to stay home in the previous twelve months either because they were sick or to care for a sick family member (table 7.3). Prime working-age individuals (twenty-five to fifty-four years old), women, whites, college graduates, parents, and workers with a chronic health condition were more likely than other groups to have needed PSL.[13]

The PSLO allows workers to use PSL when they are sick, to care for ill family members, and to get preventive care. Most workers can use paid sick days when they are ill (79.3 percent; data not shown), but far fewer—just over half—reported that they can take sick days for all three required circumstances. Workers are least likely to be able to use PSL to care for their families. One of five workers accrues fewer leave days than the PSLO requires. Considering the required uses and accrual rate, only two of five workers reported having access to PSL as provided by the PSLO (see table 7.1). Nearly one-third lacked one or more parts of the required policy, and more than one-fourth did not know if they could use PSD as established by the PSLO.

Access to PSL varies substantially by demographic characteristics. Young workers (under age twenty-five) have the least access to PSL, followed by part-time, temporary/seasonal, and low-wage workers.[14]

---

[13] "Chronic health conditions" are conditions such as heart disease, asthma, and diabetes that are not curable and require continuous treatment.

[14] Low-wage workers here are those in the bottom wage quartile, earning less than $15 per hour (2010 dollars).

Table 7.3   Workers' Access to and Use of PSL

Worker Characteristics (%)	Needed Sick Leave in Past 12 Months	Has Some PSL	Has Full PSL	Workers with Some PSL Who Used PSL in Past 12 Months	Median Days of PSL Used in Past 12 Months		Employer Not in Full Compliance with PSLO*
					ALL WORKERS	WORKERS WITH SOME PSL WHO TOOK LEAVE	
All	68.9	84.2	44.1	72.5	2	4	23.7
Age							
18 to 24	68.5	69.6	11.7	65.9	1	3	28.6
25 to 54	73.4	85.4	46.4	77.3	2	4	25.2
55 and over	51.5	82.9	43.2	60.4	1	4	16.8
Sex							
Women	74.4	87.1	48.6	74.7	2	4	29.3
Men	64.4	81.9	40.4	70.7	2	4	18.6
Race and ethnicity							
White	71.8	83.5	46.9	73.9	2	4	17.3
Black	63.2	93.2	40.1	77.1	3	4	40.6
Latino	60.8	77.6	33.5	70.2	2	4	44.9
Asian	68.8	88.9	43.7	73.6	2	3	26.1
Other	72.2	84.9	51.6	72.8	2	2	30.0
Educational attainment							
High school or less	56.6	81.5	37.8	70.4	2	4	26.2
Some college	64.8	81.4	38.1	70.7	2	4	37.6
College degree	73.1	87.0	47.9	73.8	2	3	18.7
Parental status							
Parent	72.8	83.3	47.6	78.9	2	4	27.1
Not a parent	67.3	84.6	42.7	70.0	2	3	22.4
Health status							
Chronic health condition	78.1	84.4	41.7	72.8	2	5	26.2
No chronic condition	66.5	84.8	45.0	72.2	2	3	23.3
Wage quartile							
Bottom	63.1	78.1	25.8	63.0	1	4	44.2
Second	68.1	86.3	46.0	76.4	2	4	25.4
Third	75.2	88.1	52.0	75.6	2	4	19.5
Top	69.9	85.1	54.5	75.0	2	3	15.3

Table 7.3   (continued)

Worker Characteristics (%)	Needed Sick Leave in Past 12 Months	Has Some PSL	Has Full PSL	Workers with Some PSL Who Used PSL in Past 12 Months	Median Days of PSL Used in Past 12 Months		Employer Not in Full Compliance with PSLO*
					ALL WORKERS	WORKERS WITH SOME PSL WHO TOOK LEAVE	
Work hours							
Part-time	64.0	61.2	19.1	59.2	0	3	32.0
Full-time	69.8	88.7	49.0	74.3	2	4	22.7
Work schedule							
Temporary or seasonal	53.7	72.0	24.5	52.6	0	3	33.8
Other workers	70.9	86.3	47.1	75.2	2	4	23.2

* Of workers who used PSL in the past 12 months.

SOURCE: Author's analysis of worker survey.

NOTES: Differences in shares of workers within each category are statistically significant at the $p < .01$ level, based on Chi-squared tests, with the exception of the difference between workers with and without chronic health conditions regarding employer noncompliance with the PSLO.

Latinos are much less likely to have PSL for their own health needs, family care, and doctor visits and much less likely to accrue as many days as required by the PSLO, compared to whites, blacks, and Asians. Only one-third of Latino workers have PSL that fully reflects the PSLO. Men, workers with lower educational attainment, nonparents, and workers with chronic health conditions are also less likely than others to have full PSL.

Workers' Use of PSL

Workers' use of PSL was fairly modest. More than one-third did not take any PSL in the twelve months before the survey (data not shown); the median worker used 2.0 days. In comparison, the PSLO provides that full-time workers in small firms accrue a maximum of five days, while full-time workers in larger firms accrue up to nine days.[15] Among the workers likely to have accrued the most leave—full-time workers with at least one year of job tenure in firms with 10 or more employees—PSL use averaged 3.0 days in the year before the survey. In this group, older workers and temporary/seasonal workers averaged even fewer days of PSL.

More than four of five workers who took PSL used the time to address their own health needs (data not shown).[16] One-third needed PSL to visit a doctor or dentist, one of five cared for a child, and nearly as many cared for an adult relative. One of ten workers who took PSL used the time for another purpose, such as a mental health day, death of a family member, or vacation.[17] Not surprisingly, workers used PSL for different reasons at different points in their lives. Prime working-age individuals were the most likely to use PSL for their own health or to care for a child but the least likely to take PSL to care for an adult or visit a doctor. Men were more likely than women to use PSL to care for their own health, to care for an adult family member, or to see a doctor, while women used PSL to care for a child more often than men.

Parents were much less likely than other workers to use PSL for their own health, but three-fifths of parents who used PSL in the previous year took time to care for children. This finding suggests that parents may try not to use PSD for themselves, saving their leave for when their children need care. Parents were also more likely to take PSL to care for an adult relative. One in ten parents reported using PSL to care for both a child and a parent in the previous twelve months.

[15] More specifically, the ordinance allows workers to accrue up to nine days of PSL (five days in firms with fewer than ten employees). If a worker uses some of that leave, accrual begins again, with the same cap on accrual.

[16] The percentages taking different types of leave sum to more than 100 percent because survey respondents were asked to report a reason for every leave they took.

[17] These uses may or may not have been authorized by these workers' PSL policies. For instance, PSL may be provided under a general paid time off plan that can also be used for vacations.

Benefits and Costs for Workers

Workers with full PSL who worked for the same employer before and after implementation of the PLSO reported that the ordinance substantially improved their ability to manage their health needs (table 7.4). One of four of these workers reported that they were better able to care for their own and their families' health needs because of the PSLO. Workers of color, older workers, women, parents, workers with chronic health conditions, and low-wage workers were more likely to report this benefit, with two of five workers in the bottom wage quartile noting this change. One of six workers with full PSL gained additional days of leave through the PSLO. Low-wage workers and those in small firms were the most affected by this benefit—that is, workers in the firms that had been least likely to offer PSL before the PSLO was adopted. For more than one-third of workers with full PSL, their employer became more supportive of their taking PSL. Workers without a college degree, women, workers in the bottom half of the wage distribution, workers of color, and workers in smaller firms were the most likely to report this change.

Overall, half of these workers benefited directly from the PSLO. The gains were most striking among young adults, workers with no schooling beyond high school, those in the bottom wage quartile and temporary workers.

Reports by workers of negative impacts from the PSLO were less common. One of six workers with full PSL reported that their employer increased workload to compensate for workers taking PSL. Young workers, those without a college degree, Latino and Asian workers, and workers in the bottom wage quartile were especially likely to experience higher productivity demands. Workers with no education beyond high school, Latinos, and low-wage workers were also more likely to report that their employers reduced compensation in response to the PSLO. Few employers laid workers off or reduced work hours because of the PSLO: less than one in ten, according to workers' reports. Altogether, one quarter of workers with full PSL who worked for the same employer before and after implementation of the PSLO reported

Table 7.4   How Workers Benefited from the PSLO

Worker Characteristics (%)	Better Able to Care for Health	More Leave	Employer More Supportive	One or More Benefits
All	25.3	15.9	37.8	49.8
Age				
18 to 24	100.0	100.0	0.0	100.0
25 to 54	20.9	14.9	39.8	49.0
55 and over	31.6	17.0	40.3	54.5
Sex				
Women	31.1	16.6	41.0	53.6
Men	19.7	15.2	35.0	46.2
Race and ethnicity				
White	23.7	14.2	32.1	46.3
Black	27.6	14.9	53.9	56.6
Latino/a	29.0	27.9	46.4	61.4
Asian/PI	27.2	14.9	49.1	55.1
Other	47.2	8.2	53.6	69.1
Educational attainment				
High school or less	33.5	24.0	47.9	77.7
Some college	28.6	8.4	31.8	55.6
College degree	18.2	9.4	27.5	41.3
Parental status				
Parent	26.3	13.1	39.6	49.2
Not a parent	24.8	17.2	36.9	50.1
Health status				
Chronic health condition	26.9	7.9	34.0	52.1
No chronic condition	25.3	18.3	39.5	50.1
Wage quartile				
Bottom	41.0	48.0	54.2	77.9
Second	27.3	15.4	54.1	61.5
Third	24.2	11.3	33.6	44.3
Top	18.8	6.3	23.2	34.6
Work hours				
Part-time	31.9	31.9	34.7	56.2
Full-time	24.7	14.5	38.1	49.3
Work schedule				
Temporary or seasonal	43.9	51.7	72.7	79.2
Other workers	23.1	13.5	35.7	47.7

SOURCE: Author's analysis of worker survey.

NOTES: Differences in shares of workers within each category are statistically significant at the p < .01 level, based on Chi-squared tests, with the exception of work hours for "better care" and gender and parent status for "more days."

that their employer passed on perceived costs of PSL to workers in at least one way.

Impact of the PSLO on the General Public

The PSLO made it easier for sick workers and children to stay home and avoid spreading germs and viruses to customers and other students. Employer support for using PSL increased disproportionately in jobs that involve contact with the public: More than one-third of workers who deal directly with the public—in food service, health care, and education, for example—reported that their employers were more supportive of workers using PSL because of the PSLO.[18] One in eight workers with public contact reported that the PSLO reduced presenteeism in their workplace—a somewhat larger effect than other workers reported. However, one in ten workers who dealt with the public said that the PSLO *increased* presenteeism. Increased presenteeism was more likely to be reported in the education and health sectors, while workers in the hospitality industry were more likely to report lower presenteeism. Workers with public contact were more than half again as likely as other workers to go to work sick, even after adoption of the PSLO.

Most parents had allowed a sick child to go to school in the previous year, but parents with PSL were more likely to stay home with their sick children.

According to workers' reports, few employers raised prices because of the PSLO. Workers in the education, health care, and leisure and hospitality fields and low-wage workers were more likely to note higher prices than other workers.

Employers' Compliance with the PSLO

Some workers reported that their employers penalized employees for using PSL or engaged in other practices that violate the PSLO. Low-wage

---

[18] Close to half of workers who interacted with the public were employed in the education and hospitality industries.

workers reported substantially more noncompliance than others, including having to "make up" time they took as PSL or find a replacement for their leave or being threatened with losing pay or being written up. More than two in five black and Latino workers reported at least one of these problems, as did approximately one-third of temporary/seasonal and part-time workers. Women, parents, and younger workers were disproportionately likely to note these problems as well.[19]

The PSLO allows employers to require confirmation from a health care practitioner when workers use more than three consecutive days of PSL. Fewer than one quarter of workers were asked to supply such documentation. However, worker reports suggest that some are required to document their need for PSL more frequently than the PSLO allows. For instance, 38.6 percent of low-wage workers and 39.8 percent of part-time workers reported being asked for documentation, but only 25.5 percent of low-wage workers and 16.1 percent of part-timers took four or more leave days.[20]

A majority of workers (65.5 percent) said they would feel comfortable filing a complaint if their employer violated the PSLO. Reports of policies that constitute noncompliance were very high—44.8 percent of surveyed workers reported at least one violation. Yet less than three hundred complaints were filed, suggesting that workers were less than fully aware of the PSLO.[21] They may not realize that there are specific PSL requirements or that there *is* a complaint process. Alternatively, some workers may fear employer retaliation or simply have more pressing workplace concerns.

8.   HOW WELL IS THE PSLO WORKING?

San Francisco's PSLO expanded sickness leave to more than 59,000 private sector workers, according to employer reports. While most San

---

[19] Data are for workers who had used PSL in the previous twelve months.

[20] Data on the share of workers taking more than three consecutive days of PSL are not available.

[21] Data on complaints are for the period February 5, 2007, through September 14, 2012 (SF Office of Labor Standards Enforcement, pers. com., Oct. 2, 2012).

Francisco firms offered PSL two and a half years after the ordinance went into effect, 15 percent—more than 4,000 firms, employing a total of more than 16,500 workers—did not. In addition, one-third of firms with PSL said that their policy excluded some employees. These findings suggest that greater attention to education and enforcement may be needed.

Two of five San Francisco workers benefited directly from the PSLO in terms of their ability to use PSL, and many reported being better able to manage their and their families' health because of the PSLO. Workers reported very little direct punitive behavior by employers for use of PSL. Those in jobs that involve contact with the public appear to have benefited from the PSLO more than other workers.

San Francisco's business community has been surprisingly positive about the PSLO. The majority of firms surveyed reported that the law is easy to implement, though a sizable minority reported difficulties understanding or administering the law. Three-fourths of employers participating in the employer survey were supportive of the PSLO.

Other researchers found similar results. Interviews with twenty-six employers in March 2008 found that "most employers were able to implement [the PSLO] with minimal impacts on their business in the first year" (Boots, Martinson, and Danziger 2009, 12). Based on its work with employers and its handling of worker complaints, the agency charged with overseeing the PSLO agrees. And the Golden Gate Restaurant Association has stated that "sick leave is one issue where people just looked at adjusting their policies and moved on. It hasn't been a big issue."[22]

The results of the surveys suggest significantly lower costs to employers than predicted by PSL opponents. Workers reported using less than one-fourth of their available sick days. Only a small fraction of employers reported that they generally replaced workers when they were out sick. Some costs of providing sick leave were absorbed through higher prices, reductions in other forms of compensation, lower profits, and improved productivity.

[22] Kevin Westlye, quoted in DeBare 2008.

Despite these gains by workers overall, Latinos, low-wage workers, and part-timers continue to have less access than other workers—despite targeted efforts to craft a PSL policy that would include all part-time workers, as discussed above. Although several public agencies and non-profit organizations conducted outreach to employers and workers to familiarize them with the law, many workers remain poorly informed about their rights under the PSLO, suggesting that workers are not taking full advantage of their PSL benefit.[23]

9. ENACTING PSL ELSEWHERE: LESSONS FROM SAN FRANCISCO

San Francisco was not the first place to consider universal PSL—a proposal was presented to the city council in Madison, Wisconsin, in 2005 and Sen. Ted Kennedy introduced a federal proposal in Congress in 2004—but it was the first to succeed. Several other jurisdictions have done so since, and campaigns are under way in many others.

Washington DC was the second jurisdiction after San Francisco to adopt PSL. The District Council adopted a provision in March 2008 allowing workers to earn PSL after one year on the job.[24] Leave accrual is capped, with fewer days allowed for workers in smaller firms. The law excludes food service workers who receive both wages and tips, most work-study students, health care workers choosing premium pay programs instead of benefits, and independent contractors. In 2011, Connecticut adopted a PSL law that applies to service workers in firms with fifty or more workers, and the Seattle City Council approved a PSL policy for workers in firms with

[23] For example, OLSE conducted a public rule-making process for the PSLO; OLSE and San Francisco's Mayor's Office of Economic and Workforce Development distributed informational brochures and employee fact sheets to employers and advertised the PSLO in local newspapers and in bus shelters; OLSE and the San Francisco Department of Public Health worked with community-based organizations to educate workers about the PSLO (Donna Levitt, OLSE enforcement officer, letter to New York City Council member Gale A. Brewer, Nov. 16, 2009, 1; Delwiche 2009, 4).

[24] Gibson Dunn (2008) notes that the law's language about the waiting period is ambiguous but will likely be interpreted as being one year.

five or more workers. In 2013, Portland, Oregon, adopted PSL for workers in firms with six or more employees and unpaid sick leave for those in smaller firms, and New York City mandated a phase-in of PSL for workers in firms with fifteen or more workers. All five policies allow workers to use PSL for services related to domestic violence and stalking.[25]

As of April 2013, state-level PSL campaigns have been active in Arizona, California, Colorado, Hawaii, Illinois, Iowa, Maine, Maryland, Massachusetts, Michigan, Minnesota, New Jersey, New York, North Carolina, Oregon, Pennsylvania, Vermont, Washington, and Wisconsin, and local campaigns have been working in Denver, Colorado; Miami, Florida; Orange County, Florida; and Philadelphia, Pennsylvania (National Partnership for Women and Families 2013). Advocates in Washington DC are also pursuing improvements to that city's PSL law.

Unlike the campaign for the PSLO, efforts to enact PSL in other places have been very contentious, with national organizations funding opposition campaigns.[26] PSL is still frequently characterized as a job-killer, especially for small businesses, and requiring too much red tape. Employer representatives express concern that employees will abuse their leave, calling in sick on Mondays and using every allotted hour of leave. And opponents argue that PSL policies will be too costly to enforce.[27]

San Francisco's PSLO is unique not only in being the nation's first such universal policy but also in following a relatively mild campaign that was successful in a very short time. While efforts elsewhere may take longer and face substantially more opposition, the PSLO offers the best available guidance on how universal paid sick leave would affect employers, workers, and the public in other cities and states. The key

[25] Milwaukee, WI, adopted a PSL law in 2008, but it was enjoined and eventually overturned by the state legislature.

[26] For example, the National Restaurant Association and national restaurant chains donated to opposition campaigns in Denver.

[27] To the contrary, Donna Levitt of the OLSE observed that "we were able to easily incorporate enforcement of paid sick leave into our enforcement of minimum wage and we hired no additional staff to enforce the paid sick leave ordinance" (Community Service Society 2012, 12).

lessons from employers' and workers' reports of their experiences with the PSLO are:

- Implementation of PSL is not burdensome for employers. The PSLO had minimal negative impacts on profits, and employers had relatively little difficulty understanding and implementing the ordinance. More than one-third of surveyed employers were "very supportive" of the PSLO and another third were "supportive." Two-thirds of employers that made significant changes to their PSL policies or created new policies favored the ordinance.

- Workers tend to use PSL conservatively. One-fourth of full-time workers who had been with their employer for at least a year did not use any PSL in the twelve months before they were surveyed. Of full-timers with one year of tenure who did use some PSL, the typical worker took four days.

- More than 59,000 workers gained job-protected PSL through the ordinance, along with a mechanism for reporting compliance issues.

- Workers are better able to deal with health issues as a result of the PSLO.

- San Francisco's most vulnerable workers—including low-wage workers, workers of color, and part-time workers—experienced the largest gains in access to PSL through the PSLO.

- Universal PSLO provides public health benefits by making it easier for workers and schoolchildren to stay home when they have a contagious disease.

Challenges to providing adequate support to sick workers remain after enactment of the PSLO: some employers are not fully in compliance with the ordinance, and many workers are unaware of their new leave rights. Nevertheless, the findings reported here offer a clear endorsement for those concerned about the business impact of universal PSL while confirming that PSL policies bring concrete benefits to workers.

REFERENCES

Artz, Benjamin. 2008. "Fringe Benefits and Job Satisfaction." *International Journal of Manpower* 31, 6: 626–44.

Asfaw, Abay, Regina Pana-Cryan, and Roger Rosa. 2012. "Paid Sick Leave and Nonfatal Occupational Injuries," *American Journal of Public Health* 102, 9 (Sept.): e59–e64.

Boots, Shelley Waters, Karin Martinson, and Anna Danziger. 2009. *Employers' Perspectives on San Francisco's Paid Sick Leave Policy.* Washington DC: Urban Institute.

CCH. 2007. "CCH Survey Finds Most Employees Call in "Sick" for Reasons Other than Illness; Poor Morale Adds Up to Even More No-Shows" (Oct. 10), www.cch.com/press/news/2007/20071010h.asp (accessed Oct. 12, 2010).

Clemans-Cope, Lisa, Cynthia D. Perry, Genevieve M. Kenney, Jennifer E. Pelletier, and Matthew S. Pantell. 2008. "Access to and Use of Paid Sick Leave among Low-Income Families with Children." *Pediatrics* 122: e480–e486.

Community Service Society. 2012. "The Impact of Paid Sick Days on Jobs: What's the Real Story?" (Sept.). http://b.3cdn.net/nycss/d53aaf5763daaa089b_8bm6bluvr.pdf.

ComPsych. 2004. "Vast Majority of Employees Work While Sick, According to ComPsych Survey" (Mar. 8). www.compsych.com (accessed Mar. 17, 2005).

Cooper, Philip F., and Alan C. Monheit. 1993. "Does Employment-Related Health Insurance Inhibit Job Mobility?" *Inquiry* 30: 400–416.

DeBare, Ilana. 2008. "S.F. Sick Leave Law Celebrates 1 Year." *San Francisco Chronicle*, Feb. 6.

Delwiche, Alexa. 2009. "Memo on the Implementation Status of the Paid Sick Leave Ordinance." City and County of San Francisco Board of Supervisors, Office of the Legislative Analyst (Aug. 24).

Dornhelm, Rachel. 2006. "Sick Days for All." American Public Media, *Marketplace AM*, Oct. 5. www.marketplace.org/topics/economy/sick-days-all (accessed Sept. 23, 2012).

Dow, William H., Arindrajit Dube, and Carrie Hoverman Colla. 2010. *Bay Area Employer Health Benefits Survey: Health Benefits Report 2009.* University of California, Berkeley, School of Public Health.

Drago, Robert, and Vicky Lovell. 2011. "San Francisco's Paid Sick Leave Ordinance: Outcomes for Employers and Employees." Washington DC: Institute for Women's Policy Research. www.iwpr.org/publications/pubs/San-Fran-PSD.

Drago, Robert, and Kevin Miller. 2010. "Sick at Work: Infected Employees in the Workplace during the H1N1 Pandemic." Washington DC: Institute for Women's Policy Research (Feb.).

Flocks, Sara. 2012. Personal communication. Sept. 30.

Gibson Dunn. 2008. *Washington, D.C. Passes Paid Sick Leave Law* (June 30). www. gibsondunn.com/publications/pages/Washington,DCPaidSickLeaveLaw. aspx?printpreview=true (accessed Oct. 7, 2012).

Grinyer, Anne, and Vicky Singleton. 2000. "Sickness Absence as Risk-Taking Behavior: A Study of Organizational and Cultural Factors in the Public Sector." *Health, Risk and Society* 2: 7–21.

Harter, James K., Frank L. Schmidt, and Theodore L. Hayes. 2002. "Business-Unit-Level Relationship between Employee Satisfaction, Employee Engagement, and Business Outcomes: A Meta-Analysis." *Journal of Applied Psychology* 87: 268–79.

Heymann, Jody. 2000. *The Widening Gap: Why America's Working Families Are in Jeopardy and What Can Be Done about It.* New York: Basic Books.

Heymann, Jody, Alison Earle, and Brian Egleston. 1996. "Parental Availability for the Care of Sick Children." *Pediatrics* 98: 226–30.

Heymann, Jody, Hye Jin Rho, John Schmitt, and Alison Earle. 2009. *Contagion Nation: A Comparison of Paid Sick Day Policies in 22 Countries.* Washington DC: Center for Economic and Policy Research (May).

Li, Jiehui, Guthrie S. Birkhead, David S. Strogatz, and R. Bruce Coles. 1996. "Impact of Institution Practices on Communicable Disease Outbreaks in New York State Nursing Homes." *American Journal of Epidemiology* 143: 1042–49.

Lifsher, Marc. 2008. "Feeling Ill over Sick Leave." *Los Angeles Times,* July 5.

Lovell, Vicky. 2006. *Valuing Good Health in San Francisco: The Costs and Benefits of a Proposed Paid Sick Days Policy.* Washington DC: Institute for Women's Policy Research (July).

———. 2013. "The San Francisco Paid Sick Leave Ordinance: Impacts on Employers and Workers." Paper presented at the University of California, Berkeley, Institute for Research on Labor and Employment Spring 2013 Colloquia, Feb. 11.

Miller, Stephen. 2008. *Beware the Ill Effects of Sick Employees at Work.* Alexandria, VA: Society for Human Resources Management (Jan.).

National Partnership for Women and Families. 2013. *State and Local Action on Paid Sick Days.* Washington, DC: National Partnership for Women and Families (Apr.).

NPR/Kaiser Family Foundation/Harvard School of Public Health. 2008. *Health Care and the Economy in Two Swing States: A Look at Ohio and Florida* (July). http://kaiserfamilyfoundation.files.wordpress.com/2013/01/7794.pdf.

Partnership for New York City. 2010. *Impact of Paid Sick Leave on NYC Businesses: A Survey of New York City Employers.* New York (Sept.).

Peipins, Lucy A., Ashwini Soman, Zahava Berkowitz, and Mary C. White. 2012.

"The Lack of Paid Sick Leave as a Barrier to Cancer Screening and Medical Care-Seeking: Results from the National Health Interview Survey." *BMC Public Health* 12, 520: 1–9.

Phillips, Bruce D. 2008. *AB2716, The CA Healthy Workplaces Act of 2008: Economic and Small Business Effects.* Nashville, TN: National Federal of Independent Business Research Foundation (June).

Phillips, Douglas J. 1990. "The Price Tag on Turnover." *Personnel Journal* 2162: 58–61.

Rankin, Nancy. 2012. *Still Sick in the City: What the Lack of Paid Leave Means for Working New Yorkers* (Jan.) New York: Community Service Society. http:// b.3cdn.net/nycss/d76bb0cbb411222dd8_bim6yhxso.pdf.

Restaurant Opportunities Centers United. 2010. *Serving While Sick: High Risks & Low Benefits for the Nation's Restaurant Workforce, and Their Impact on the Consumer.* New York (Sept. 10).

Towne, Sarah, Rhiana Gunn-Wright, Kevin Miller, and Barbara Gault. 2011. *Denver Paid Sick Days Would Promote Children's School Success.* Washington DC: Institute for Women's Policy Research (Oct.).

U.S. Bureau of Labor Statistics. 2010. "Paid Sick Leave in the United States." *Program Perspectives* 2, 2: 1–4. www.bls.gov/opub/perspectives/program_perspectives_vol2_issue2.pdf.

U.S. Centers for Disease Control and Prevention. 2011. *Benefits of Health Promotion Programs* (Apr. 11). www.cdc.gov/workplacehealthpromotion/businesscase/benefits/index.html.

Van Kammen, Ben. 2013. *Sick Leave Mandates and Employment.* https://pantherfile.uwm.edu/bjv2/www/Sick%20Leave%20Mandate%20Paper%2001292013.pdf.

Williams, Claudia, Robert Drago, Kevin Miller, and Youngmin Yi. 2011. *Access to Paid Sick Days in the States, 2010* (Mar.). Washington DC: Institute for Women's Policy Research.

WoltersKluwer/CCH. n.d. *Survey Says Unscheduled Absence Costs Employers 8.7 Percent of Payroll.* www.employmentlawdaily.com/index.php/news/survey-says-unscheduled-absence-costs-employers-8–7-percent-of-payroll/.

PART THREE **Making the Mandates Work**

EIGHT Enforcement of Labor Standards

Miranda Dietz, Donna Levitt, and Ellen Love

1. INTRODUCTION

The best labor laws are only as good as the enforcement that supports them. Nevertheless, enforcement considerations are often an afterthought, and adequate enforcement is far from a given. San Francisco's employer mandates stand out not just for their strength and breadth as written but also for the City's commitment to on-the-ground enforcement.

While living wage laws have been widely adopted by jurisdictions across the country, their enforcement is uneven. A review in eighty locations classified more than half of living wage laws as having "narrow" implementation: no full-time staff person assigned to administer the law or answer questions and no monitoring of compliance unless a complaint is filed. Implementation in only a few cities—14 percent of the sample, San Francisco among them—was classified as "expansive." In these cities, implementation was characterized by knowledgeable and accountable staff, data collection and monitoring processes that support evaluation and improvement of original ordinance language, and a focus on public outreach and education (Luce 2005).

As San Francisco's set of employment laws has grown beyond the living wage, so too have its enforcement practices and policies continued to expand. Since 2000, San Francisco's Office of Labor Standards Enforcement (OLSE) has worked to make the City's extensive laws meaningful in the lives of workers. OLSE also offers lessons for combating labor standards violations at any level. Components of OLSE's enforcement strategy may provide a model for other agencies. Key components are education and outreach; building trust with workers; thorough, company-wide investigations; and cooperation with other departments.

This chapter begins by describing OLSE's mandate, resources, approach, and accomplishments, including a comparison with enforcement agencies elsewhere. Section 3 outlines OLSE's efforts in education and outreach, including the role of community-based organizations, that are crucial to compliance and enforcement. Section 4 discusses the key components of OLSE's strategy and illustrates their results with stories from the field. Section 5 concludes by looking at lessons for other jurisdictions and remaining challenges.

2.   OVERVIEW OF SAN FRANCISCO'S OFFICE OF LABOR STANDARDS ENFORCEMENT

The OLSE Mandate

The City of San Francisco's Office of Labor Standards Enforcement was founded in 2001 in response to union concerns that the City's purchasing department, in charge of enforcing public works construction contracts, was motivated to complete projects on time and on budget but without regard for enforcing prevailing wage laws. The office's three employees began with the narrow mandate to enforce these laws. Between 2001 and 2007, San Francisco adopted a series of innovative new labor laws, and OLSE's mission and staff expanded.

OLSE now enforces seven local labor laws and has an annual budget of $3 million that includes eighteen positions: a manager, fifteen investigators (or contract compliance officers), a clerical position, and an analyst. The budget also supports three professional services contracts—for labor law outreach and education, for a web-based system used by contractors and departments for submittal of certified payroll records, and for monitoring factory conditions in the global supply chains that produce uniforms purchased by the City.

Three of the labor laws that OLSE enforces apply to all employers with employees performing work in San Francisco. These broadly applicable laws are:

- *Minimum Wage Ordinance (MWO):* San Francisco's minimum wage, unlike the federal or state minimum wage, adjusts annually with inflation. It applies to all San Francisco employers and to employees who work two or more hours per week and are subject to California's minimum wage, including tipped workers, teenagers, and part-time workers.

- *Paid Sick Leave Ordinance (PSLO):* Adopted by San Francisco voters in November 2006, the PSLO established the first paid sick leave law in the United States. Employees covered by the ordinance accrue one hour of paid sick leave for every thirty hours worked. This law applies to all employers and all employees for work performed in San Francisco.

- *Health Care Security Ordinance (HCSO):* Adopted unanimously by the San Francisco Board of Supervisors in August 2006, the HCSO requires that employers with twenty or more employees must spend a minimum amount per hour (adjusted annually) on their employees' health care. Employers can choose how to spend the required funds as long as they are used for health care services.

OLSE also conducts robust enforcement of labor standards on City contracts and leases. These laws ensure that businesses that benefit from City contracts pay workers a living wage. OLSE enforces the following laws.

- *Prevailing Wage:* OLSE works with City departments that award public works contracts in order to effectively enforce local, state, and federal prevailing wage requirements. In addition to public works construction contracts, City contracts for janitorial services, parking lot attendants, movers, biosolid hauling, and theatrical workers on events on City property are subject to prevailing wage rates.

- *Minimum Compensation Ordinance (MCO) / Health Care Accountability Ordinance (HCAO):* The MCO requires businesses to pay a living wage (adjusted each year) on professional service contracts and on leases at the airport. The HCAO applies to these same businesses, as well as to leases at the Port of San Francisco, and requires that employers offer employees a health plan that meets the minimum standards set by the Department of Public Health or pay the City an hourly amount to care for the uninsured.

- *Sweatfree Contracting Ordinance:* Enacted in 2005, the Sweatfree Contracting Ordinance aims to prevent goods purchased by the City from being manufactured in sweatshops. Currently, the law pertains only to apparel, garments, and textiles.

The Need for Enforcement and Outreach

OLSE plays a role in education and outreach for each of the ordinances described above. But despite extensive outreach, compliance is still an issue. While the underlying prevalence of labor law violations is difficult to assess, recent evidence suggests that labor standards violations are still a significant if not a growing problem. National estimates made in 2008 found that 26 percent of low-wage urban workers in Chicago, Los Angeles, and New York were paid below minimum wage at some point in the previous week (Bernhardt, Milkman, Theodore, et al. 2009), though critics argue that the respondent-driven sampling methodology likely led to an upward bias (Gile and Handcock 2010). Local estimates from a survey of restaurant workers in San Francisco's Chinatown also found evidence of high rates of violation: 50 percent of restaurant workers surveyed reported being paid below minimum wage, and 42 percent were not being paid for sick days (Chinese Progressive Association 2010). Evidence from broader employer and employee surveys conducted after implementation of the Paid Sick Leave Ordinance also indicates gaps in workplace compliance levels. Overall, 82 percent of employers reported providing paid sick leave, though this figure was only 70 percent among low-wage firms; and while a similar share of workers (84 percent) reported having some paid sick leave, only 44 percent indicated their employer was in full compliance (see Lovell, chap. 7 this volume).

Budgeting

Securing adequate funding for the enforcement of San Francisco's progressive labor laws has been an ongoing challenge, especially in tight budget years. While about one-third of OLSE's budget comes from other City departments that pay the OLSE to enforce prevailing wage laws on their public works projects, the budget for the enforcement of laws of general application (minimum wage, sick leave, and health care) is supported by the City's General Fund. The Minimum Wage and Paid Sick Leave Ordinances were passed at the ballot box with no provisions for funding enforcement. The San Francisco Board of Supervisors eventually established new positions to enforce the new citywide minimum wage. In fiscal year 2012–13, after ten years of persistent advocacy for adequate funding, OLSE had 6.5 full-time employees specifically dedicated to the enforcement of the PSLO and minimum wage. Given their funding battles, OLSE staff and advocates strongly recommend that new local labor laws include provisions for enforcement staffing and identify dedicated funding when possible.

Basic Approach and Capacity

With current resources OLSE can respond to complaints from workers and conduct in-depth investigations of their workplaces to assess violations of labor law. The office can also conduct proactive investigations of City contractors based on tips from City staff, worker complaints, and the contractors' electronic payroll records. Given current funding, however, OLSE cannot audit businesses at random or take a more proactive, targeted, city-wide approach to assess compliance with the labor laws. Enforcement of the laws of general application are driven by worker complaints.

When a worker submits a complaint to OLSE, it initiates a thorough investigation of that employer, interviewing the employer and other employees, auditing payroll records, and reviewing other relevant documents to determine whether the employer violated the labor rights of the original claimant or any other employee. If OLSE investigators find violations, the office develops a case against the employer on behalf of all the employees whose rights were violated. Conducting these broad investigations is typically more time-consuming than reviewing one claimant's case, but violations are rarely isolated to a single employee. By looking beyond the primary complaint, OLSE has been able to recover back wages for many more employees and correct the employer's business practices going forward.

OLSE organizes its caseload so that the same compliance officer handles a case from start to finish—including the initial investigation, settlement negotiations, and collection and disbursement of back wages. This contrasts with wage claim adjudication at the California Department of Labor Standards Enforcement (DLSE), where different individuals handle the separate steps of the process. As a result of San Francisco's procedures, it is less likely that the enforcement agency will lose contact with the claimant, a common reason wage claims go unresolved. OLSE also collects backup contact information for a friend or relative, which helps the agency find claimants who move.

OLSE maintains contact with claimants across international borders, sending back wages to employees who have returned to their countries of origin and even coordinating hearing schedules so that claimants can testify against former employers via video conference. In one large minimum wage case, an owner of a restaurant thought he could end an OLSE investigation by bribing his Mexican immigrant workers to return to Mexico. At least two employees who were owed back wages took the opportunity to return to their hometowns in Mexico. OLSE was able to verify that the employer had distributed large sums of cash and airplane tickets to his employees. Despite the employer's hope that convincing workers to leave the country would end the case, the former employees stayed in touch with OLSE and continued to provide evidence against the employer and to support the case. As a result, the employer eventually settled and agreed to pay the full amount of back wages owed to all affected employees, including those who had left the country. These strong relationships and the dedication to pursuing a case across international borders is unusual; according to staff who have previously worked at the California DLSE, that agency does not typically send back wages across international borders and does not pursue a case if the primary claimants leave the country.

Key Components of Laws That Support Enforcement

Certain elements of the laws themselves can help address three of the most common challenges for labor enforcement agencies: collection of wages owed, prompt processing of claims, and the threat of retaliation.

One perennial problem in wage cases is that employers who are found to owe back wages may go out of business or reorganize their businesses to avoid paying workers. Restaurants fail fairly often, more than 25 percent within the first year and 60 percent within three years (Parsa et al. 2005). If they rent space and equipment, there may be little capital and few assets to seize if they do declare bankruptcy while owing back wages. San Francisco's minimum wage law defines "employers" broadly to include individuals, such as owners and officers, who exercise "control over the wages, hours or working conditions of any Employee."[1] This strong definition of liability discourages reorganization to protect assets and has resulted in employers paying back wages even after their business has closed or reorganized. In one recent case, a restaurant

---

[1] "'Employer' shall mean any person, as defined in Section 18 of the California Labor Code, including corporate officers or executives, who directly or indirectly or through an agent or any other person, including through the services of a temporary services or staffing agency or similar entity, employs or exercises control over the wages, hours or working conditions of any Employee" (San Francisco Administrative Code Section 12R.3(b), 2003).

restructured and claimed that only the original corporation was liable for back wages owed. OLSE subpoenaed the corporate records, identified the individuals who owned the business, and held the owner and a successor corporation liable. The owner finally signed a settlement agreement and is now paying $65,000 in back wages to workers.

Employers sometimes refuse to provide payroll documents; in these circumstances OLSE issues penalties for nonsubmission of records. In the absence of records, OLSE relies on worker testimony, and it usually takes more than one session with each claimant to carefully reconstruct his or her employment history. OLSE's practice of conducting company-wide audits and reviewing compliance in previous years is labor-intensive. If an employer disagrees with the OLSE finding of a minimum wage violation or simply ignores the letter of determination, the office must initiate a formal hearing process, which can take many additional months to complete. The minimum wage law does provide that large cumulative penalties ($50 per day to the employee for every day that the violation continues and $50 per worker per day to the City to compensate for the cost of investigation) may be assessed after a due process hearing. Largely due to this penalty provision, OLSE is able in all but a few cases to reach settlements with employers for wages, interest, and the City's costs without going to a hearing. Other San Francisco laws, such as the prevailing wage law and the HCSO, provide that the employer must either comply with OLSE's determination or file a request for a hearing within a fifteen-day period, in contrast to the minimum wage law, which defaults to a hearing. If the employer fails to file a timely appeal, the agency's determination is final.

All of the laws that OLSE enforces include strong antiretaliation language. Retaliation against workers who file a complaint or cooperate with investigators is illegal but remains a serious problem for labor enforcement everywhere. In San Francisco, however, there is a rebuttable presumption that retaliation did take place if any "adverse action" is taken within ninety days.[2] Enforcement officers are careful not to overstate the

---

[2] "Taking adverse action against a person within ninety (90) days of the person's exercise of rights protected under this Chapter shall raise a rebuttable presumption of having done so in retaliation for the exercise of such rights." In, for example, the Health Care Security Ordinance, San Francisco Administrative Code, Ch. 14.4d.

protection that this affords, and the risk of losing a job or facing other retaliatory measures remains very real. The minimum wage law and the Paid Sick Leave Ordinance also specifically allow workers to report a violation without disclosing their identity to the employer, which can alleviate fears of retaliation. The MWO states, "[OLSE] shall encourage reporting pursuant to this subsection by keeping confidential, to the maximum extent permitted by applicable laws, the name and other identifying information of the Employee or person reporting the violation,"[3] and the PSLO includes an identical provision.[4] Although other San Francisco labor laws do not affirmatively instruct OLSE to protect claimants' identities, in practice, when the claimant does not wish to be identified, the office does its best to protect anonymity in those cases as well. This type of confidentiality is not possible in the standard wage claim process, such as that used at the California DLSE, where an employee must face her employer in person at a hearing adjudicated by the enforcement agency.

Overview of Accomplishments

The Office of Labor Standards Enforcement has recovered millions of dollars in back wages and penalties in its cases. It has responded to more than 1,300 complaints from employees regarding the three citywide laws and recovered more than $13 million in back wages and health care expenditures for employees in the city.

In addition to back wages and health care expenditures, OLSE has recovered $385,000 in administrative penalties for noncompliance with these citywide ordinances. In prevailing wage cases, OLSE has also recovered $4.4 million in back wages and $1.6 million in penalties since 2002, and four contractors have been debarred from City contracting.

Comparison with Other Labor Enforcement Offices

Enforcement at the local level ideally complements rather than replaces state and federal enforcement. State and local offices work together and

---

[3] San Francisco Administrative Code Sec. 12.R.7(b).
[4] San Francisco Administrative Code Sec. 12.W.8(b).

Table 8.1   Enforcement of Citywide Labor Laws

San Francisco Ordinance	Year Enacted	Worker Complaints	Wages / Health Care Expenditures Recovered	Workers Paid Back Wages / Health Care Expenditures
Minimum Wage	2003	616	$5,820,000	3,004
Paid Sick Leave	2006	293	$100,000	434
Health Care Security	2006	439	$6,915,000	6,251

SOURCES: San Francisco Administrative Code and OLSE case records through mid-2012.

refer cases to one another. OLSE refers cases involving overtime, meal and rest breaks, and other issues that are not covered under San Francisco laws; cases that come to the state related to paid sick leave and other San Francisco–specific laws are referred to the City. In cases where there is potential overlap, for example, minimum wage, California DLSE enforces San Francisco's minimum wage, though in previous gubernatorial administrations all minimum wage cases were referred to the City.

The creation and development of OLSE occurred in the context of decades of stagnant or declining federal and state labor enforcement resources. Nationally, the workforce and the number of workplaces grew by 11 percent from 1998 to 2008, while the number of investigators in the federal Department of Labor's Wage and Hour Division (WHD) fell by 22 percent; the number of investigations also fell, and as a result the rate of investigations per establishment declined by 53 percent (Weil 2010). In California from 1980 to 2000, the workforce increased by 48 percent, while staffing levels at the Department of Labor Standards Enforcement declined by 7.6 percent (Bar-Cohen and Carrillo 2002). Combined with decreasing unionization, a greater variety of work arrangements, and expanding regulatory responsibilities, these trends have weakened labor standards enforcement. Fewer investigations result in fewer cases of back wage and penalty assessments, decreasing the deterrent effect of enforcement and the incentive to comply.

Enforcement staffing levels in San Francisco are around 31,000 workers per OLSE staff member, a level similar to the state's during the first Brown administration in the late 1970s (Bar-Cohen and Carrillo 2002). But resources for enforcement have declined at the state level since then. In the mid-1990s, state enforcement staff ratios climbed to around 50,000 state workers per staff member and have only recently begun to come back down, now standing at a proposed 37,000 workers per staffer for 2012–13 (California Department of Finance 2012).

Similarly at the federal level, resources for enforcement did not keep pace with growth in the size of the workforce and the number of employers. In 2007, the Wage and Hour Division had 750 investigators, or one investigator for every 173,000 American workers (see table 8.2). Kim Bobo, founder and executive director of Interfaith Worker Justice, looks at enforcement staffing levels in 1941 and 1962 in the federal WHD, when workers per investigator stood at 8,800 and 18,000 respectively, and asks how many investigators would be needed today to provide comparable coverage. She first calculates that 12,500 investigators would be needed to maintain the 1941 level of workers per investigator. She then takes into account productivity increases of 373 percent over that period and arrives at an estimate of 3,350 investigators needed to maintain these early enforcement staffing levels. Similar calculations for 1962 produce an estimate of 2,834 investigators needed. Thus her estimates suggest that the number of investigators would need to be about four times larger than it was in 2007—resulting in a ratio of about 43,000 workers per investigator—to provide a level of enforcement coverage similar to that which existed in either 1941 or 1962 (Bobo 2009).

Under the Obama administration, 300 new investigators were hired in the Wage and Hour Division.[5] This hiring has brought down the ratio of workers per staff, but it remains far from the equivalent of historical staffing levels. OLSE's staffing level is not as robust as productivity-adjusted historical levels but is above current federal levels. With 6.5

[5] Though as the Wage and Hour Division's deputy administrator pointed out in congressional testimony, those extra enforcement personnel are still being trained, and their impact has not yet been felt (Leppink 2011).

Table 8.2   U.S. Department of Labor, Wage, and Hour Division, Resources over Time and in Comparison with San Francisco

	1941	1962	2007	2012	SF OLSE, 2011
MW* investigators	1,769	1,544	750	ca. 1,050	6.5
Workers covered	15.5m	28m	130m	130m	559,000
Workers per Investigator	8,800	18,000	173,000	124,000	86,000

* MW = minimum wage.

SOURCES: Department of Labor data from Bobo 2009, 120; 2011 and 2012 data from OLSE and California Quarterly Census of Employment and Wages.

investigators for minimum wage cases at OLSE in 2011, each investigator was responsible for approximately 86,000 workers; with the extra position added for 2012–13, the number drops to 75,000 workers per investigator.[6]

In addition to staffing levels, metrics on cases processed and wages collected can help compare results across agencies. Focusing on minimum wage cases in the period 2008–11,[7] OLSE opened an average of seventy-four cases per year. As of 2012, 55 percent of cases were resolved, meaning back wages had been paid, and 3 percent were in the process of paying. Another 11 percent of cases were referred to either the state or the federal government. A quarter of cases had been closed, meaning that either no violation was found or the claimant stopped pursuing the claim—a share similar to the federal WHD percentage of "no violation" cases (Weil 2010). Another 5 percent of cases, most of them from 2011, were still under investigation. Of those cases that were resolved or in the process of paying in 2011, OLSE had recovered an average of more than $13,000 per case, or $3,300 per claimant.

[6] Workers per *investigator* (the federal comparison) and workers per *staffer* (the state comparison) are both relevant metrics, but available data limit the ability to compare on both metrics across all jurisdictions and all time periods.

[7] The minimum wage went into effect in 2004, but OLSE administrative data are most complete for these years.

One analysis of enforcement across states looks at the number of cases opened in a given year (regardless of outcome) and the amount of money collected in back wages (Lurie 2011). On this metric, OLSE opened seventy-seven cases in 2011, collected $638,171 in wages (not necessarily for those cases, since some cases are completed in a different calendar year), and paid those back wages to an average of 4.1 workers per case, for an average of $8,300 per case, or just over $2,000 per claimant (table 8.3). In comparison, a survey of seventeen states found most with collections at or below $1,000 per case, and only two states, Connecticut and New York, had averages significantly above $1,000 (Lurie 2011). The California Bureau of Field Enforcement (BOFE), whose operations make it the state agency most like OLSE, reported collecting $3.1 million in wages owed and issuing 294 minimum wage and overtime citations, an average of about $10,500 per citation (Su 2011). In part this number is higher because BOFE takes only those cases that involve multiple workers. Wages per case or citation is a useful metric but ignores the importance of small claims. Small claims may not increase the average value of wages collected per case but are nevertheless vital for the workers involved.

Wages collected can differ substantially, however, from *wages due.* The $3.1 million collected by California's BOFE represented just 40 percent of the total wages found due; the current California labor commissioner reports that collections are a focal point for improvement (Su 2011). In contrast, San Francisco's OLSE has a much stronger collections record. In cases where wages are owed the office collects the wages or agrees with the employer on a payment plan. While cases may take some time to be fully paid off, only a handful of cases have failed to result in full back wages paid to workers.

Such comparisons suggest that OLSE has a strong record on finding and collecting back wages, as well as staffing levels that are relatively high but not out of line with either historical staffing levels or recent efforts to strengthen enforcement. These comparisons are illustrative and do not account either for geographic factors, such as the difference in enforcement for a forty-nine-square-mile city and a large dispersed geographic region, or for prevalence of violations, which may differ over time and by area. A deeper discussion of prevalence, enforcement

Table 8.3   Minimum Wage Cases, Wages Collected, and Wages per Case
Various jurisdictions

Place	Laws*	Year	Cases	Wages Collected	Wages Collected per Case**	Source
Full employer investigations						
SF OLSE	MW, WP	2011	77 opened	$638,171	$8,288	OLSE
					($2,041 per claimant)	
CA BOFE	MW, OT	FY 2010–11	294 citations	$3,088,895	$10,506	Su
Wage claims (brought by individuals and adjudicated by the agency)						
New York	MW, OT, WP	2009	7,588 opened	$20,270,323	$2,671	Lurie
Connecticut	MW, OT, WP	FY 2009	3,906 claims	$6,020,431	$1,541	Lurie
CA DLSE	MW, OT, WP	2009	42,205 opened	$42,001,340	$995	Lurie
Washington DC	MW, OT, WP, LW	2011	634 claims	$485,782	$766	DC budget & report

*Laws for which the statistics apply; MW = minimum wage, OT = overtime, WP = wage payment (e.g., not receiving a final paycheck), LW = living wage.

** Wages collected per case includes cases that were opened in other years; wages collected per case is simply the result of dividing wages collected in a given year by the number of cases opened or claims filed.

SOURCES: OLSE internal records; Lurie 2011; Su 2011; DC Department of Employment Services 2012.

metrics, and sufficient staffing models is beyond the scope of this chapter, however. Below we explore in more depth OLSE's policies and practices for successfully deploying the resources they have.

3. EDUCATION AND OUTREACH

OLSE has made educating the public a priority. Without education and outreach, employers may not comply and employees may not report violations simply because they do not understand the law. All staff members devote time to answering questions via hotlines and emails as well as setting up meetings to educate and take questions from employers and workers. The OLSE website provides copies of San Francisco labor laws and their respective regulations, fact sheets, FAQs, brochures on labor laws in six languages, multilingual complaint forms, information on regular trainings on electronic payroll records, and a video on construction contracting requirements. In order to share information on workers' rights, staff members have done radio shows in English, Spanish, and Cantonese, and have spoken at community college vocational and ESL classes and at labor and community forums. The Minimum Wage and Health Care Security Ordinances specifically mention and require outreach efforts, but the office has made public education a priority for all laws.

After the passage of the Health Care Security and Paid Sick Leave Ordinances, some members of the Board of Supervisors were concerned that businesses might not have the knowledge and tools needed to voluntarily comply with the law. To remedy this, they provided supplemental funding that OLSE used for employer-focused outreach material, merchant walks in business corridors in every district, and ads in bus shelters and community newspapers. To make sure businesses are informed about the laws, especially since the minimum wage increases annually with inflation, OLSE sends out required notices for posting to all businesses with employees every year. In addition, posters announcing the new minimum wage rate are posted in City buses at the beginning of each year. OLSE staff regularly make presentations and conduct webinars in conjunction with the City's Office of Small Business and employer organizations, with a focus on providing tools for success to San Francisco's small businesses.

The Role of Community-Based Organizations

OLSE contracts with a collaborative of community-based organizations to provide education and outreach to low-wage and immigrant communities. In fiscal year 2011–12, the office provided $190,000 in funding to three organizations: the Chinese Progressive Association, which works closely with restaurant workers in Chinatown and develops worker organizers; La Raza Centro Legal, which offers a drop-in legal clinic; and the Filipino Community Center, which provides workers' rights information and has developed a strong network of workers employed at nursing homes. As part of their contracts these organizations are also responsible for resolving or referring to OLSE a certain number of cases each year. Many of the claimants referred to OLSE by community groups may not have otherwise found their way to a government agency or had the support needed to file a claim.

In addition to informing workers of their rights, community organizations play critical political roles in supporting effective enforcement generally. Outside pressure, whether from unions or community-based organizations, has been documented to improve implementation and enforcement of employment laws (Weil 1991; Luce 2005). The sociologist Stephanie Luce's study of implementation of living wage laws across the country notes the many ways in which community groups influence implementation: pressuring bureaucracies as the Solidarity Sponsoring Committee, a workers' rights organization, did when it helped school bus aides file living wage complaints in Baltimore; exerting legislative pressure to force more expansive implementation, as the Los Angeles Alliance for a New Economy did in advocating for amendments to Los Angeles's living wage law to explicitly cover workers at the airports; and supporting budget allocations for enforcement work, the absence of which may have doomed the one living wage enforcement position in Tucson, which was cut as the result of a budget shortfall (Luce 2005).

Community groups in San Francisco, whose support and advocacy were crucial to the passage of the laws, continue to advocate for strong enforcement. Most recently this support has resulted in creation of the multidepartment Wage Theft Task Force and an increase in funding for community-based worker education and outreach. The task force brings together representatives from seven relevant departments—OLSE, the Police Department, the Department of Public Health, the City Attorney's Office, the District Attorney's Office, the Office of the Treasurer and Tax Collector, and the Office of Small Business—and eight community members: four from community nonprofits, one from labor, and three representing employers in industries where wage theft is prevalent (San Francisco Board of Supervisors 2012). In addition, an extra $296,000 per year were allocated for community organizations to conduct worker education and outreach to target additional communities.

Clarifying and Revising the Laws

Clarifying and revising legislation, like education and outreach, is an important part of effective enforcement. For the pathbreaking PSLO and HCSO, the OLSE had statutory authority to issue regulations clarifying areas of ambiguity. With paid sick leave in particular, OLSE conducted hearings and solicited comments from both Young Workers United, a group that drafted and fought for passage of the ballot initiative, and opponents from the Chamber of Commerce and Golden Gate Restaurant Association. By involving a broad range of stakeholders in the rule-making process, the office was able to take their concerns about implementation of the new law into account and perhaps win more support for the legislation from employers. Many of the resulting rules, including the procedures for notification of employers about sick leave usage or the verification of an illness, have been used across the country as other jurisdictions work to propose and implement their own paid sick leave legislation.

Revisions and updates to laws have also been required. Three years after the Health Care Security Ordinance went into effect, community advocates expressed concerns that employers were complying with the law by setting up Health Reimbursement Accounts that had extremely low reimbursement rates and that restaurants and others were collecting extra revenue through menu surcharges but not spending it on worker health care. In response, the Board of Supervisors amended the Health Care Security Ordinance to address both issues, though advocates suspect employers may still be limiting access to health reimbursement benefits and potentially profiting from health care surcharges not spent on employee health care (Grady 2012).

4. COMPONENTS OF THE OLSE ENFORCEMENT STRATEGY

Building Trust with Workers

Overcoming mistrust and building relationships with workers is key to building successful cases against labor law violators, and staff members with relevant experience and skills are the office's greatest asset in this area. When complainants can relate to the officer responsible for their cases, they are more likely to participate in the (sometimes painstaking) process of providing testimony and developing a case against the alleged violator. The majority of OLSE minimum wage violation cases involve workers paid in cash, typically a set amount per pay period, regardless of hours worked. Because employers do not maintain accurate records of actual hours worked, in these cases OLSE must rely on workers' testimony to prove or correct pay received and hours worked. Developing strong working relationships with claimants therefore is critical to OLSE's success. Unscrupulous employers may threaten to contact Immigration and Customs Enforcement (ICE) to scare workers and dissuade them from filing complaints and may instruct workers to lie to investigators in order to save their jobs.

Recent research corroborates what labor advocates have long known—that trust of government institutions is low in the immigrant and minority communities where wage theft is most likely to occur. Shannon Gleeson (2009) has demonstrated that racial and ethnic minorities are more likely to report low levels of trust in government institutions and are less likely than other workers to report labor law violations. Gleeson

(2010) has also highlighted the reluctance of undocumented workers to stand up for their labor rights. Whether that mistrust is based on prior experiences or an abundance of caution, overcoming it is a central challenge in enforcing San Francisco's labor laws.

The industries where violations of San Francisco's labor laws appear to occur most frequently, such as food service and construction, also have a large proportion of workers of racial and ethnic minorities and immigrant workers. By far the largest proportion of OLSE's minimum wage complaints are filed against employers in the food service industry (56 percent from workers in restaurants, cafés, and coffee shops in 2011). While PSLO and HCSO cases are not concentrated in any single industry, food service businesses are still the most common target of sick leave complaints and the second most common target of HCSO cases. Because prevailing wage laws apply to public works contracts, OLSE's prevailing wage cases involve the construction industry.

Since Latino and Asian immigrants are disproportionately represented in both the food service and construction industries, OLSE has designed its enforcement programs to attempt to overcome mistrust and minimize the cultural and institutional barriers to building cases against labor law violators. Nine OLSE staff members speak languages other than English, including Spanish, Cantonese, Mandarin, Tagalog, and Thai. Spanish and Cantonese are by far the most commonly spoken languages in San Francisco after English, and sharing a common language has been shown to be a key factor in building trust (Office of Civic Engagement and Immigrant Affairs 2011). In addition, five OLSE staff members were born outside the United States and speak a language other than English as their first language. These individuals may share common threads of an immigrant experience with immigrant workers, and this could help build trust in the compliance officers, the claims process, or the agency as a whole.

OLSE's contract compliance officers also have knowledge and experience specific to the laws they enforce. The OLSE manager worked for ten years in the construction trades and for ten years as a carpenters' union representative. She and others on staff speak the language of construction and are comfortable on a work site. When enforcement staff share a common language, background, and/or experience with workers and employers, it becomes easier to bridge the gap between bureaucrat and client and to humanize the claims process.

OLSE tries to be particularly sensitive to the concerns of undocumented workers who come forward to report violations. In interviews and throughout the enforcement process, the OLSE staff never ask about immigration status, and staff ensure all employees know they are entitled to rights under San Francisco laws, consistent with state law and the fact that San Francisco is a sanctuary city. It is impossible to prevent retaliation against undocumented workers who do come forward in all cases, but OLSE staff members have gone to great lengths to support claimants when OLSE suspects employers of retaliation.

In one case, a claimant's husband was detained by ICE soon after OLSE determined that her former employer had failed to pay minimum wage. The claimant strongly suspected that her employer, Si Señor Taqueria, had notified immigration authorities to retaliate against her. An ICE employee in Eloy, Arizona, informed the OLSE that they had picked up the claimant's husband after receiving an anonymous letter that alleged he was undocumented and a criminal. OLSE wrote a letter to the judge in the case asking that he be released because of the pending minimum wage case and the possibility that ICE was notified in retaliation for the claimant asserting her right to minimum wage. The claimant's husband was released and given a copy of the anonymous letter and its envelope. OLSE was able to trace the postal meter stamp on the envelope to a location connected to the employer (Hendricks 2006). Although ICE required that the couple return to Mexico, with OLSE's support they were able to successfully settle a lawsuit for retaliation.

As noted above, OLSE collaborates with partner organizations based in immigrant communities to conduct education and outreach. All of those community based organizations provide counseling and referral services for victims of labor standards violations. Workers fearful of coming to a government agency (because of immigration status or attitudes towards government) also have the option of bringing their claim to a community group, which they may be more likely to trust.

Finally, perhaps the most effective way to gain the trust of communities most affected by violations is to succeed in recovering back wages and to empower the recipients of those who recovered wages to refer their friends and colleagues when their rights are violated. OLSE staff report that word-of-mouth referrals make up a large segment of minimum wage cases.

Thorough, Company-Wide Investigations

When OLSE receives a complaint, it launches an investigation of the company as a whole rather than just adjudicating a dispute between one worker and the employer. The office investigates for all workers and checks for compliance with all applicable ordinances. About 40 percent of successfully resolved minimum wage cases end up expanding to cover more workers than originally brought the complaint. In some notable cases, most recently a case against Tower Car Wash, investigations sparked by complaints related to one law exposed extensive violations in other areas. While this policy of company-wide investigations may mean that cases can take longer, the goal is to correct business practices going forward, ensuring that all employees' rights are protected and that the employer implements proper record keeping processes. In addition, company-wide investigations can help protect workers from retaliation, since in the initial stages of the investigation it is easier for the identity of the claimant to remain protected.

The level of investigation also distinguishes OLSE. For minimum wage complaints, the office conducts a site visit for every case. OLSE officers first conduct an interview with workers to know what to look for, for example, a phony sign-in sheet, and then make an unannounced site visit to the workplace. This contrasts with the practice of both state and federal labor law enforcement agencies. A significant number of complaints at the federal level are dealt with through reconciliation, often involving a phone call to the employer, and at the state level through an informal settlement conference (Weil 2010; Rose 2011).

In addition, OLSE has subpoena power, which enables investigators to call in source documents, obtain evidence more quickly, and find violations that would not show up, for example, in the certified payroll records submitted pursuant to the prevailing wage law. OLSE audits require employers to provide pay stub details and copies of the front and back of canceled checks. On several occasions, insisting on these documents has resulted in the OLSE being able to uncover pay schemes involving forged endorsements on the backs of paychecks and kickbacks to the employer.

In a case involving a painting contractor who had performed City contracts for twenty years, workers told OLSE that they were paid less than half of the hourly wage rate that the company reported paying on the certified payroll records they submitted to the City. Unable to get source documents from the contractor, OLSE issued subpoenas for pay stub details from a payroll service used by the contractor and for canceled checks from the contractor's bank. OLSE determined that the contractor had underpaid workers on City contracts by more than $600,000 over three years. Based on these findings, the San Francisco District Attorney arraigned the owner on fifty-seven felony counts "related to wage theft, filing false instruments, offering fraudulent documents, and workers' compensation insurance premium fraud" (Organized Labor 2012).

Cooperation with Other Departments

OLSE cooperation with other departments increases the office's efficiency and effectiveness. In addition to working together on the newly formed Wage Theft Task Force, the Department of Public Health, contracting departments, the Treasurer and Tax Collector's office, the City Attorney, and the District Attorney all collaborate with OLSE. Together they are able to reach more employers, uncover more violations, and recover larger amounts of back pay.

Court cases undertaken with the help of the district or city attorney usually take significantly longer to complete than the administrative process, but litigating a case can be an effective way to deal with intransigent employers and especially egregious cases. For example, in one recent case OLSE and the City Attorney's Office filed for a prejudgment writ of attachment that froze a restaurant owner's assets, preventing him from moving assets into family members' names. In July 2011 the city attorney sued a couple whose restaurant the OLSE had found was paying less than $4 an hour for eleven-hour days, six days a week. The lawsuit introduced the possibility that the City would seize and sell two properties owned by the couple to collect the wages owed. In January 2013 the case was settled; the owners agreed to pay penalties to the City and full back wages to the workers, a total of more than half a million dollars (Coté 2013). City attorney involvement has also been important in cases against car washes in both San Francisco and Los Angeles (Larrubia 2009; Coté 2012). Criminal prosecution of labor laws is rare, though worker advocates have argued that state attorneys general should be more involved in labor law enforcement, as were District Attorney Eliot Spitzer and Labor Commissioner Patricia Smith in New York (Romer-Friedman 2005). The district attorney in San Francisco has filed criminal and felony charges in two prevailing wage cases. In one, the district attorney charged executives at a trucking firm with grand larceny for wage theft violations, as well as numerous instances of fraud (Marzotto 2006).

Cooperation with the Department of Public Health (DPH) is another important interdepartmental relationship. DPH engages in investigations and administrative hearings regarding health permits for restaurants, an industry with a high proportion of low-wage workers and a history of employment law violations. The department understands its purview as including local labor laws;[8] it therefore can incorporate evidence of noncompliance with labor laws in hearing procedures associated with health permits.[9] In a handful of cases, OLSE has used DPH hearings and the threat of revocation of health permits to enforce existing agreements with employers for back pay. The threat of health permit revocation has also helped resolve matters with intransigent employers engaged in negotiations with OLSE.

---

[8] CA Health and Safety Code §113715: "Any construction, alteration, remodeling, or operation of a food facility shall be approved by the enforcement agency and shall be in accordance with all applicable local, state, and federal statutes, regulations, and ordinances, including but not limited to, fire, building, and zoning codes."

[9] CA Health and Safety Code §114405.

Finally, collaboration with other departments can help uncover violations. This is particularly true with prevailing wage violations. Contracting department staff are trained to review payroll records and alert OLSE to disparities between reports and actual job site activity. For example, work site construction inspectors and project managers who know that work is going on during the weekend can look at certified payroll records to make sure that the proper hours are being reported. If not, they alert OLSE to the discrepancy. This site-specific knowledge enables the office to develop more cases than they would otherwise find from worker complaints or payroll record reviews alone.

5. CONCLUSION

San Francisco's OLSE provides a noteworthy example of effective labor standards enforcement. Robust staffing levels and impressive results collecting back wages for workers are the consequence of strategic policies internally and a network of external relationships. Outreach and education efforts aim to increase awareness among workers and employers to support compliance. OLSE works with community groups, collaborates with other departments, and builds trust with workers themselves. Staff members conduct thorough investigations of an entire employer in response to complaints, uncovering violations well beyond the initial complaint. Negotiations with employers have resulted in the payment of millions of dollars in back wages and benefits, and thousands of workplaces have come into compliance with the City's array of groundbreaking labor laws.

However, the office is for the most part constrained to investigations in response to complaints. Staffing levels are not high enough to do strategic proactive enforcement or random inspections that would help to both establish underlying rates of violation and enforce the laws for workers who still, despite the efforts of OLSE and community organizations, either do not know their rights are being violated or are too afraid of retaliation to speak up. Battles for funding will continue, as will efforts of the newly created Wage Theft Task Force to increase compliance. But as the local standards and mandates passed in San Francisco spread, whether to other localities, states, or the nation, the fight for the changes these laws promise will not be complete without serious attention to how they are implemented and enforced.

REFERENCES

Bar-Cohen, Limor, and Deana Milam Carrillo. 2002. "Labor Law Enforcement in California, 1970–2000." *State of California Labor*, 135–70. Available at www .escholarship.org/uc/ile_scl2002.

Bernhardt, Annette, Ruth Milkman, and Nicholas Theodore, et al. 2009. *Broken Law, Unprotected Workers: Violations of Employment and Labor Laws in America's Cities*. Chicago, New York, and Los Angeles: Center for Urban Economic Development, National Employment Law Project, UCLA Institute for Research on Labor and Employment.

Bobo, Kim. 2009. *Wage Theft in America: Why Millions of Working Americans Are not Getting Paid—and What We Can Do about It*. New York: New Press.

California Department of Finance. 2012. *Labor and Workforce Development*. Retrieved Oct. 4, 2012, from 2012–13 Salaries and Wages, www.dof.ca.gov /budget/historical/2012–13/salaries_and_wages/documents/7000.pdf.

Chinese Progressive Association. 2010. *Check, Please!* San Francisco: Chinese Progressive Association.

Coté, John. 2012. "Tower Car Wash Pays $500,000 to Settle Wage Theft Lawsuit." *San Francisco Chronicle*, July 6, City Insider.

———. 2013. "SF Restaurant Pays Back Wages, Fines." *San Francisco Chronicle*, Feb. 13. www.sfgate.com/default/article/SF-restaurant-pays-back-wages-fines-4273029.php.

DC Department of Employment Services. 2012. "Fiscal Year 2011–2012 Performance Hearing Responses." www.dccouncil.us/files/user_uploads /budget_responses/fy11_12_agencyperformanag_deptofemploymentser-vices_responses.pdf.

Elliott, Robert H. 1981. "The Policy Adoption-Implementation Spiral." *International Journal of Public Administration* 3, 1: 113–41.

Gile, Krista J., and Mark S. Handcock. 2010. "Respondent-Driven Sampling: An Assessment of Current Methodology." *Sociological Methodology* 40, 1: 285–327.

Gleeson, Shannon. 2009. "From Rights to Claims: The Role of Civil Society in Making Rights Real for Vulnerable Workers. *Law & Society Review* 43, 3 (Sept.): 669–700.

————. 2010. "Labor Rights for All? The Role of Undocumented Immigrant Status for Worker Claims Making." *Law & Social Inquiry* 35: 561–602.

Government of the District of Columbia. 2012. *FY 2013 Proposed Budget and Financial Plan: Volume 2 Agency Budget Chapters—Part I*. Washington DC: Government of the District of Columbia.

Grady, Barbara. 2012. "S.F. Civil Grand Jury Slams Restaurant Health Care Surcharges." *San Francisco Public Press*, July 19. http://sfpublicpress.org /news/2012–07/sf-civil-grand-jury-slams-restaurant-health-care-surcharges#mayor.

Hendricks, Tyche. 2006. "Worker Wins Her Rights but Loses Hope; Someone Told Feds She's Here Illegally." *San Francisco Chronicle*, May 11. www.sfgate. com/restaurants/article/Worker-wins-her-rights-but-loses-hope-Someone-2535290.php.

Larrubia, Evelyn. 2009. "Criminal Charges Filed against Car Wash Owners." *Los Angeles Times*, Feb. 10, L.A. Now.

Leppink, Nancy J. 2011. "Examining Regulatory and Enforcement Actions under the Fair Labor Standards Act." *Hearing before the Subcommittee on Workforce Protections, Committee on Education and the Workforce, U.S. House of Representatives*. Washington DC: U.S. Government Printing Office.

Luce, Stephanie. 2005. "The Role of Community Involvement in Implementing Living Wage Ordinances." *Industrial Relations* 44, 1: 32–58.

Lurie, Irene 2011. "Enforcement of State Minimum Wage and Overtime Laws: Resources, Procedures, and Outcomes." *Employee Rights and Employment Policy Journal* 15, 2: 411–42.

Marzotto, Mary. 2006. "Workers Receive $274,000 in Back Wages from Unscrupulous Contractor." Retrieved Sept. 24, 2012, from San Francisco Building and Construction Trades Council, www.sfbuildingtradescouncil. org/content/view/121/71/.

Office of Civic Engagement and Immigrant Affairs. 2011. "Language Matters: Language Access Ordinance Annual Compliance Summary Report" (July). Retrieved from http://sfgsa.org/modules/showdocument. aspx?documentid=8196.

Organized Labor. 2012. "Non-Union Contractor Charged with Cheating." Retrieved Dec. 4, 2012, from San Francisco Building and Construction Trades Council, www.sfbuildingtradescouncil.org.

Parsa, H.G., John T. Self, David Njite, and Tiffany King. 2005. "Why Restaurants Fail." *Cornell Hotel and Restaurant Administration Quarterly* 46, 3: 304–22.

Romer-Friedman, Peter. 2005. "Eliot Spitzer Meets Mother Jones: How State Attorneys General Can Enforce State Wage and Hour Laws." *Columbia Journal of Law and Social Problems* 39, 4: 495–553.

Rose, Harvey M. 2011. *Legislative Analyst Report: Enforcement of the Minimum Wage Ordinance in San Francisco*. San Francisco: Board of Supervisors.

San Francisco Administrative Code. 2011. Ch. 6–12R-17-d. *Chapter 12R Minimum Wage, 17d Violation* (Sept. 16). Retrieved from www.amlegal.com /nxt/gateway.dll/California/administrative/chapter12rminimumwage?f=t emplates$fn=default.htm$3.0$vid=amlegal:sanfrancisco_ca.

San Francisco Board of Supervisors. 2012. *BOS ord 102–12* (May 1). Retrieved from Administrative Code—Establishing a Wage Theft Task Force, www. sfbos.org/ftp/uploadedfiles/bdsupvrs/ordinances12/00102–12.pdf.

Su, Julie A. 2011. *2011 Annual Report on the Effectiveness of the Bureau of Field Enforcement*. State of California: Department of Industrial Relations.

Weil, David. 1991. "Enforcing OSHA: The Role of Labor Unions." *Industrial Relations* 30, 1: 20–36.

———. 2010. *Improving Workplace Conditions through Strategic Enforcement: A Report to the Wage and Hour Division*. Boston: Boston University.

NINE Labor Policy and Local Economic Development

Miriam J. Wells

1.   INTRODUCTION

As the fabric of globalization has become more densely woven, the consequences for organized labor have alarmed many scholars. Some scholars hold that globalization threatens workers' rights because it erodes the state's inclination and capacity to guarantee them (Brecher and Costello 1994; Mander and Goldsmith 1997; Tilly 1995). Without challenging the pattern of declining federal protections that these authors document or disagreeing that global action has merit, I sug-

*Portions of this chapter are based on or appeared in Miriam Wells, "When Urban Policy Becomes Labor Policy: State Structures, Local Initiatives, and Union Representation at the Turn of the Century," *Theory and Society* 31 (2002): 115–46. Reprinted with kind permission from Springer Science+Business Media.

gest here that their despondence about local action and state involvement is unwarranted and that it reflects an overly simplistic concep-
tion of the state. The American federal state, because of the relative
autonomy of city, county, and state governments from the federal government, adds more layers, complexity, and openings for challenge
than are found in more centralized systems, such as those of France or
England.[1] Postwar urban development processes have further elaborated this complexity, increasing the variety of functions that local
jurisdictions have taken on and devolving many responsibilities from
the federal to the local level.

In this chapter I argue that a multilayered state structure has created
openings for local actors, frustrated by the federal retreat from labor
protection, to activate the resources of the local level on behalf of workers' rights. Such initiatives make the nature of the locality and the strategies of local actors key to the protection of labor's rights. They bring
U.S. labor unions, which have a long history of engagement with the
law, to a more concerted focus on policy and into broad-based alliances
at the local level (Forbath 1991). Finally, they render industries that are
bound to or dependent on a locality especially subject to state constraints.

The ensuing analysis is based on a case study of local politics in San
Francisco, California.[2] It examines a particular initiative and controversy:
passage of a local ordinance, the San Francisco Employee Signature
Authorization Ordinance (ESAO), which shifted significant authority
over labor relations from the federal to the local level. I show that in at

[1] Germany and Switzerland, however, are quite decentralized, and Canada probably
even more than the United States.

[2] This chapter is based on a larger research project funded by the Cultural Anthropology
Program of the National Science Foundation and the University of California, Davis, that
explores the relationship between unionization and globalization in the San Francisco
hotel industry. Between October 1996 and June 2001, the author conducted 85 interviews,
from one to four hours long, with government officials and staff, attorneys, hotel workers
and managers, union staff, employers' association spokespersons, representatives of community and immigrant organizations, and the staff of several firms that do research on the
hotel industry. Attendance at the meetings of governmental bodies that considered the
ordinance provided useful data on the positions and self-presentations of vested actors, as
has perusal of local newspapers for the duration of the project.

least one global industry, the hotel industry, some local workers are being freed from national strictures in adjudicating labor decisions. The movement thus initiated, however, is not toward weaker labor protections and greater global dominance but toward more effective state protection rooted in localities.

I present in the next section a brief history of how federal law has become much less effective in defending workers' rights and how an alternative route—using card check elections—has gained in importance. Section 3 discusses the evolution of this process in San Francisco, in particular, in the hotel industry. Section 4 shows how local governments have become enabled to regulate labor-management relations, particularly in instances when a city has a proprietary stake in labor peace. The ensuing local context of political activity is discussed in Section 5, and its culmination, the Employee Signature Authorization Ordinance, is the subject of Section 6. The concluding section reviews the implications of these developments for other ordinances, both in San Francisco and elsewhere.

2. FEDERAL LAW AND WORKERS' RIGHTS

During the New Deal and with modifications thereafter, the U.S. government declared its intent to protect the right of workers to organize and bargain collectively, within the broader goal of keeping the industrial peace (Gorman 1976). It assigned implementation of this goal to the federal government through the National Labor Relations Act (NLRA) and its implementing body, the National Labor Relations Board (NLRB). At the same time it precluded local jurisdictions from acting in the same area, stating that their right to action was "pre-empted" by the federal monopoly on labor relations regulation. The NLRA set out employees' rights regarding organizing and collective bargaining, established the mechanisms and procedures through which union certification elections were to be conducted, and defined as unfair labor practices employer acts that could constrain workers' ability to organize freely and to bargain collectively.

The National Record

Although the NLRA boosted union organizing and representation until the mid-1970s, its effectiveness has declined significantly since that time. Even more than in other advanced industrial nations, U.S. regulatory controls on private industry have been relaxed or dismantled in the name of fostering market competitiveness.[3] Antiunion sentiment has gathered force among politicians and the public, and twenty years of Reagan and Bush appointees to the NLRB, along with earlier amendments that reduced the strength of NLRA protections, have compounded the difficulty of securing union recognition through the NLRB. Faced with rising costs and initially falling profits in the world market and given the alternative of cheaper labor elsewhere, U.S. employers have scapegoated unions for undercutting profitability.

Research shows that the overwhelming majority of U.S. private sector employers now aggressively oppose unionization, constituting a—if not *the*—major impediment to the implementation of the NLRA. Their coercive and illegal antiunion tactics have proliferated, ranging from intense intimidation and propaganda campaigns to firing employees who support union representation drives in nonunion firms and permanently replacing those who strike in support of collective bargaining in unionized firms. With startling frequency, employers threaten plant closure, border patrol raids, and job loss; they use electronic surveillance, intimidation, bribes, interrogation, and captive audience speeches.[4] Thousands of employees—about one in twenty in 1980—are illegally fired each year for participating in union organizing drives (Weiler 1983). Sanctions are unevenly and slowly applied and an

---

[3] Belying claims that nation-states are uniformly unwilling or unable to protect labor's rights, U.S. law provides less protection from attacks than do the laws of most other advanced industrial countries because of administrative features that increase its vulnerability to unsympathetic political leadership and diminish the speed and fairness with which it expedites unfair labor practice litigation (Edwards 1986; Jenson and Mahon 1993). Lengthy election procedures and the law's permission to replace striking employees permanently are also impediments.

[4] A "captive audience" speech refers to an antiunion speech given at a meeting employees are required to attend (Bronfenbrenner and Juravich 1995).

insignificant deterrent, given the substantial gains derived from intimidation and election delays.

Alternative Routes to Union Recognition

As a result of this experience, U.S. unions and employers have done an
about-face in their orientations toward the NLRA. Whereas employers
vehemently denounced it at the outset, they now applaud its "even-
handedness" and moderate implementation. Union leaders, initially
enthusiastic and galvanized by the federal government's unprecedented
foray into protecting labor's rights, have since declared that labor would
be better off if the NLRB were disbanded and the act repealed (Weiler
1986).

In the wake of these changes, union interest in alternative means of
securing recognition has grown, and the AFL-CIO has initiated a national
campaign to develop "non-Board" recognition strategies. The NLRA sets
out two ways in which unions can be recognized without going through
the cumbersome and resistance-ridden federally supervised election process: the NLRB may order an employer to recognize a union if he has
unlawfully refused to bargain or has committed enough unfair labor
practices, and a union may request recognition from an employer if it
secures a majority (51 percent) of voluntarily signed union authorization
or membership cards from employees. A union may also negotiate a collective bargaining agreement or secure a verbal agreement for recognition once a card majority is obtained. Given such an agreement, the
employer cannot back out or later insist on an election.

To reduce their exposure to employer intervention, unions pursuing
the card-signing approach usually organize clandestinely and then conduct the card-signing campaign as rapidly as possible (Greenhouse
1997). Keeping an organizing and card-signing campaign under wraps is
difficult, however, and employer intimidation and countertactics constitute major stumbling blocks to securing union representation through
this method as well. As a result, many unions have turned to "card check
neutrality agreements," in which the employer agrees to remain neutral
while the union conducts a card-signing campaign for union member-

ship or collective bargaining representation. For its part, the union agrees not to picket or boycott the employer while the campaign is being conducted, thus ensuring a climate of industrial peace in which the true preferences of workers can be ascertained.

This approach has yielded gains in union membership in recent years because it averts the intensive campaigns of employer intimidation and harassment that have so crippled the NLRB election process. In Las Vegas alone, the Hotel Employees and Restaurant Employees union (HERE) increased its membership from 18,000 to over 60,000 by using cards instead of NLRB elections (Greenhouse 1997).[5] Nationally, unions have pursued this strategy through the Employee Free Choice Act, which would have streamlined card check recognition and facilitated initial collective bargaining agreements. Though it passed the House in both 2007 and 2009, it was blocked by a filibuster in the Senate in 2007 and failed to pass the Senate again in 2009.

3. THE VIEW FROM SAN FRANCISCO

San Francisco's hotel unions have a long and militant history, beginning with craft locals in the 1860s (Josephson 1956). When hotel workers engaged in a protracted and bitter strike during World War II, the War Labor Board stepped in and mandated a settlement that created virtually 100 percent union representation in the industry. This settlement initiated a strike-free period of continuous labor-management contracts that lasted for almost forty years, during which hotel employers routinely accepted union recognition as a necessary precondition for operation (Cobble and Merrill 1994; Josephson 1956; Wells 2000). In the mid-1970s, however, the conditions underlying this accord began to crumble, and union structure and policy underwent an epochal reconfiguration. Increasingly, chains and multinational corporations began to replace locally based hoteliers, some of which resisted union recognition.

---

[5] Also, Ian Lewis, research director, UNITE HERE Local 2, interview by M. Dietz, July 12, 2012.

In 1975, as part of a national effort to counter the leverage of large corporations, HERE merged its five San Francisco craft locals (food servers, cooks, bartenders, bellmen and room cleaners, and kitchen help) into a single industrial union, Local 2. This merger made Local 2, with a membership of 25,000, the largest union local in the city and shattered the preestablished power hierarchy among the hotel crafts, creating an upwelling of demands for contract revisions, rank-and-file democracy, and ethnic and gender equality (Russell 1978). These demands were seized and promoted by activists from the women's, ethnic, farm labor, New Left, and antiwar movements, whose members had joined the union in considerable numbers over the previous decade to push for their vision of a more democratic union movement. These tensions and the new industrial union structure led to the ousting of the union's longtime leadership in 1978 and a citywide hotel strike in 1980. The strike produced dramatic improvements in wages and contract terms, signaling an end to the era of conservative contracts negotiated in closed rooms by business and labor leaders and the advent of unpredictable and growing demands by a militant and widely participatory organization.

In this context, hotel and restaurant owners began to resist unionization seriously. New hotels opened in record numbers in the 1980s, several without union contracts. In 1984, restaurant owners defeated Local 2 in a citywide restaurant strike that decimated the union's restaurant membership. In the same year, hotel owners successfully challenged the union's practice of negotiating top-down collective bargaining agreements with hotel employers, forcing it to undertake direct organizing in order to maintain or expand its membership. In 1985, the large hotel owners' collective bargaining association disbanded, allegedly at the urging of a major international hotel company, forcing the union to negotiate separately with each owner. Also in 1985, the city's restaurants followed suit. Faced with this organizing crisis, Local 2 restructured its organization to foster member participation, shifted one-third of its staff and financial resources to organizing, and launched an aggressive campaign to organize nonunion hotels (Wells 2000).

Beginning in the late 1980s, Local 2 undertook a series of bitterly fought hotel organizing campaigns that became emblematic of the consequences of unfettered labor-management conflict. Its first target, in 1989, was the 1,003-room Parc 55, flagship of the Park Lane Hotels International chain and the city's first nonunion Class A hotel, which had opened in 1984. Seeking to avoid the lengthy delays and potential for employer coercion of an NLRB election, Local 2 decided on a card check campaign and began to organize clandestinely. In June 1989, it publicly announced its campaign and set about polling workers. A hotel owner, Larry Chan, responded with a concerted effort to discredit the union and intimidate workers out of supporting it. In July, the union filed an unfair labor practice suit against the hotel with the NLRB. In September, despite its hostile operating environment, the union announced that a majority of the employees had signed cards.

Hotel management refused to accept them, however, insisting instead on an NLRB election. Local 2 countered by filing a massive NLRB complaint against the hotel, listing over eighty violations of federal labor laws, including threatening employees with loss of jobs and benefits, wrongfully disciplining employees for union activity, spying on employees and assigning security guards to follow union activists both inside and outside the hotel, stopping employees from distributing union literature, interrogating employees about their union activity, bribing employees with wage increases and other benefits to discourage union organizing, and creating a company union. The complaint charged that the violations were so serious and the atmosphere within the hotel so poisoned that a fair union election could not be held.

At the same time, Local 2 launched an intensive public influence campaign and international boycott of the hotel. It undertook corporate research on the hotel's holdings, partners, and financial circumstances, and it strengthened ties to the city's Asian and Latino communities to secure their support of their hotel worker compatriots. It also began regular, often flamboyant, picketing of the hotel. Hotel guests were greeted by lines of up to seventy people beating pans and chanting. Influential local and national figures took part, including the chair of the Board of Supervisors, an array of local religious leaders, even the Reverend Jesse Jackson.

As a result of these tactics, the hotel's business plummeted. Even before the end of the fray, it had lost more than $3 million in business and racked up hundreds of thousands of dollars in legal bills, according to court filings and interviews with hotel officials (Calbreath 1992). In September 1993, the NLRB judge found against the hotel, confirming most of the union's charges. Citing "pervasive, serious, and continuing widespread unfair labor practices prompted by the union organizing campaign," she imposed the maximum penalty and ordered the hotel to recognize and bargain with Local 2 (Brazil 1993). In March 1993, a contract was signed, ending the four-year union representation battle. At the signing, union president Sherri Chiesa announced Local 2's intent to take on another nonunion hotel immediately.

Several sustained and economically damaging organizing campaigns followed, most notably against the Marriott Corporation. Overall, through its organizing pressure and flexible tactics, Local 2 has been able to maintain collective bargaining agreements with a striking 90 percent of the city's Class A hotels and unionize 75 percent of the city's hotel workers, at a time when union representation nationally is flagging. This record has been achieved at tremendous cost, however, and Local 2 leaders regard the NLRA's ineffectual protections and ponderous procedures as a serious impediment. In this context, they see card check neutrality agreements as a valuable alternative route to union representation.

4.   LABOR PROTECTIONS AND THE MULTIPLE LEVELS OF THE STATE

Until recently, the formal federal monopoly on labor regulation meant that local governments were not expected to play a role in this process. In practice, however, the elaboration of city functions and evolving legal interpretations as to their impact on city prerogatives have created an opening for cities to intervene. Local redevelopment agencies have accumulated large amounts of independent legal, financial, and technical powers and resources. Through such agents and on their own, cities became *financial participants* in urban renewal: they became managers of redevelopment projects, owners of redevelopment property, and lenders and loan guarantors to private entrepreneurs and developers. These developments set the stage for local governments to play an increasingly important role in labor policy.

The City as Regulator versus the City as Proprietor

The multiple functions of local governments, along with the overlapping and competing authorities of the different levels of the state, heighten the ambiguity as to where state authority lies. In the case of labor protections, although formally the NLRA reserves sole authority over labor relations to the federal level, in practice case law has identified certain circumstances under which local governments can get involved. The crux of this determination is whether the locality's action is based on its status as a *regulator* or as a *proprietor*. The Supreme Court has articulated two distinct NLRA preemption principles, both of which speak to the actions of local governments as regulators.

The *Garmon* preemption, developed from *San Diego Building Trades Council v. Garmon* (1959), prohibits states from regulating activity that the NLRA protects, prohibits, or arguably protects or prohibits The *Machinists* preemption, developed from *Machinists v. Wisconsin Employment Relations Commission* (1976), precludes state and municipal regulation concerning conduct that Congress intended to be unregulated and left up to the free play of market forces. The issue here is that although the NLRA structures the labor-management relationship, it intentionally tries to leave it as unrestricted as possible to foster the free play of the market. It does not want to limit either party's use of its economic power to get the best bargaining concessions possible.[6]

A series of cases followed *Garmon* and *Machinists,* applying their principles to the resolution of particular disputes and in the process refining the conditions of their application. In 1992, however, the court in *Associated Builders v. Seward,* a case in the Ninth Circuit in which San Francisco is located, determined that a city's intervention in labor

---

[6] Both *Machinists* and *Garmon* allow localities to regulate the conduct of industrial relations in two specific circumstances: when the conduct is of peripheral concern to the NLRA and when the conduct implicates interests deeply rooted in local feeling and responsibility.

relations could be justified on the basis of its status as a market participant. In this case, the court permitted the city of Seward to require the
successful bidder for work on a city project to agree to a work preservation clause, in order to foster labor stability by bringing labor treatment
on the project in line with customary city practice (*Associated Builders v.
Seward,* 1992). In 1993, the reasoning behind this notion that the proprietary functions of cities can justify their involvement in labor relations
was elaborated in the landmark case known as *Boston Harbor.* In this case,
an organization representing nonunion construction industry employers
in the cleanup of the Boston Harbor filed suit against the Massachusetts
Water Resources Authority directive that successful bidders agree to
abide by the terms of a labor agreement designed to assure labor stability
over the length of the project.

After a series of appeals, the suit went to the U.S. Supreme Court. The
Court observed that there is an important and protected place for local
governance: Congress did not intend to displace state law, so the Court
was reluctant to infer preemption. Thus local regulations are to be sustained where there is no express provision for preemption, unless they
conflict with federal law or would frustrate the federal scheme or unless
the totality of circumstances indicates that Congress intended to occupy
the field exclusively.

The Supreme Court dismissed the relevance of *Garmon* and *Machinists*
for the circumstances of *Boston Harbor* because it applied to a local government's regulatory activity, not to its interactions with private participants in the marketplace.

> A State may act without offending . . . [*Garmon* and *Machinists*] when it
> acts as a proprietor and its acts therefore are not tantamount to regula-
> tion or policymaking. . . . Our decisions in this area support the distinc-
> tion between government as regulator and government as proprietor.
> We have held consistently that the NLRA was intended to supplant
> labor *regulation,* not all legitimate state activity that affects labor.
> (*Building and Trades Council v. Associated Builders,* 1993)

With this distinction, the Court appropriated to public property owners
the extensive body of U.S. law and tradition that establishes the rights

and responsibilities of private property owners (Jacobs 1998). One of the most important of these is property owners' right to make sound economic decisions regarding their investments.

Following *Boston Harbor*, a series of cases reaffirmed and refined the distinctions between the regulatory and proprietary activities of local governments (*Babler Brothers, Inc. v. Roberts*, 1993; *Alameda Newspapers, Inc. v. City of Oakland*, 1996; *Colfax Corporation v. Illinois State Toll Highway Authority*, 1996); and several cases struck down their actions on the basis of *Garmon* and *Machinists* (*Cannon v. Edgar*, 1994; *Chamber of Commerce of U.S. v. Reich*, 1996; *Chamber of Commerce of U.S. v. Bragdon*, 1995). Together these cases forged an opening for shifting the locus of state authority over labor relations from the federal to the local level, making the protection of labor's rights highly dependent on the political and economic characteristics of the locality and on the interests and strategies of local actors.

5. THE LOCAL CONTEXT OF POLITICAL ACTIVITY

A number of factors make San Francisco a propitious site for a confluence of municipal and labor interests that could foster the protection of workers' rights. First, the city's politics have long been marked by exceptionally weak municipal government institutions whose support is based on broad and loose coalitions of local interests (Castells 1983). Thus political leadership in San Francisco is unusually fragile, so that alliances of politicians, unions, and community groups are well placed to promote policy.

This political fragmentation is exacerbated by, and enhances the import of, a second aspect of the local setting: the historical strength of organized labor and the political efficacy of the affected union, HERE Local 2. Whereas uncontested business interests controlled many U.S. communities into the 1970s, political power in San Francisco has long been divided between corporate business and an alliance of organized labor and the Catholic Church (Castells 1983). Public restrictions on business conduct are well-established practice, and labor's concerns are widely legitimate. Many of the city's major economic sectors are unionized, and trade unions are strong, mutually supportive, and linked by joint labor councils and a powerful central labor council. Unions contribute substantially to political campaigns, and their representatives sit on city commissions and hold city offices. In addition, despite the loss of its restaurant membership in the mid-1980s, Local 2, with a membership of about thirteen thousand, is still the largest private sector union in the city, an active political participant, and one of the dominant unions on the San Francisco Labor Council. It has links to a wide range of community groups and deploys what is perhaps the city's most substantial get-out-the-vote apparatus for candidates and political issues.

Third, as noted earlier, Local 2 has maintained a high market share of unionized hotels and has proved its ability to inflict economic damage. This record makes its threat to the economic interests of the city highly credible. It also reduces established hotel employers' opposition to policy constraints on new operators, since these would help level the economic playing field for all firms in the city.

Fourth, the city's post–World War II economic development both legitimates policy intervention in labor relations and makes such intervention particularly constraining for certain firms. After the war, the long-term flight of traditional manufacturing gathered force and the city blossomed as a center of finance, banking, business services, and global tourism. Of these, the income and jobs generated by tourism are major contributors to the city's economy (Economic Research Associates 1987; Potepan and Barbour 1996; Walker 1996). Moreover, the key industries in this sector, hotels and restaurants, are especially sensitive to labor disturbances and subject to city constraints. Their business depends on face-to-face relations, and they cannot relocate to avoid labor conflict.

In addition, San Francisco's nucleated pattern of development exposes these firms especially to city policy. Unlike cities such as Los Angeles in which development is dispersed into several geographic submarkets, some containing undeveloped land and not part of a redevelopment district, San Francisco has a single urban center within which its tourist facilities and historical and cultural attractions are concentrated. The city center is entirely built up, and most of the land is part of a redevelopment zone.[7] Thus firms that want to capitalize on the city's unique attractions must locate there, and to do so they will probably have to tear down, renovate, or erect a new structure on City-owned or City-managed land. Consequently they have little choice but to accede to the strictures of local government.

Fifth and finally, since the early 1950s, San Francisco has undergone a process of urban development that has not only intensified the fragmentation of political power holding, but has involved the city in the kinds of proprietary economic roles that legal precedent has established can justify a city's intervention in labor relations. Community resistance to urban growth was triggered by the experienced harshness of redevelopment and shaped by the network of policies and programs surrounding it. In 1976, shortly after the election of Mayor George Moscone on a slow-growth platform with the support of high-rise opponents, minorities, gays, and neighborhood activists, Proposition T, a proposal to create district-based rather than citywide elections to the Board of Supervisors, was passed. This proposition altered the face of city politics permanently: It sharply curtailed the influence of downtown business, increased that of minorities and neighborhood groups, and ensured that subsequent boards would be widely representative of local interests (De Leon 1992; Hartman 1984). Although the ordinance was repealed in 1980, district representation was reinstated in 2000, and the pattern of constituency representation has become institutionalized.

By 1980, San Francisco's present multisectoral political dynamic was firmly ensconced. In place of the traditional division of political power between organized labor and corporate business, a wide and varied range of interest groups had become established political participants. These joined in shifting and often fleeting alliance with a weakened union movement, forming a coalition from which corporate business was largely excluded (Castells 1983). Downtown developers were

---

[7] Redevelopment zones were dissolved in 2011 but were in place for decades, including when San Francisco's card check ordinance was debated and passed. Redevelopment agencies are technically state entities, but the San Francisco agency made a habit of mirroring city laws, including card check, in response to land use campaigners' activism (Lewis, interview, 2012).

increasingly forced to shoulder some of the burden for the social impacts of urban redevelopment.[8] Such requirements met with little resistance from developers. "Call it extortion or blackmail," observed an official of Canada's Marathon Corporation, "but we're pragmatic. We've come to San Francisco to build quality projects and when you come to a community, you observe the rules" (quoted in Hartman 1984).

6. SAN FRANCISCO'S EMPLOYEE SIGNATURE AUTHORIZATION ORDINANCE

San Francisco skyrocketed out of the real estate slump of the early 1990s. By the late 1990s, hotel vacancy rates were at an all-time low, profits were at a record high, and new hotels and restaurants were opening apace. The City had a financial stake in many of these, and it used the income from such projects to cover other expenses. As a result, the fact that many nonunion hotels were opening in a city where the major union had a record of financially damaging campaigns against nonunion operators and the fact that these businesses were the largest contributors to the city's economy and especially vulnerable to labor-management strife were major concerns for local politicians.

Thus, in late 1996, liberal Democratic County Board of Supervisors member Leslie Katz began to draft a local ordinance that would protect the city's proprietary interests in real estate developments from the threat of labor-management conflict. As an attorney specializing in employment and business law, and as vice-chair of the board's Economic Development, Transportation, and Technology Committee, Katz worked closely with local business and saw herself as a guardian of the city's economic interests.[9] These she viewed as particularly at risk in the late

---

[8] For example, hotel developers in the Tenderloin district agreed to create a housing subsidy and a social services fund for the neighborhood and to give priority to residents in half of the jobs at the new hotels.

[9] Katz was appointed to the Board of Supervisors by Mayor Willie Brown in June 1996 and elected in November 1996. Her involvements exemplify the diverse bases of support that successful city leaders must develop. She was also vice chair of the Health, Family and Environment Committee; former president and member of the San Francisco

1990s, in that San Francisco had entered a period of intense urban revitalization in which the City was financially implicated and that promised to be conflictual. Thus on October 27, 1997, she introduced the San Francisco Employee Signature Authorization Ordinance (ESAO) to the county Board of Supervisors. This bill endeavored to shift authority over labor relations from the federal to the local level. Its passage and survival under challenge legitimated, and in effect *created*, new authority for the local level of the state.

In brief, the ESAO required that, as a condition of the City's proprietary involvement in a hotel or restaurant project by virtue of its role as a landlord, lender, or loan guarantor, employers in such projects had to agree to remain neutral while labor unions conducted a card check to determine whether employees wanted to be unionized. Unions had to agree to refrain from picketing, boycotts, strikes, demonstrations, and other destructive economic actions during the card check. The ESAO's stated goal was to protect the city's financial interests from the threat of damaging labor-management conflict. It disavowed concern with the outcomes of card checks; rather it aimed to foster labor peace while workers' representation preferences were ascertained.

Supporters and Opponents

The bill was strongly supported by organized labor and its allies and vigorously opposed by local business (Gordon 1997; Diaz 1997). Mayor Willie Brown enthusiastically endorsed it and even urged its extension to a wider range of firms than ordinance sponsors thought was defensible. Nine of the eleven Board of Supervisors members cosponsored it.[10] The San Francisco Labor Council, with HERE Local 2 at the forefront, also expressed its support, as did a range of community groups. However,

---

Community College Board; vice chair and member of the San Francisco Democratic County Central Committee; president of the local chapter of the National Women's Political Caucus; and a member of the Planned Parenthood and Jewish Community Relations boards.

[10] These included Leslie Katz, Amos Brown, Mabel Teng, Sue Bierman, Susan Leal, Michael Yaki, Leland Yee, Tom Ammiano, and Jose Medina.

the mayor's Small Business Advisory Commission strongly opposed the bill and at the board's Finance Committee hearing a number of business associations spoke against it. These included the San Francisco Chamber of Commerce, the city's major overarching business association representing over two thousand small, medium, and large businesses; the San Francisco Council of District Merchants; the Golden Gate Restaurant Association, a group of some 350 business owners organized to protect the interests of the local restaurant industry; and the Committee on Jobs, a coalition of thirty-two of the city's major employers employing about fifty thousand workers, described by a local newspaper as "an umbrella organization for corporate San Francisco" (Gordon 1997). Hotel employers were notably absent from the roster of hearing speakers and kept a low profile on the issue in the community, a practice probably attributable to the high proportion of union operators among them and their desire to level the playing field.

Constraints on the Discourse of Contestation

As the ordinance campaign played out, both supporters and opponents had to craft their cases so as to garner support in the context of local politics and survive challenges based on legal precedent. First, to survive preemptory challenges, the ordinance had to chart its way through the maze of reefs and shoals developed over time by case law. To avoid being found regulatory, it could not be perceived as coercive, punitive, or attempting to enforce certain behavior. Nor could it be construed as setting broad policy or establishing general rules. To qualify as necessary to protect the city's proprietary interests, it had to be narrow in scope and tailored to a particular and limited set of circumstances, or a specific project, in which the city's financial involvement was clear and the threat to it demonstrable.

Second, to secure the wide base of support required by San Francisco's political system and to legitimate the city's stance both supporters and opponents had to represent their positions as "in the general interest" (Johnston 1994). The legitimacy of public institutions depends on a definition of their actions as benefiting the collectivity. This representation was especially important for supporters, since an appearance that the ordinance intended to promote unionization would open it to the challenge that it aimed to foster certain behavior: that is, regulate.

Third, given San Francisco's history as a union town and its acceptance of public restrictions on the conduct of business, opponents could not afford to speak negatively of unions or labor organizing. Nor could they appeal to norms vaunting unfettered private property rights, as they might in a city with a noninterventionist local government and a weak labor tradition. Rather they had to argue that their position promoted the general good and also took labor into account.

In addition to these structural constraints establishing the ways that local actors could represent the ordinance to mold an outcome to their advantage, there were strategic choices of meaning for both sides. Union and business responses to the "economic threat" contention that was required to justify the ordinance exemplified their selective appropriation of meaning. This contention placed both Local 2 and local business leaders in awkward positions.

While unions often show muscle by pointing out that strikes and labor-management conflict can cause economic damage, Local 2 relied on community support and did not want to portray itself as harming the public. Similarly, although business leaders were incensed at the economic damage that the union was able to inflict and distressed by an ordinance that could give it an edge, they also wanted to portray their firms as strong and impervious to harm from a union. This position represented both a negotiating stance and signal to the other side, and a reassurance to their investors, since their representation of unions as too dangerous could undermine perceptions of their stability. Ironically, but not surprisingly, these constraints led unions to frame their support for the bill as "good business" and protecting property rights, and business groups to frame their opposition in terms of protecting workers' rights.

The Representation of Legitimacy

About seventy individuals attended the above-mentioned Finance Committee hearing, including hotel and restaurant workers, employers, attorneys, and spokespersons from business and labor organizations. At this hearing, as in press audiences and the preceding mayor's Small Business Advisory Commission hearing, supporters and opponents made cases as to the *identity* of the city in relation to the law and the *principled grounds* on which its involvement was or was not justified (Gordon 1997; Diaz 1997). In her verbal presentation at the hearing and in the packet of materials she presented in support of the ordinance, Supervisor Katz represented the ESAO as good business practice for the city and as neither favoring nor discounting organized labor (Katz 1997). She characterized it as her independent introduction, designed in consultation with experts and interested parties representing both sides of the issue.[11] She argued that the bill was legally defensible on the basis of *Boston Harbor:* it was the legitimate action of a local government to protect its proprietary interests. She discounted herself as a labor ally and underscored her concern for the economic well-being of private business and the City.

> This Ordinance is not motivated by an effort to assist unions, although we need to forthrightly recognize that the Hotel Workers' Union is likely to benefit from it. Our purpose in sponsoring and passing this Ordinance is to save the City, and the particular hotel and restaurant projects in which we have an interest beyond the usual regulatory interests, from disruptive labor disputes, and thereby protect the City's financial interests from harm resulting from such disputes. (Katz 1997)

Katz documented the aggressive organizing campaigns that HERE locals had conducted, including the costly campaign against the Parc 55, the bitter labor dispute at the Marriott that elicited a $6 million suit against then-Mayor Art Agnos, and the politically charged corporate campaign against the Japanese owners of the New Otani Hotel in Los Angeles. She presented written testimony from four labor scholars attesting to the

---

[11] Experts cited included attorneys for the City, the chamber of commerce, and HERE Local 2, as well as the labor scholars Kate Bronfenbrenner, Adrienne Eaton, Jill Kriesky, and Michael Reich. Interested parties cited included the Chamber of Commerce, the San Francisco Committee on Jobs, the Golden Gate Restaurant Association, and the San Francisco Building Owners Management Association, as well as the San Francisco Labor Council and HERE Local 2.

severe economic damage caused by labor-management conflict and the stabilizing impact of card check agreements. She provided newspaper articles and statements from a Nevada state assemblywoman and the general counsel and senior vice president of the Circus Circus Hotel in Las Vegas affirming the efficacy of card check agreements in fostering labor peace in Las Vegas and underscoring the economic losses and damage to the city's reputation caused by labor strife at companies that refused to enter into such agreements.

Katz also cited, as local precedent for the ESAO, the city's 1980 requirement that the Marriott Corporation sign a card check neutrality agreement with Local 2 as a condition of its receiving a contract to build a hotel on City land. This agreement was breached by Marriott when the hotel opened, brought to court by Local 2, and upheld in 1993 on the basis of *Boston Harbor* (*Hotel Employees and Restaurant Employees Union, Local 2, AFL-CIO, Plaintiff, v. Marriott Corporation, Defendant*, 1993).

Further aligning herself with private business and the financial interests of the city, Katz referred sympathetically to testimony before the mayor's Small Business Advisory Commission the previous month describing the "terribly disruptive" role that Local 2 played in the 1984 citywide restaurant strike. She warned that not only would the city's reputation and thus its income stream from tourism be damaged by such labor-management strife, but that the city, as the hotels' partner in development, would likely be attacked in the process. As a result, she concluded, "We need this ordinance not to curry favor with the Hotel Workers' Union but to protect our business and related interests from them!" (Katz 1997). After establishing the threat posed by union organizing, Katz circled back to affirm her belief in unionization and praise unions for their salutary impact on the community, in terms of helping reduce poverty and crime and assuring wage levels that fostered stability and home ownership. She also distanced herself from some employers' antiunion stance.

> We understand, of course, that certain hotel operators or developers may prefer to operate non-union, either because of a philosophical opposition to unions or a mere preference to avoid dealing with them on a day to day basis. We do not share such a philosophical opposition to unions. . . .

No one is forcing any of these developers to do business with us or to seek our economic or other participation in their projects. (Katz 1997)

Finally and importantly, Katz reviewed the reasons that the ordinance could not be construed to set broad policy and therefore regulate. This demonstration was especially crucial and difficult because, unlike *Boston Harbor* and other prior cases of permitted local involvement in labor relations, the ESAO was prospective: it applied to situations that had not yet arisen rather than being initiated after the advent of a specific threat to a locality's economic interests. This feature made it especially vulnerable to the claim that it set general policy.

To deflect this claim, the ESAO required a case-by-case determination of applicability, established by the presence of a particular and limited set of circumstances. Most important, the City had to have a demonstrated and substantial proprietary interest in a hotel or restaurant project based on a lease, loan, or loan guarantee. Only firms with at least fifty employees were covered, so that the extent of the threat was assured to be substantial.[12] Seven categories of exemption were detailed, including firms in operation before the bill was enacted and those operating with a union contract. Finally, the ordinance applied only in the initial startup period of an enterprise, when labor strife could do the most damage and when the subsequent tenor of labor relations was established.

All of the business groups opposing the ordinance noted earlier were represented at the hearing. In different ways but with common themes, their spokespersons argued that the bill was unnecessary and illegal because the NLRA already adequately protected workers' rights and preempted local interference in such matters. Moreover, they insisted, the bill was a threat to employees' right to a secret and private ballot and potentially exposed them to unfair pressure and coercion by union organizers.

---

[12] The size of the firm was a matter of political negotiation. The ordinance was initially written with a 25-employee cutoff; pressure from the mayor's Small Business Advisory Commission and the city attorney, as well as pragmatic recognition that larger firms were more defendable as posing a significant economic threat, led to the cutoff being raised to 35, then to 50.

Subsectors of the business community articulated their concerns at the hearing. The executive director of the Committee on Jobs announced that his group would strongly oppose extending the ordinance to other sectors, such as the city's nonprofits. The president of the San Francisco Council of District Merchants read a letter from the Golden Gate Restaurant Association arguing that the ordinance addressed a problem that did not exist in the restaurant industry, where union contracts were rare because workers had to depend on each other as a family does. Moreover, restaurants were too small and had too narrow an operating margin to support unionization, so that "dragging restaurants under [the] ordinance" could "lead to unintended, unnecessary, and expensive consequences for the city and its tourism industry."[13]

Several spokespersons expressed labor's support for the ordinance. Michael Reich, a labor economist from the University of California, Berkeley, presented the results of his research documenting the substantial economic damage that labor-management conflict can inflict.[14] Lorraine Powell, a former waitress and Local 2 organizer, detailed the creative and costly union tactics employed in the Parc 55 union recognition battle. Local 2 president Mike Casey articulated the overall position of organized labor. Casey began by aligning himself and his organization with the economic concerns of private business and the public. He praised the ordinance as making good business sense—as providing an opportunity for the city to follow the advice of a recent "economic summit" of the city's business interests: that is, to "operate in a more businesslike manner." Casey observed that many hotel giants around the country have embraced card checks as a peaceful and cost-effective way to recognize a union.

Next, Casey obliquely dismissed the charge—unspoken at the hearing but freely articulated by business and its advocates in the community at large—that the bill was a "political gift to labor" that would upset the

[13] The quotations in this section are from the transcript of the hearing, at which the author was present.

[14] Reich found a permanent drop in shareholder equity of about 4 percent and a per-strike cost of about $80 million in 1980 dollars for 700 industrial strikes studied between 1968 and 1982. He indicated that losses in service sector firms would likely be much higher.

already labor-friendly balance of power between San Francisco unions and management in labor's favor (Diaz 1997; Gordon 1997). Casey pointed out that the bill took away the armory of pressure tactics that unions could deploy—a restriction they did not suffer gladly. His organization, he emphasized, was "not ecstatic about all the terms of this legislation. We are conceding a considerable leverage by giving up the right to picket, protest, demonstrate, boycott, and strike over recognition issues. And no union does that blithely." He underscored that it only concurred with this limitation in light of the common good. At the same time, he firmly signaled his organization's determination to organize, implying that any resultant strife or economic damage would be due to management intransigence.

> I think that, in the interest of a secure industry future, secure labor relations are useful. Because the reality is, it is our commitment that these new hotels will be organized. Local 2 is committed to organizing and we can do it in one of two ways. We can do it in the way in which we have traditionally organized, which is like at the Parc 55, a four-year fight, or the Mark Hopkins in 1994, a 73-day strike, or the four-year strike going on right now at the Sir Francis Drake. Or we can do it in a peaceful, more civil manner as Supervisor Katz refers to it, and bring an environment conducive to fair and cooperative labor relations and avoid that war over recognition.[15]

In the absence of further public comment, the only committee member opposing the ordinance, Barbara Kaufman, spoke briefly. She reiterated the points made by business speakers, questioning the ordinance's legality, expressing concern that it deprived workers of a secret ballot and exposed them to intimidation, and pointing out that the mayor's Small Business Advisory Commission voted strongly against it. The vote was then called and the ordinance passed, with two members supporting it and one opposed. The Board of Supervisors enacted the ordinance in early January. Mayor Willie Brown signed it, and it went into effect on February 15, 1998.

---

[15] Mike Casey, Presentation at the hearing before the Finance Committee of the San Francisco Board of Supervisors in Support of the San Francisco Employee Signature Authorization Ordinance, San Francisco, CA, Dec. 17, 1997.

Aftermath

Unsurprisingly, the ordinance was immediately challenged in court. Two days after its enactment, the Golden Gate Restaurant Association (GGRA) filed suit to overturn it on the grounds that it was regulatory, a veiled excuse to promote unionization, and therefore preempted by the NLRA (*Golden Gate Restaurant Association v. City and County of San Francisco*, 1998). On May 26, 1998, the suit was dismissed on the basis that it was not yet ready for federal review: application of the ordinance depended on the evaluation of specific circumstances, so its impact and legitimacy could not be determined in the abstract. Moreover, as it had not yet been applied, GGRA members had suffered no damage, so had no standing to bring a suit. More legal challenges were attempted, but in early July 2000, as part of the negotiations surrounding the passage of the living wage law, the GGRA agreed to withdraw its suit to overturn the ESAO for three years in return for the port being excluded from that law.

Meanwhile, labor peace agreements have been put into effect across San Francisco. Within the city, card check was used at two completed hotel development projects in which the City had a proprietary interest, Hotel Vitale and the St. Regis. Local 2 has also obtained card check neutrality agreements from some new restaurants opening on port land. In addition, the ordinance has had a penumbral effect: despite not being directly affected by ESAO, most of the ten large hotel chains in the city organized since 2000 have voluntarily signed card check neutrality agreements. UNITE HERE estimates that membership has grown by 3,500 in that time, with only 800 the direct result of the ordinance.[16]

Involved politicians and labor leaders attribute these non-card check agreements to several factors: the perception by employers that the City made a policy statement with the ESAO that card checks are locally approved business practice; the same developers work on both private and public projects, so if they oppose the union in a private development, they may face increased opposition to future public ones; and the high union density in hotels, which creates a relatively level playing field

[16] Lewis, interview, 2012.

for all operators whether or not they operate under union contract. Given these conditions, as one individual put it, "Employers say, 'Let's not have a fight we don't have to.'"

Contrary to the claims of the restaurant association and the chamber of commerce that card check would kill jobs and destroy development in San Francisco, a number of major projects subject to card check were successfully developed, including downtown attractions such as the Westfield shopping mall, the Ferry Building, and the Giants' baseball stadium. Developers did not abandon San Francisco for Oakland, and in fact the Port of Oakland passed its own labor peace agreement. Moreover, labor peace agreements have spread beyond San Francisco and Oakland to ports, school districts, airports, and dozens of other local governmental entities.

The interplay between federal and local power has continued to evolve, as NLRB rulings on procedures related to card check have altered its strategic benefit in organizing. The Bush NLRB's 2007 *Dana Corp* decision ruled that workers in companies recognizing a union via card check could immediately petition for a secret vote to reject the union (*Dana Corp.*, 2007). This meant that employers could sign a card check agreement for labor peace, then work immediately to nullify it, a tactic especially powerful in small workplaces, where employers generally exert more influence over workers. This tactic, however, has not precluded unionization where local conditions and strategies have countervailed. For example, at the San Francisco International Airport, HERE chose to reject a card check campaign and preserve its potential for interrupting labor peace because it suspected that the employer intended to nullify the card check once enacted. In the end, disruption was unnecessary and workers were organized without a protracted battle, due to the involvement of the company's unionized employees from other terminals. In 2011, the Obama NLRB overturned *Dana* in *Lamons Gasket Company*, so that a waiting period is again required before workers can challenge unions recognized through card check (*Lamons Gasket Company*, 2011). This ruling too is vulnerable under future administrations, as federal regulations continue to constrain the legal space in which local labor organizers operate.

7. CONCLUSION

Cities are simultaneously spatial, cultural, regulatory, and economic units and actors: they occupy and regulate a distinctive physical space; they are the repositories and defenders of traditions and cultural meaning associated with political participation and residency; and they create their own ordinances and guidelines to govern activities within their boundaries. Most important for the issue examined here, cities are financial entities and market participants with expenses, assets, and incomes, as well as rights and responsibilities to their investors, here the citizenry.

This study reveals the continued, even enhanced import of locality in a globalizing system. Although the federal protection of U.S. workers' rights has indeed dwindled over the past three decades, it has fostered an interest by unions in initiatives at the local level. San Francisco's card check ordinance is part of a wider push by U.S. labor unions and their allies toward what are termed "non-Board strategies." These include a range of policies passed by state and local jurisdictions and public agencies that apply to firms that contract with such entities or operate on their land. They include "labor peace" rules such as the ESAO passed by cities and municipally run agencies like airports; responsible contracting policies that consider a firm's law compliance history in making procurement decisions; successorship laws stipulating obligations to existing employees when a new employer takes over a firm; and various labor standards rules, such as health insurance and living wage ordinances.

All of these measures are an explicit response to the federal retreat from labor protection and Congress's failure to raise the minimum wage in step with the cost of living (Talwani and Kronland 2001; Uchitelle 1999). Living wage ordinances are the most widely dispersed of such initiatives, springing up in numerous localities across the country since 1994. They often reach far beyond the issue of wages to mandate labor organizing protections, union access rules, labor peace measures, and incentives to unionize, as well as health insurance, vacations, sick pay, and job security (Sharpe 2001; Zabin and Martin 1999).

Thus though legal arguments may express local values, they must ultimately refer to legal sources of authority. This requirement can result in strange bedfellows, as in labor's support for San Francisco's card check ordinance on the basis of private property rights and employers' opposition to it based on workers' rights. Finally, the influence of legally embedded power contests is far-reaching, in that decisions made in one venue can be deployed on behalf of groups both socially and physically distant. It is this last consequence that raises the import of the local conflict studied here to the level of the general and begs for attention to its unfolding over time and space.

ACKNOWLEDGMENTS

I would like to thank John Dale, Jack Goldstone, and the editors and reviewers of *Theory and Society* for their thoughtful advice on an earlier version of this chapter, as well as my research assistants Michael Flota, Anna Muraco, and Karen Leventhal. I am particularly indebted to Ian Lewis for his valuable suggestions regarding the current status and implications of this policy and to Miranda Dietz for her excellent editorial work on the article for this book.

REFERENCES

Court Cases

San Diego Building Trades Council v. Garmon, 359 (Supreme Court, 1959).
Machinists v. Wisconsin Employment Relations Commission, 427 (Supreme Court, 1976).
Associated Builders v. Seward, 140 (Ninth Circuit, 1992).
Babler Brothers, Inc. v. Roberts, 995 (Ninth Circuit, 1993).
Building and Trades Council v. Associated Builders, 113 (Supreme Court, 1993).
Hotel Employees and Restaurant Employees Union, Local 2, AFL-CIO, Plaintiff, vs. Marriott Corporation, Defendant, C-89–2707 (Third Circuit Court of Appeals, August 24, 1993).
Cannon v. Edgar, 33 (Seventh Circuit, 1994).
Chamber of Commerce of U.S. v. Bragdon, 64 (Ninth Circuit, 1995).
Alameda Newspapers, Inc. v. City of Oakland, 95 (Ninth Circuit, 1996).

Chamber of Commerce of U.S. v. Reich, 74 (DC Circuit Court, 1996).

Colfax Corporation v. Illinois State Toll Highway Authority, 79 (Seventh Circuit, 1996).

Golden Gate Restaurant Association v. City and County of San Francisco, C-98–0642-VRW (Northern District of California, 1998).

Golden Gate Restaurant Association v. City and County of San Francisco, First Amended Complaint for Declaratory and Injunctive Relief, C-98–2342-VRW (Northern District of California, 1999).

Dana Corp., 6-RD-1518 (National Labor Relations Board, September 29, 2007).

Lamons Gasket Company, 16-RD-1597 (National Labor Relations Board, August 26, 2011).

Publications

Bodenheimer, Thomas. 1980. *An Introduction to the Anglo-American Legal System.* St. Paul: West Publishing Co.

Brazil, Eric. 1993. "Hotel, Union End Long Battle." *San Francisco Examiner,* Mar. 30, A1.

Brecher, Jeremy, and Timothy Costello. 1994. "Global Village or Global Pillage: A One-World Strategy for Labor." International Labor Rights Education and Research Fund, Washington DC.

Bronfenbrenner, Kate, and Thomas Juravich. 1995. *The Impact of Employer Opposition on Union Certification Win Rates: A Private/Public Comparison.* Working Paper 113. Washington DC: Economic Policy Institute.

Calbreath, Dean. 1992. "Union-Hounded Parc Fifty-Five Cuts Back Staff." *San Francisco Business Times,* July 17, 1.

Castells, Manuel. 1983. *The City and the Grassroots: A Cross-Cultural Theory of Urban Social Movements.* Berkeley: University of California Press.

Clemens, Elisabeth S. 1997. *The Peoples' Lobby: Organizational Innovation and the Rise of Interest Group Politics in the United States, 1890–1925.* Chicago: University of Chicago Press.

Cobble, Dorothy S., and Michael Merrill. 1994. "Collective Bargaining in the Hospitality Industry in the 1980s." In *Contemporary Collective Bargaining in the Private Sector,* ed. P. Voos, 447–89. Madison, WI: Industrial Relations Research Association.

De Leon, Richard. 1992. *Left Coast City: Progressive Politics in San Francisco, 1975–1991.* Lawrence: University Press of Kansas.

Diaz, John. 1997. "Tilting the Field." *San Francisco Chronicle,* Dec. 22, A22.

Economic Research Associates. 1987. *The Economic and Employment Impacts of Visitors to San Francisco.* San Francisco: Economic Research Associates.

Edwards, Richard, Paolo Garonna, and Franz Todlting. 1986. *Unions in Crisis and Beyond: Perspectives from Six Countries.* Dover: Auburn House.

Forbath, William E. 1991. *Law and the Shaping of the American Labor Movement.* Cambridge, MA: Harvard University Press.

Glendon, Mary Ann, Michael W. Gordon, and Christopher Osakwe. 1994. *Comparative Legal Traditions.* St. Paul: West Publishing Co.

Gordon, Rachel. 1997 "Joining Union Would Be Easier under Katz Plan." *San Francisco Examiner,* Oct. 28, A4.

Gorman, Robert A. 1976. *Basic Text on Labor Law, Unionization, and Collective Bargaining.* St. Paul: West Publishing Co.

Greenhouse, Steven. 1997. "Bruised Unions Trying an End Run." *New York Times,* Mar. 10, sec. A.

Hartman, Chester. 1984. *The Transformation of San Francisco.* Totowa, NJ: Rowman and Allanheld.

Jacobs, Harvey M. 1998. *Who Owns America? Social Conflict over Property Rights.* Madison: University of Wisconsin Press.

Jenkins, J. Craig. 1985. *The Politics of Insurgency: The Farmworker Movement in the 1960s.* New York: Columbia University Press.

Jenson, Jane, and Rianne Mahon. 1993. *The Challenge of Restructuring: North American Labor Movements Respond.* Philadelphia: Temple University Press.

Johnston, Paul. 1994. *Success While Others Fail: Social Movement Unionism and the Public Workplace.* Ithaca, NY: ILR Press.

Josephson, Matthew. 1956. *Union House, Union Bar: The History of the Hotel and Restaurant Employees and Bartenders International Union, AFL-CIO.* New York: Random House.

Katz, Leslie. 1997. Packet Submitted to the Finance Committee of the San Francisco Board of Supervisors in Support of the San Francisco Employee Signature Authorization Ordinance. San Francisco.

Lazarus-Black, Mindie, and Susan F. Hirsch. 1994. *Contested States: Law, Hegemony, and Resistance.* New York: Routledge.

Mander, Jerry, and Edward Goldsmith. 1997. *The Case against the Global Economy and for a Turn toward the Local.* San Francisco: Sierra Club Books.

Merryman, John H. 1985. *The Civil Law Tradition: An Introduction to the Legal Systems of Western Europe and Latin America.* Stanford: Stanford University Press.

Potepan, Michael, and Elisa Barbour. 1996. *San Francisco's Employment Roller Coaster: A Report on the City's Employment Economy from 1980 to 2000.* San Francisco: Mayor's Office of Community Development.

Russell, James. 1978. "Letter from San Francisco: Rank-and-File Union Victory." *Radical America* 12, 5: 70–74.

Sewell, William H. 1992. "A Theory of Structure: Duality, Agency, and Transformation." *American Journal of Sociology* 98, 1: 1–29.

Sharpe, Rochelle. 2001. "What Exactly Is a 'Living Wage'?" *Business Week,* May 28, 78–79.

Swidler, Ann. 1986. "Culture in Action: Symbols and Strategies." *American Sociological Review* 51, 2: 273–86.

Talwani, Indie, and Scott Kronland. 2001. *Organizing-Related State and Local Legislation.* Paper presented at the Lawyers Coordination Conferece, AFL-CIO, San Francisco, May 24, 2001.

Tilly, Charles 1978. *From Mobilization to Revolution.* Reading: Addison-Wesley.

———. 1995. "Globalization Threatens Labor's Rights." *International Labor and Working Class History* 47: 1–23.

Tomlins, Christopher L. 1985. *The State and the Unions: Labor Relations, Law, and the Organized Labor Movement in America, 1880–1960.* New York: Cambridge University Press.

Uchitelle, Louis. 1999. "Minimum Wages, City by City; as More Local Laws Pass, More Businesses Complain." *New York Times,* Nov. 19, A10.

Walker, Richard 1996. "Another Round of Globalization in San Francisco." *Urban Geography* 17, 1: 60–94.

Walton, John 1992. *Western Times and Water Wars: State, Culture, and Rebellion in California.* Berkeley: University of California Press.

Weiler, Paul. 1983. "Promises to Keep: Securing Workers' Right to Self-Organization under the NLRA." *Harvard Law Review* 96, 8: 1769–86.

———. 1986. "Milestone or Tombstone: The Wagner Act at Fifty." *Harvard Journal on Legislation* 23, 1: 1–31.

Wells, Miriam J. 1996. *Strawberry Fields: Politics, Class, and Work in California Agriculture.* Ithaca, NY: Cornell University Press.

———. 2000. "Unionization and Immigrant Incorporation in San Francisco Hotels." *Social Problems* 47, 2: 241–65.

Zabin, Carol, and Isaac Martin. 1999. *Living Wage Campaigns in the Economic Policy Arena.* Berkeley: Center for Labor Research and Education, University of California, Berkeley.

TEN Community Benefit Agreements and Economic Development at Hunters Point Shipyard

Ken Jacobs

1. INTRODUCTION

Over the past twenty years debates about urban economic development in the United States have shifted markedly. Environmentalists used to oppose development as intrinsically bad for the environment. Now environmentalists have come to see smart growth, with a focus on reclaiming brownfields, as an important way to reduce the environmental impacts of development, achieve energy efficiency, and combat global warming. This position is strongly supported by empirical evidence (Norman,

*Portions of this chapter are based on or appeared in Ken Jacobs, "Raising the Bar: The Hunters Point Shipyard and Candlestick Development Community Benefits Agreement," University of California, Berkeley, Center for Labor Research and Education, 2010, available at http://laborcenter.berkeley.edu/livingwage/.

MacLean, and Kennedy 2006; Golub and Brownstone 2009). Community organizations and unions now recognize that dense urban development is more likely to lead to living wage jobs (LeRoy n.d.). Economists point to the benefits of clustering for the development and retention of high road industries (Rogers and Luria 1999). At the same time, the failures of traditional urban economic development strategies have become more widely recognized. Cities were routinely trading off the future tax benefits of development in order to attract any jobs, with little evaluation of how many net new jobs would actually be created in the region, who would have access to those jobs, and the quality of those jobs (Gross, LeRoy, and Janis-Aparicio 2005).

In previous decades, urban renewal disrupted communities and displaced local residents. In more recent years, investors found new opportunities in urban areas as middle-class professionals flocked back into cities, sending land and housing prices soaring. While development projects bring new tax revenue into a city, the costs to local residents from displacement and rising rents became a central concern for community organizations (Wolf-Powers 2010). Although affordable housing and other mitigations became standard parts of community development projects, the level of affordable housing production is well below demand. Local residents in high-cost cities have fewer affordable options if their incomes increase beyond the point that they are eligible for subsidized housing.

As a result, stakeholders that were previously on opposite sides of development conflicts have created new coalitions to promote accountable development. Accountable development brings the community into the decision-making process and places conditions on development projects to ensure broad community benefits, including affordable housing, living wage jobs, job access for local residents, parks and open space, and environmental mitigation. These goals may be achieved through a combination of broad public policies, such as living wage and inclusionary zoning laws, and negotiated conditions tailored to specific development projects.

Many of these new coalitions are also using a new tool: community benefits agreements (CBAs). CBAs are legally binding agreements between developers and private community organizations. Under CBAs, developers agree to provide specific community benefits as part of a proposed project and in exchange obtain broader community support and reduced risk of litigation. CBAs enable local residents to gain legal rights to direct benefits from the development project, while the developer gains a valuable benefit by eliminating potential disruptions and gaining support for a more rapid approval process.

In this chapter I first describe CBAs and discuss their emergence and evolution since the early 2000s. I then turn to the history of economic development policies in San Francisco, tracing how they evolved in a direction that led to CBAs. In Section 4 I discuss changes in the Bayview–Hunters Point section of San Francisco that gave rise to the most expansive CBA in the United States. Section 5 reviews this CBA in some detail. Section 6 asks whether the affordable housing mandates have been successful. I conclude in Section 7 with some of the lessons that the Hunters Point Shipyard and Candlestick Point CBA offers to other locations in the United States.

2.   WHAT ARE COMMUNITY BENEFITS AGREEMENTS?

The first CBAs were negotiated in Los Angeles in the early 2000s, most notably at the Staples Center, and they have since been used in San Jose, San Diego, Oakland, Seattle, Denver, Pittsburgh, and New Haven (Partnership for Working Families n.d.). While policy makers, community organizations, unions, and environmental groups have long bargained with developers over specific issues (affordable housing, environmental mitigations, project labor agreements), the CBAs that emerged in the late 1990s and early 2000s have unique attributes. They are usually negotiated by a coalition of community-based organizations and include agreements covering a range of issues rather than a single issue. The Figueroa Corridor Coalition for Economic Justice, which negotiated the Staples Center CBA, was composed of more than twenty member organizations (Gross 2009).

Typical CBA provisions concern local hires, job quality, job training, environmental mitigations, and affordable housing. The community organizations are parties to the agreement, which is enforceable through private right of action. In the past, legal agreements directly between developers and community organizations came from settlements of lawsuits. CBAs are developed through negotiations between the community coalition and the developer at the outset of the development process. Gross (2009, 197) describes this process as a "proactive, optimistic engagement strategy," in contrast to the more reactive strategy that is often seen in conflicts over development.

Critics of CBAs question the role of private parties in negotiating community benefits, arguing that such agreements on this topic should be a public function, since public officials are elected to represent the community as a whole (Wolf-Powers 2010). Community organizations may put their narrow self-interests above the broader community, or developers may find willing partners that do not represent broader community interests. Gross (2009, 198) argues that "community groups are well within their rights to support a project only when conditions they feel are important are met." The main benefit that developers gain from CBAs is reduced opposition to development projects. While there is no guarantee that private community groups reflect the needs of the community, a developer will gain little by negotiating with organizations that do not have weight with governmental decision makers. In order to avoid conflicts of interest and preserve the credibility of the process, Gross (2009) further argues that community-based organizations that are party to the contract should not take contributions or receive service contracts from the developer.

3. ECONOMIC DEVELOPMENT IN SAN FRANCISCO: A SHORT HISTORY

To understand the political and economic context of the Hunters Point Shipyard CBA it is instructive to review the long history of conflicts in San Francisco over economic development. This history has been chronicled by Chester Hartman (2002). As I review below, conflicts at first focused on protesting redevelopment projects that displaced local residents and reduced the supply of low-income housing. Later, conflicts were resolved by including mitigating conditions on particular projects. More recently, they led to setting inclusionary zoning policies on all new developments.

In the 1960s, about four thousand families were displaced from the Fillmore and Western Addition neighborhoods by urban renewal. Most of the displaced were African Americans and Asians. In San Francisco's Mission district, organizations such as the Mission Council on Redevelopment and the Mission Coalition Organization successfully stopped plans for urban renewal in the neighborhood. When the San Francisco Redevelopment Agency planned a massive development program south of Market Street, in the Yerba Buena area, Tenants and Owners Opposed to Redevelopment successfully sued for replacement housing for the single-room occupancy units demolished in the process. This settlement generated a pattern for future development projects.

Starting in the 1970s, community organizations and land use attorneys sued large-scale developments and gained concessions on funding for affordable housing, parks, and libraries. In the early 1980s, the North of Market Planning Coalition won a series of mitigations from hotel developers that included funding for a child care center, preferential hiring for Tenderloin residents, monies for a neighborhood community fund, and a housing subsidy fund. They are reportedly the first such agreements with hotel developers in the United States (Robinson 1995). The deals are a precursor to what would later become known as community benefit agreements, including both a wide range of mitigations and private legally binding agreements between a community organization and developers.[1]

In the 1980s many of these policies became codified in law. In 1981, the San Francisco Planning Condition established guidelines for an Office-Housing Production Program. Developers of office buildings over 50,000 square feet were required to contribute to the construction of housing, in

[1] Mark Aaronson, email communication, May 16, 2013.

an amount that was proportional to the size of the office building (Goetz 1989). In 1985, the city passed the Office Housing Linkage Ordinance, requiring developers to pay a mitigation fee per square foot of office development. In subsequent years, the city added linkage fees on developers for open space, child care, street trees (in lieu of planting), and transit and infrastructure impacts. In the 1980s, as Proposition 13 reduced the growth of city property tax revenues, mitigation fees provided an increasingly important avenue to finance needed infrastructure improvements (Calavita and Grimes 1998).

In 1986, San Francisco voters approved Proposition M, which imposed a permanent annual citywide limit on new office construction. Proposition M further established priority policies in San Francisco's master plan for preservation of neighborhood-serving retail businesses, as well as existing housing and neighborhood character; preservation of affordable housing; protection of industrial and service sectors from displacement by office construction; and protection of parks and open space (DeLeon 1992).

In 1990, the Council of Community Housing Organizations (CHCO) won approval of a city mandate that 50 percent of tax increment financing by the San Francisco Redevelopment Agency be spent on affordable housing. This mandate compared to a 20 percent requirement under California state law. In the Mission Bay Redevelopment Area, Catellus Development Corporation agreed to make 28 percent of the six thousand housing units available at a range of income levels (City and County of San Francisco 2012). Importantly, the affordable housing would have to be built on the same time line as the market-rate units (Rosen and Sullivan 2012). The Mission Bay project reflected a new, inclusive vision for large-scale developments in San Francisco.

A New Direction for Economic Development Policy

In the 1990s, San Francisco's economic development policy began to turn in a new direction by incorporating labor standards conditions. In 1996, the City passed an ordinance providing for card-check procedures for union recognition for hotels on city property (see chapter 9 this volume).

In 2000, after the passage of San Francisco's general living wage ordinance, the Redevelopment Agency followed suit with a living wage policy for redevelopment projects. The conditions on economic development projects now expanded to include labor standards beyond the construction phase. However, the redevelopment living wage policy was ambiguously worded and weakly enforced.

DeLeon (2002) describes three distinct Left subcultures that make up progressivism in San Francisco. *Liberals* focus on redistribution and public intervention in the economy to promote social and economic equality; *environmentalists* seek to regulate the private sector and place limits on growth; and *populists* seek to protect their neighborhoods from incursion by corporations and government. Progressives in San Francisco, he argues, share each of these values. The Proposition M campaign united all three groups into a coalition of neighborhoods against downtown businesses. The progressive coalition was central to the passage of rent control, San Francisco's many environmental and labor standards policies, and the establishment of district elections in the City and the subsequent election of progressive majorities on the Board of Supervisors.

DeLeon discusses the danger in the creation of what he terms an "antiregime" that is capable of saying no but is unable to unite around a common positive vision. When it comes to economic development, San Francisco's progressive coalition has often been more successful at stopping development than putting forward a viable economic alternative, even as it has extracted important concessions on housing. The Hunters Point Shipyard case demonstrates how community benefits agreements, in combination with broad labor standards policies, have the potential for a more proactive, positive, progressive approach to economic development that promotes growth with equity.

4.   HUNTERS POINT SHIPYARD INTEGRATED DEVELOPMENT PROJECT

Hunters Point Shipyard and Candlestick Point are located in the southeastern part of San Francisco, in the neighborhood of Bayview–Hunters

Point. In 1868 the California legislature designated the northern Bayview area "Butcher Town" (it was where livestock was slaughtered). In 1903, the largest dry dock on the West Coast was built in Hunters Point. In the 1930s, Bethlehem Steel opened a new shipyard, which was acquired by the U.S. Navy in 1940. The population grew rapidly during World War II as thousands of people flocked into the district for work, including large numbers of African American migrants from the South. The last of the slaughterhouses closed in the early 1960s, and the shipyard closed in 1974. The industrial history of the district resulted in significant environmental degradation (SF Planning Department 2010). The shipyard was listed as a Superfund site in 1989 (EPA 2012).

After the displacement of African American families from the Western Addition and Fillmore, Bayview–Hunters Point became the most predominantly black neighborhood in the city. In 1970, San Francisco was home to just under 100,000 African Americans, 13.6 percent of the city's population (San Francisco Planning Department 2010). By 2010, the number had fallen to 58,000, 7.2 percent of the population. In 1980, nearly three of four residents of Bayview were black; this proportion fell to slightly under half (48 percent) in 2000. By 2010, the neighborhood was a diverse mix. African Americans still made up a slim plurality (33 percent), followed by Asians (30 percent), Latinos (25 percent), and whites (6 percent). Bayview residents are more than twice as likely to be in households with children under eighteen (34 percent) than is San Francisco as a whole (16 percent). Nearly half (49 percent) of the housing units in the neighborhood are owner occupied, compared to slightly over one-third (36 percent) in the city as a whole (U.S. Census Bureau 2010). African Americans in San Francisco are 1.5 times more likely than the city's population as a whole to live in or near poverty, with 44.5 percent in families with incomes under 200 percent of the federal poverty level, compared to 29.7 percent for the general population (Ruggles et al. 2012).

In June 1997, after a contentious and expensive campaign, San Francisco voters approved measures providing revenue bonds and zoning changes for a new stadium and shopping mall at Candlestick Point. The deal fell apart after San Francisco Forty-Niners owner, Edward DeBartolo, resigned as chair of the team over a scandal related to riverboat gambling licenses in Louisiana. With his sister in control of the team, the family decided not to pursue the project and later set their sights instead on moving to Santa Clara (Hartmann 2002).

In 1999, the Lennar Corporation won the bid to redevelop the Hunter Point Shipyard and Candlestick Point area (Selna 2007). Lennar's draft Design and Development Agreement (DDA) contemplated 10,500 residential homes, 635,000 square feet of regional retail, 2.65 million square feet of office and research and development space, a hotel, art studios, and significant open space. The project also included a new stadium, with alternative plans if the Forty-Niners did not agree to relocate there. In order to integrate the area into the rest of the city, existing streets would be extended and a new bridge would connect the shipyard area with Candlestick Point. This conceptual framework was endorsed by the Board of Supervisors.

Supporters of the development placed Proposition G on the June 2008 ballot. This initiative provided a policy statement in favor of the development framework and authorized the City of San Francisco to sell, convey, or lease park land at Candlestick Point for nonrecreational uses. A coalition of community-based organizations, including several that had worked to pass San Francisco's minimum wage and living wage policies, joined some progressive members of the Board of Supervisors in opposing the development. They argued that the environmental cleanup was insufficient, that the housing would "benefit new luxury condo owners" and not the neighborhood, and that the plan only encouraged affordable housing and local hiring but had no real teeth. The longtime neighborhood activist Espanola Jackson expressed the issue succinctly: "G is for Gentrification" (San Francisco Department of Elections 2008). Opponents placed an alternative initiative on the ballot that would require 50 percent of the new housing to be affordable for low-income families. Development supporters argued that the requirement was a backdoor way to scuttle the project altogether, since there was no source of financing for the high requirement of affordable housing.

Another group of unions and community-based organizations had a different angle on the development. The San Francisco Labor Council, the San Francisco Organizing Project (SFOP), and San Francisco ACORN joined together to negotiate a community benefits agreement with Lennar. Together these organizations represent a cross section of the affected community. The San Francisco Labor Council represents about 100,000 members from 150 unions; 10,000 of these members live in the southeast area of the city. Both SFOP and ACORN had a history of organizing in the area and answer to a broad membership base of community residents with substantial Bayview concentration. SFOP works in thirty congregations and schools in San Francisco representing 40,000 people. At the time, San Francisco ACORN had 6,500 members and program participants, of which 1,300 were in the southeast part of the city. This coalition reached agreement with Lennar in May 2008, one month before the issue went on the ballot.

The new CBA established legally binding conditions for the redevelopment of the Hunters Point Shipyard and Candlestick Point that included requirements, detailed below, related to affordable housing and economic development. In June 2008, San Francisco voters overwhelmingly passed Measure G (62 percent to 38 percent), making it City policy to encourage the Hunters Point Shipyard and Candlestick Point development and making necessary legal changes to allow it to go forward. By an equally wide margin, the voters rejected the alternative measure containing the 50 percent affordable housing requirement, which was deemed a "poison pill" by the developer (San Francisco Department of Elections 2008). The opponents of the development project thus failed to stop approval of the agreement. However, the very possibility that the project could be defeated provided greater leverage for labor and community supporters of the development who sought strong conditions in the agreement.

5. ELEMENTS OF THE COMMUNITY BENEFITS AGREEMENT

Through the CBA, the developer agreed to a wide range of commitments for the project concerning housing, labor standards, and work access that went well beyond what was required by the Redevelopment Agency, existing law, or similar agreements in other jurisdictions. These agreements are legally binding on the developer and enforceable by the signing community representatives.

Affordable Housing

The Hunters Point Shipyard and Candlestick Point CBA addresses San Francisco's need for affordable rental housing for low- and very-low-income households, as well as its need for affordable for-sale housing for moderate-income families. The development of housing that would be affordable to working families was a high priority for the community coalition in its negotiations with the developer.

The development of below-market-rate for-sale housing would meet a dire need for housing that is both affordable and available to moderate-income families in San Francisco. The California Budget Project estimates that a San Francisco family would need an annual income of $140,000 to purchase a median-priced home, which was $725,000 in 2008, or $66,000 more than the median household income (California Budget Project 2010). While the share of low-income residents of San Francisco declined only slightly (2 percent points) from 1990 to 2010, the share of middle-income families fell more sharply. In 1990, 4 of 10 San Franciscans were in families with incomes between 200 and 500 percent of the federal poverty level; by 2010, the share of the population in the middle-income group had fallen to only 31.7 percent (Ruggles et al. 2012). The lack of workforce housing cannot be solved simply through longer commutes as this shortage is not unique to San Francisco but is a problem across the nine Bay Area counties (Urban Land Institute 2012).

California law requires that 15 percent of housing built in redevelopment areas be affordable for low-income families, defined as below 60 percent of area median income (AMI). In 2002, San Francisco passed an ordinance requiring that all developments with more than ten units set aside no less than 10 percent of the units as affordable housing under the same standard. In 2006, this requirement was amended to 15 percent. The Bayview–Hunters Point Redevelopment Plan sets the bar at 25 percent, with at least half of the tax increment finance funding going to support affordable housing for low- and very-low-income residents.

The Hunters Point Shipyard CBA goes well beyond both the legal requirements applicable to the project and the affordable housing requirements of other CBAs. Lennar committed to ensuring that no less than 31.86 percent of the new housing units would be below-market-rate housing; 15.66 percent would be affordable rentals for families with incomes below 60 percent of AMI.[2] An additional 16.2 percent would be for-sale units for families with incomes between 80 and 160 percent of AMI, with 3.45 percent for families with incomes between 80 and 100 percent of AMI and 4.25 percent each affordable to families at 120 percent of AMI, 140 percent of AMI, and 140 to 160 percent of AMI.[3] The AMI in San Francisco in 2008 when the agreement was signed was $82,900 for a four-person household. The developer is required to ensure an average of 2.5 bedrooms in affordable housing units, excluding senior and disabled housing. These averages must be maintained in each phase of the project. This goes further than the original Design and Development Agreement and is designed to ensure the development of a significant supply of affordable family housing.

The community and labor organizations that negotiated the CBA were concerned about the ability of African American families to stay in the community, as well as the ability of families that had previously been displaced from the city to return. The CBA provides affordable housing preferences to families displaced during the redevelopment of the Fillmore district and other redevelopment agency projects, to residents of Bayview–Hunters Point, to families with unaffordable rents, and to residents, prior residents, and family members of residents of District 10, the supervisorial district encompassing the Bay View, Hunters Point, Visitacion Valley, and Potrero Hill neighborhoods. The CBA commits the developer to rebuild the Alice Griffith public housing development, commonly known as Double Rock, as part of the first phase of development

---

[2] AMI is defined in the agreement as the median income in the city.

[3] In comparison, the landmark Staples Center CBA in Los Angeles required 20 percent affordable units.

and to ensure that its current residents have the opportunity to move directly from their current residences to the replacement units. Residents will also have the option to move to interim public housing during construction to the extent that it can be made available by the City. Lennar will contribute to funding the relocation of the tenants if the City's fund for this purpose is not sufficient. The affordability requirements under the CBA apply to each specific phase of housing development so that the affordable units are built simultaneously with the market-rate housing. Compared to the requirements being imposed by the Redevelopment Agency, this generates a much more aggressive time line for the development of affordable housing. Construction may not begin on the second phase of housing development for market-rate units until the proportional development of affordable housing for the first phase has been completed, with the units ready for occupancy.

In addition to the construction of affordable housing, Lennar committed to contributinge $27.3 million to a "Community First Housing Fund." The amount will be proportionally adjusted if the developer builds more or fewer than ten thousand housing units. The funds will be used to assist community residents in purchasing market-rate units in District 10 through a combination of down payment assistance, rent-to-own, housing counseling, and additional services. This fund may also be used to support construction of additional affordable units outside the project. The Community First Housing Fund is expected to bring the total share of affordable housing achieved through the project to more than 35 percent, or 3,500 units. Organizations party to the CBA or helping direct fund expenditures will not be eligible to receive funds.

Workforce Development

Lennar committed to a contribution of $8.5 million for workforce development in the Bayview–Hunters Point area. The Mayor's Office of Economic and Workforce Development agreed to match those funds, for a total of $17 million. The funds will be administered by a local foundation, with advice from an implementation committee composed of key stakeholders. The funds will support a wide range of job training and job readiness programs needed by the Bayview community. As with the affordable housing fund, organizations party to the CBA or helping direct fund expenditures will not be eligible to receive funds.

Union Recognition

Current San Francisco law requires a simplified process for union recognition once a majority of workers choose to join a union and pursue collective bargaining (see chapter 9 this volume). The ordinance applies to restaurants and hotels on City-owned land or where the City otherwise has a proprietary interest in labor peace. The CBA applies this policy to hotel and restaurant projects in the development area, expands the industries covered under the agreement to grocery stores, and includes security and custodial workers where the contract exceeds $25,000 a year and to stationary engineers where the contract exceeds $50,000 a year. Construction jobs are covered under a separate project labor agreement. This policy will enable workers to exercise their rights to organize and bargain collectively while minimizing labor strife in the development area. By enabling workers to more easily enter into collective bargaining agreements, the CBA will serve both to improve labor standards and to tailor the conditions to each specific industry. Voice on the job also plays an important role in reducing occupational health and safety problems (Baugher and Timmons 2004). In addition to expanding the coverage of the City policy to more businesses and industries in this project, the CBA gives community groups a private right to action to enforce City policy in cases of noncompliance.

Living Wage

The CBA codifies the existing Redevelopment Agency living wage policy and the application of that policy to subsequent purchasers, contractors, or lessees of land located in the project site. San Francisco law requires a minimum wage of $10.55 for any work performed within the geographic boundaries of the city. The Redevelopment Agency's minimum compensation policy applies a higher minimum wage rate of $12.43 to firms with twenty or more workers. The rate for nonprofit organizations is $11.03. Employers are also required to provide twelve days of paid vacation per year (or cash equivalent) and ten days off without pay per year. The policy generally applies to Redevelopment Agency contracts, leases, and development agreements where there is a proprietary interest (SFRDA 2009).

The precise scope of the businesses that would be covered by the policy in the Hunters Point Shipyard project, however, was not clear. When the San Francisco Board of Supervisors approved the project in July 2010, Supervisor David Campos and the board amended the approval legislation to state clearly that all firms with twenty or more employees are required to meet the higher standard for any employee working in the project area.[4] This condition makes the economic development project the largest in the United States to date to have such far-reaching wage standards for all employees operating within the project.

Again, a comparison with the Staples Center agreement is useful. The Staples Center CBA included a "Living Wage Goal" of 70 percent of jobs in the project, which would be measured at five and ten years from the date of the agreement. It also set a process to meet and confer on steps to reach the goal. If the goal is not met, however, the developer will still be considered in compliance with the agreement as long as the other provisions are met (Community Benefits Program for the Los Angeles Sports and Entertainment District Project 2001).

First Source Hire

The project is subject to the Redevelopment Agency's Bayview Hunters Point Employment and Contracting Policy. In addition, all nonconstruction employers within the project are required to abide by a first source hiring program set forth in the CBA.

The CBA's first source policy establishes a goal of hiring 50 percent of entry-level jobs from the local community. First priority is given to individuals whose housing was displaced by the project, who are San

---

[4] Julian Gross, interview by author, July 2, 2010.

Francisco Housing Authority residents or rent-assisted residents living within District 10. Second priority is given to low- and moderate-income individuals living within the district. Next priority is given to low- and moderate-income individuals living in low-income zip codes within the city. The policy requires employers to notify the first source referral system of any job postings. During the initial hiring phase before the employer begins operation, employers must first hire priority individuals for entry-level positions for the first three weeks after opening the job. Once operations have begun they will follow the same procedure for the first five days of hiring, after which they are required to make good faith efforts to hire locally.

6.   DO AFFORDABLE HOUSING MANDATES WORK?

One of the most notable features of the Hunters Point Shipyard CBA is the high level of affordable housing required from the developer. There are inherent difficulties in studying the impacts of project-specific agreements, since they vary according to the particular circumstances. The literature on inclusionary zoning policies does offer instructive insights into how affordability requirements affect housing production and cost. Inclusionary zoning policies require or encourage developers in an area to meet minimum standards for the share of new units that are affordable to low- or moderate-income residents (Armstrong et al. 2008). Opponents of inclusionary zoning argue that affordable housing requirements will lead to fewer housing units produced and increased prices for market-rate housing. Powell and Stringham (2005–6) suggest that inclusionary zoning functions like a tax on development. In order to pay for the cost of below-market-rate units, developers must increase the prices of the market-rate units. This price increase will in turn reduce demand for homes and thereby reduce supply.

Proponents counter that the costs of inclusionary zoning in high-cost cities provides a tool to fill the gaps in needed affordable housing that are not met by the market (Kautz 2001–2; Calavita and Grimes 1998). In practice, the cost of the policies can be offset by incentives for developers. The most common incentive is density bonuses, which allow developers to increase the number of units that would normally be allowed under zoning laws. Other incentives include fast track reviews, which speed the time of permit approvals, fee waivers, subsidies, and reduced parking requirements. Inclusionary zoning policies and housing requirements in CBAs may also lower development costs by building community support for development, reducing litigation, and speeding up approval processes. These savings would be significant in jurisdictions like San Francisco that have a history of conflict over development. Finally, to the degree that it is not entirely offset by incentives, the cost of inclusionary zoning is likely to be borne by landowners as developers are willing to pay less for land. Kautz (2001–2, 987) argues that since landowners benefit from zoning policies that raise land costs and from infrastructure investment, inclusionary zoning allows "for the public to share in the windfall profits it created."

The empirical research on inclusionary zoning requirements suggests that affordable housing requirements can result in increased affordable housing without negative impacts on overall housing production but that policy specifics and the market context matter. The research is based on inclusionary zoning policies that apply to a range of projects in a geographic area, not on affordable housing agreements in specific community benefit agreements. Knapp, Bento, and Lowe (2008) found that inclusionary zoning policies in Northern California had no impact on the number of housing permits issued and resulted in a shift toward multifamily units. They further found that while inclusionary zoning policies increased the price of more expensive homes, they decreased the price and size of less expensive homes.[5] Schuetz, Meltzer, and Boon (2011) examine the effects of inclusionary zoning in the San Francisco metropolitan area and suburban Boston. They find a small increase in housing prices and reduction in permits in Boston as a result of the policy, during times when housing prices were appreciating generally. By contrast, in the San Francisco Bay

[5] From a smart growth prospective, increased density might be considered a positive outcome of the policy, along with greater affordability for low- and moderate-income families.

Area they find no statistically significant effect on housing production. Inclusionary zoning in the San Francisco area was associated with increased prices during periods of price growth, when it is easier for developers to pass costs on to consumers, and decreased housing prices during declines. Policies that include density bonuses and exempt small developments appear to produce more affordable housing units. Interestingly, the San Francisco Bay Area housing policies were broader in scope and more likely to be mandatory than those in the suburban Boston area.

Inclusionary zoning policies such as across-the-board labor standards policies have the advantage of setting a common floor and a standard set of rules for firms competing in a geographic area. CBAs have the advantage of allowing for the standards to be set based on the conditions of a given development project. The two methods of establishing standards may also work in tandem, with the broader policies setting a floor from which the CBA may be negotiated based on the specifics of the development proposal and the needs of the community.

7. CONCLUSION

The community benefits agreement for Hunters Point Shipyard is far-reaching and surpasses many of the standards both in existing San Francisco law and in similar laws and agreements elsewhere. In the San Francisco Bay Area, inclusionary zoning policies for affordable housing range from 10 percent in many communities to a high of 20 percent in East Palo Alto (California Affordable Housing Law Project and Western Center on Law and Poverty 2002). Nationally, CBA requirements fall within the same range (Partnership for Working Families n.d.). The combined 32 percent affordable rental and for-sale housing standard agreed to by the developer is a high mark for private development projects of this scale. The housing and job training funds in the agreement are likewise greatly in excess of any similar commitment in a CBA and well beyond what redevelopment agencies usually require.

The preference system for affordable housing is designed to enable existing residents of Bayview–Hunters Point to remain in the community and for family members and those displaced by previous redevelopment projects to return. The multiple affordability level tiers offer opportunities to stay in the community to families whose income improves to the point that they no longer qualify for affordable housing. In this way, the project will contribute to strengthening and preserving San Francisco's racial, ethnic, and cultural diversity.

A major strength of the CBA model is that it is legally enforceable by the community representatives. The CBA is a legally binding agreement, and the signatories have the private right of action if the agreement is not followed. This requirement is in addition to the enforcement power of the City for its related laws and the Redevelopment Agency over the DDA.

Between the CBA and San Francisco's existing laws and redevelopment agency policies, the labor standards requirements for the project surpass in important respects the standards in CBAs and economic development policies elsewhere in the country. The labor standards in the Hunters Point Shipyard CBA include a card-check union recognition policy for certain traditionally low-wage occupations, a living wage policy, and compliance with the City's across-the-board minimum wage, paid sick leave, and health care ordinances. The agreement also includes a first source hiring policy, which is a common feature of other CBAs. Together, these policies will go a long way toward ensuring both the high quality of the jobs produced and the ability of the local community to access ongoing jobs at the project.

The Hunters Point Shipyard agreement in San Francisco applies living wage conditions to the broadest scope of employers in a private commercial development anywhere in the United States. That it was achieved quietly and without fanfare stands in marked contrast to the earlier debates surrounding a living wage in San Francisco and current debates in cities like New York over living wage policies tied to economic development projects. The Lennar Corporation, one of the nation's largest housing developers, did not see the provisions as an obstacle to the success of the project.

As other cities consider the use of CBAs or affordable housing and labor standards policies that apply to large-scale development projects, the implementation of the Hunters Point Shipyard CBA will be closely watched. Lennar began the first housing construction on the project in July 2013 (Dineen 2013). The full project is expected to be developed over a twenty-year period. A large retail complex is in the planning stages to replace Candlestick Stadium (Wildermuth 2013). Some parcels may be sold off to other developers. According to the terms of the CBA, those developers would be required to abide by the conditions of the agreement. If successful, the Shipyard CBA can be expected to serve as a model for community/environmental/labor coalitions around the country.

ACKNOWLEDGMENTS

I want to thank Julian Gross, Conny Ford, Tim Paulson, Michael Theriault, and Mark Aaronson for their helpful feedback and comments on the material in this chapter.

REFERENCES

Armstrong, Amy, Vicki Been, Rachel Meltzer, and Jenny Schuetz. 2008. "The Effects of Inclusionary Zoning on Local Housing Markets: Lessons from San Francisco, Washington DC and Suburban Boston Areas." Policy Brief, Furman Center for Real Estate and Urban Policy, New York University.

Baugher, John, and Robert J. Timmons 2005. "Workplace Hazards, Unions, and Coping Styles." Labor Studies Journal 29, 2: 83–106.

Calavita, Nico, and Kenneth Grimes 1998. "Inclusionary Housing in California: The Experience of Two Decades." Journal of the American Planning Association 64, 2: 150–69.

California Affordable Housing Law Project and Western Center on Law and Poverty. 2002. "Inclusionary Zoning: Policy Considerations and Best Practices." Oakland, CA. California Affordable Housing Law Project of the Public Interest Law Project and Western Center on Law & Poverty, Dec. 2002. Accessed Oct. 29, 2012, at www.oaklandnet.com/BlueRibbonCommission/PDFs/BlueRibbon11-WCLP.pdf.

California Budget Project. 2010. Making Ends Meet: How Much Does It Cost to Raise a Family in California. Sacramento: California Budget Project.

City and County of San Francisco. 2012. *Mission Bay.* Accessed Oct. 29, 2012, at www.sfredevelopment.org/index.aspx?page = 61.

"Community Benefits Program for the Los Angeles Sports and Entertainment District Project." May 29, 2001. Accessed Aug. 26, 2013, at www.forworking-families.org/site/pwf/files/resources/CBA-LosAngelesSportsAndEntertain mentDistrictProject.pdf.

"Core Community Benefits Agreement, Hunters Point Shipyard / Candlestick Point Integrated Development Project." 2008. San Francisco, California, May 30. Available at http://juliangross.net/docs/CBA/Hunters_Point_ Agreement.pdf.

Council of Community Housing Organizations. n.d. *History.* Accessed Aug. 21, 2012, at www.sfccho.org/about/.

DeLeon, Richard Edward. 1992. *Left Coast City: Progressive Politics in San Francisco, 1975–1991.* Lawrence: University Press of Kansas.

Dineen, J.K. 2013. "Lennar Kicks off Construction at Hunters Point Shipyard." *San Francisco Business Times.* Updated June 27, 2013. www.bizjournals.com /sanfrancisco/blog/2013/06/lennar-kicks-of-construction-at.html.

EPA. 2012. "Hunters Point Naval Shipyard." U.S. Environmental Protection Agency, May 7. Accessed Oct. 29, 2012, at http://yosemite.epa.gov/r9 /sfund/r9sfdocw.nsf/db29676ab46e8081882574260074373434/23b69b19b13d3 4c488257007005e9421!OpenDocument.

Goetz, Edward. 1989. "Office-Housing Linkage in San Francisco." *American Planning Association* 55, 1: 66–77.

Golub, Thomas, and David Brownstone. 2009. "The Impact of Residential Density on Vehicle Usage and Energy Consumption." *Journal of Urban Economics* 65: 91–98.

Gross, Julian. 2009. "Community Benefits Agreements." In *Building Healthy Communities: A Guide to Community Economic Development for Advocates, Lawyers, and Policy Makers,* ed. Roger A. Clay and Susan R. Rhodes, 189–204. Chicago: ABA Publishing.

Gross, Julian, Greg Leroy, and Madeline Janis-Aparicio. 2005. "Community Benefits Agreements: Making Development Projects Accountable." Good Jobs First. Accessed Oct. 29, 2012, at www.goodjobsfirst.org/sites/default /files/docs/pdf/cba2005final.pdf.

Hartmann, Chester. 2002. *City for Sale: The Transformation of San Francisco.* Berkeley : University of California Press.

Kautz, Barbara Ehrlich. 2001–2. "In Defense of Inclusionary Zoning: Successfully Creating Affordable Housing." *USF Law Review* 36: 971–1032.

Knapp, Gerrit-Jan, Antonio Bento, and Scott Lowe. 2008. "Housing Market Impacts of Inclusionary Zoning." National Center for Smart Growth Research and Education. College Park, MD.

Kroll, Cynthia, Christina Mun, Larry A. Rosenthal, and Vishali Singal. 2010. "Below Market Rate Requirements in a Down Market: What Have We Learned from the Great Recession." Fisher Center for Real Estate and Urban Economics. Accessed Oct. 29, 2012, at http://escholarship.org/uc/item/036599mr.

Leroy, Greg. n.d. "Talking to Union Leaders about Smart Growth." Good Jobs First. Accessed Oct. 29, 2012, at www.goodjobsfirst.org/sites/default/files/docs/pdf/talking.pdf.

Norman, J., H.L. MacLean, and C. Kennedy. 2006. "Comparing High and Low Residential Density: Life-Cycle Analysis of Energy Use and Greenhouse Gas Emmisions." *Urban Planning and Development* 132, 1: 10–21.

Partnership for Working Families. n.d. "Community Benefits Agreements (CBAs)." Partnership for Working Families. Accessed October 29, 2012, at www.communitybenefits.org/article.php?list = type&type=155.

Powell, Benjamin, and Edward Stringham. 2005–6. "The Economics of Inclusionary Zoning Reclaimed: How Effective are Price Controls."*Florida State University Law Review* 33: 471–500.

Robinson, Tony. 1995. "Gentrification and Grassroots Resistance in San Francisco's Tenderloin." *Urban Affairs Review* 30: 483–513.

Rogers, Joel, and Daniel D. Luria. 1999. *Metro Futures: Economic Solutions for Cities and Their Suburbs.* Boston: Beacon Press.

Ruggles, Steven, J. Trent Alexander, Katie Genadek, Ronald Goeken, Matthew B. Schroeder, and Mathew Sobek. 2012. "Integrated Public Use Microdata Series: Version 5.0 [Machine-readable database]." University of Minnesota, Minneapolis.

San Francisco Department of Elections. 2008a. *Election Summary, Consolidated Statewide Direct Primary Election June 3, 2008.* Accessed Oct. 29, 2012, at www.sfgov2.org/index.aspx?page = 1787.

———. 2008b. "Voter Information Pamphlet, June 3, 2008 Consolidated Statewide Direct Primary Election." San Francisco, Apr. 16.

San Francisco Redevelopment Agency. 2009. "Mission Bay Affordable Housing." Sept. Accessed Aug. 12, 2012, at www.sfredevelopment.org/Modules/ShowDocument.aspx?documentid=804.

Schuetz, Jenny, Rachel Meltzer, and Vicki Boon. 2009. "31 Flavors of Inclusionary Zoning: Comparing Policies from San Francisco, Washington, DC, and Suburban Washington." *Journal of the American Planning Association* 75: 441–56.

Schuetz, Jenny, Rachel Meltzer, and Vicki Boon. 2011. "Silver Bullet or Trojan Horse? The Effects of Inclusionary Zoning on Local Housing Markets in the United States." *Urban Studies* 48, 2: 297–329.

Selna, Robert 2007. "Lennar Corp. Dominates Redevelopment in S.F. / Hunters Point; Deal Gives Firm City Hall Clout." *San Francisco Chronicle,* Apr. 10.

San Francisco Planning Department. 2010. "Bayview Hunters Point Area Plan."
    June 3. Accessed Oct. 29, 2012, at www.sf-planning.org/ftp/general_plan
    /Bayview_Hunters_Point.htm.
San Francisco Redevelopment Agency (SFRDA). 2009. "Amended Minimum
    Compensation Policy." Apr. 7. Accessed Oct. 29, 2012 at www
    .sfredevelopment.org/Modules/ShowDocument.aspx?documentid=273.
U.S. Census Bureau. 2010a. "Profile of General Population and Housing
    Characteristics, Geography: San Francisco County, California." American
    FactFinder. Accessed Oct. 30, 2012, at http://factfinder2.census.gov.
———. 2010b. "Profile of General Population and Housing Characteristics,
    Geography: ZCTA5 94124." American FactFinder. http://factfinder2.census
    .gov.
Urban Land Institute. 2012. "Priced Out: Persistence of the Workforce Housing
    Gap in the San Francisco Bay Area." June 27. Accessed Oct. 29, 2012, at www
    .uli.org/report/priced-out-persistence-of-the-workforce-housing-gap-in-the-
    san-francisco-bay-area/.
Wildermuth, John. 2013. "Neighborhood Takes Shape in Bayview-Hunters
    Point." *San Francisco Chronicle*, Sept. 6, 2013. www.sfgate.com/49ers/article
    /Neighborhood-takes-shape-in-Bayview-Hunters-Point-4790849.php#page-1.
Wolf-Powers, Laura. 2010. "Community Benefits Agreements and Local
    Government." *Journal of the American Planning Association* 76, 2: 141–59.

ELEVEN Mandates

LESSONS LEARNED AND FUTURE PROSPECTS

Miranda Dietz, Ken Jacobs, and Michael Reich

As a result of the policies discussed in this book, tens of thousands of low-wage workers in San Francisco receive higher pay. They are not as compelled to come to work when they are sick, and they are more able to take care of their loved ones when they are sick. An even larger number of workers have greater access to health care services. They no longer face discrimination in benefits based on their sexual orientation.

Adding up the results reported in each of the chapters gives us a sense of the scope of the policies' effects. An estimated 77,500 workers received pay increases as a result of the living wage, citywide minimum wage, and IHSS policies.[1] Some 59,000 workers gained access to paid sick leave. Slightly more than three-fourths (76 percent) of private employers with twenty or more workers surveyed by Colla, Dow, and Dube reported

---

[1] Includes an estimated 47,000 with increases due to the Minimum Wage Ordinance (54,000 estimated by Reich and Laitinen minus 7,000 estimated overlap with other wage policies), 8,000 at SFO, 18,000 home care workers, and 4,500 other workers on city contracts (Reich, Hall, and Hsu 1999).

making changes to health care spending or coverage. Nearly one thousand employers paid into the City health plan in 2010, contributing a total of nearly $80 million on behalf of over 55,000 participants. By 2004, 66,500 people working for companies contracting with San Francisco had taken advantage of equal benefits for domestic partners.[2]

To put these numbers in perspective, in 2012 slightly fewer than 560,000 people worked in San Francisco (U.S. Bureau of Labor Statistics 2013). Considering only those who received wage increases and work in San Francisco, the workers who benefited make up about 12 percent of the city's workforce. The benefit mandates, moreover, reached workers at higher income levels than did the wage mandates. Paid sick leave was newly offered at 15 percent of higher-wage employers; 14 percent of City health plan participants are above two times the federal poverty line (Healthy San Francisco 2012).

San Francisco may be unique in the unusual scope of these employer mandates. But it is not unique in the economic conditions that created the need for the policies or in the efforts of labor and community coalitions and local governments to address them. Rising income inequality and eroding federal protections for workers affect the country as a whole. Increased urban growth and the revival of central cities have not led to shared prosperity; the resulting increase in housing costs has left many further behind.

More than 130 cities and counties have living wage laws. Organizations such as the Los Angeles Alliance for a New Economy, Working Partnerships USA in San Jose, and the East Bay Alliance for a Sustainable Economy in Oakland were early innovators in living wage policies and community benefits agreements. Santa Fe, New Mexico, and Washington DC have long had citywide minimum wage laws and Albuquerque and San Jose have just instituted them. Cities continue to innovate. Emeryville, California, passed a living wage law for large hotels in 2005, which was followed by a similar law in Los Angeles applying to hotels near Los Angeles International Airport. Seattle, New York, and Washington DC all have adopted paid sick leave policies. The Los Angeles, Oakland, and San Jose airports all have living wage policies.

---

[2] Includes people working for those companies outside of San Francisco.

States are also taking action on low-wage work. Eighteen states have minimum wage laws above the national standard; ten of those states index their minimum wage to inflation. In 2011, Connecticut passed a paid sick leave law. New York's Domestic Workers Bill of Rights provides overtime pay for domestic workers and three paid rest days a year. In 2002, California instituted partial wage replacement for paid family leave, followed by New Jersey in 2008 (Appelbaum and Milkman 2013). In 2012, California passed legislation to create a retirement savings program for workers who do not have access to a retirement plan on the job.

The development of labor and employment policy through these methods represents part of a larger move from the federal to the local. This shift arises, as Miriam Wells reminds us in chapter 9, in response to a lack of federal action. Federal minimum wage changes have become more infrequent and the $2.13 minimum wage for tipped workers has not risen since 1991. Department of Labor resources for enforcement are well below historic levels, as we saw in chapter 8. At the same time, union organizing has been hampered by weak federal protections and increasingly ineffective national labor relations laws.

Local labor policy also represents a move from the bargaining table to the legislature (or ballot box). The policies we have reviewed here encompass some of the key elements that are traditionally found in collective bargaining agreements. The declining share of private sector workers covered under collective bargaining agreements has forced unions to look for new allies and find new avenues to raise standards. The disproportionately high prevalence of part-time and short-term work in low-wage industries like restaurants and retail creates a particular challenge to traditional organizing methods. High turnover makes it difficult to sustain organization at a particular work site when an employer can easily delay the timing of a union election.

In response to these challenges, worker centers such as Young Workers United (YWU), the Restaurant Opportunities Center (ROC), the Domestic Workers Alliance, and the Retail Action Project organize low-wage and immigrant workers outside a traditional collective bargaining framework. They rely on a combination of public pressure, litigation, and legislation to raise labor standards (Fine and Gordon 2010). YWU was the central organization behind San Francisco's Paid Sick Leave Ordinance; the National Domestic Workers Alliance led the effort to pass New York's Domestic Workers Bill of Rights.

Unions representing low-wage workers are turning to similar strategies. OUR Wal-Mart, the organization of Wal-Mart workers backed by the United Food and Commercial Workers' Union, uses a range of methods to put pressure on the company without seeking recognition for collective bargaining purposes. Similar efforts are under way by fast-food workers in New York, Chicago, and other major cities. Public policy plays an important role in all of these organizing efforts.

The Great Recession's slow employment recovery, a lingering wariness of Wall Street engendered by the banking crisis and bailouts, and calls for reducing inequality may yet result in further policy responses. Cities and states around the country and even the nation itself seem poised to implement policies discussed in this book. From the call for a higher minimum wage during President Obama's 2013 State of the Union to arguments in the Supreme Court over equal benefits for same-sex couples to the implementation of the Affordable Care Act and the recent passage of paid sick leave in New York City, elements of the social compact tested in San Francisco are being argued for and adopted on a larger scale.

What can we hope to learn from the cases discussed in this book? First, cities can take meaningful steps to address the issue of low-wage work. Second, they can do so and still remain economically strong. The San Francisco economy is not unique in its ability to incorporate employer mandates.

Dire warnings of disastrous economic and employment effects were heard each time San Francisco passed a new mandate. But San Francisco's experience and the careful empirical analysis presented in this book demonstrate that there need not be a trade-off between equity and economic growth.

In chapter 2 we saw how a citywide minimum wage law improved earnings of low-wage workers without a measurable impact on employment. Chapters 3 and 4 presented evidence that the airport's living wage policy and increased pay for home care workers improved productivity and decreased worker turnover. Chapters 5–7 presented similar evidence for policies providing paid sick leave, minimum health care spending, and equal benefits for domestic partners. These laws were not simply ignored, in large part because of the substantial enforcement and education efforts discussed in chapter 8. Instead, as chapters 9 and 10 discussed in relation to union organizing and community benefits agreements, these laws changed the norms of operation for business in the city.

Even when taken together, we find no evidence that San Francisco's series of mandates diminished the strength of its economy. While there are limits to how far employer mandates can go without creating negative employment consequences, San Francisco has not reached them. The evidence cited in this book, along with research on other state and local labor standards policies, thus suggests that the United States could go significantly further in protecting labor standards without harming employment.

At the same time, there are important limits to what cities and states can do on their own. Wages and employment both grow faster in a full-employment economy. While state and local governments can take better and worse actions to promote job creation, the strongest policy levers that affect aggregate demand lie with the federal government. Private sector labor law is likewise a federal issue, with state and local governments given limited space for intervention. While state and local labor standards are important in their own right, their success ultimately will depend on how the campaigns that pass them serve to build organization and raise the issues at higher levels of government.

Even as the research presented in this book strengthens our confidence in these policies, we recognize that there are many more unanswered questions. States and cities, to paraphrase Justice Louis Brandeis, will continue to be laboratories full of social and economic experiments. Social scientists should continue to analyze these experiments to advance our knowledge of which policies work and how to implement them effectively. The job of policy makers, organizations, and activists is to make sure that good ideas make it out of the laboratory and on to the main stages of state and national policy.

REFERENCES

Appelbaum, Eileen, and Ruth Milkman. 2013. *Unfinished Business: Paid Family Leave in California and the Future of U.S. Work-Family Policy.* New York: Cornell ILR Press.

Fine, Janice, and Jennifer Gordon. 2010. "Strengthening Labor Standards Enforcement through Partnerships with Workers Organizations." *Politics & Society* 38, 4: 552–85.

Healthy San Francisco 2012. "Annual Report to the San Francisco Health Commission, Fiscal Year 2011–2012." Healthy San Francisco. www .healthysanfrancisco.org.

Reich, Michael, Peter Hall, and Fiona Hsu. 1999. "Living Wages and the San Francisco Economy: The Benefits and the Costs." Center on Pay and Inequality, Institute of Industrial Relations, University of California, Berkeley.

Reich, Michael, and Amy Laitinen. 2003. "Raising Low Pay in a High Income Economy: The Economics of a San Francisco Minimum Wage." Policy Brief. Institute of Industrial Relations, University of California, Berkeley.

U.S. Bureau of Labor Statistics. 2013. Quarterly Census of Employment and Wages. [Data File], Series Id: ENU0607510010, San Francisco County, California, Total, all industries, all establishment sizes. Accessed May 13, 2013. www.bls.gov / cew / #databases.

Contributors

THE EDITORS

MICHAEL REICH is Professor of Economics and Director of the Institute for Research on Labor and Employment at the University of California, Berkeley. His research publications cover numerous areas of labor economics and political economy, including the economics of racial inequality, the analysis of labor market segmentation, historical stages in U.S. labor markets and social structures of accumulation, high performance workplaces, union-management cooperation, and Japanese labor-management systems. He has published fourteen books and monographs, including *Racial Inequality: A Political-Economic Analysis*, 1981; *Segmented Work, Divided Workers: The Historical Transformation of Labor in the United States*, 1982; *Social Structures of Accumulation*, 1994; *Work and Pay in the United States and Japan*, 1997; *Labor Market Segmentation and Labor Mobility*, 2009; *Labor in the Era of Globalization*, coedited with Clair Brown and Barry Eichengreen, 2010; and *Contemporary Capitalism and Its Crises*, coedited with Terence McDonough and David Kotz, 2010. He has also published over one hundred papers, including, with Arindrajit Dube and William Lester, "Minimum Wages across State Borders," *Review of Economics and Statistics* (2010); with Sylvia Allegretto and Arindrajit Dube, "Do Minimum Wages Really Reduce Teen

Employment?" *Industrial Relations* (2011); and "High Unemployment after the Great Recession: Why? What Can We Do?," *Estudios de Economía Aplicada* (2012). Reich received his PhD in economics from Harvard.

KEN JACOBS is Chair of the UC Berkeley Center for Labor Research and Education, where he has been a labor specialist since 2002. His areas of research include health care coverage, labor standards, low-wage work, and the retail industry. He is the author of more than fifty papers and policy briefs. Recent papers have examined the projected impact of the Affordable Care Act on health coverage in California and living wage policies for big-box retail. Jacobs is Co-Principal Investigator with the UCLA Center for Health Policy Research on multiple projects estimating and evaluating the impact of the Affordable Care Act in California. At the Center he has consulted for Covered California (California's Health Benefit Exchange), the California Department of Health Care Services, San Mateo County, and the City and County of San Francisco. In 2006, he served on the San Francisco Universal Health Care Council and worked on the development of the City's Health Care Security Ordinance. Before joining the Labor Center, Jacobs was with the Bay Area Organizing Committee (BAOC), an affiliate of the Industrial Areas Foundation, and served as codirector of the San Francisco Living Wage Coalition.

MIRANDA DIETZ is a researcher at the UC Berkeley Center for Labor Research and Education, working on employment and health care issues in California. She has written on temporary and subcontracted work in California as well as the implementation of the Affordable Care Act. She holds a master's degree in public policy from UC Berkeley and a bachelor's degree in government from Harvard University.

THE AUTHORS

CARRIE H. COLLA is Assistant Professor at the Dartmouth Institute for Health Policy and Clinical Practice at Dartmouth Medical School and Adjunct Assistant Professor in the Department of Economics at Dartmouth College. She is a health economist specializing in health insurance markets, insurance benefit design, provider payment, and the care and needs of the elderly. Some of her current work examines the effectiveness of a payment and delivery system reform, Accountable Care Organizations. She received a BA from Dartmouth College and an MA and PhD from the University of California, Berkeley.

WILLIAM H. DOW is Henry J. Kaiser Professor of Health Economics at the University of California, Berkeley, School of Public Health, where he is head of the Division of Health Policy and Management. He is also associate director of the Berkeley Population Center and the Center on the Economics and Demography of Aging. In addition, he is a research associate at the National Bureau of Economic Research and previously served as senior economist on the White House Council of Economic Advisers. He received his PhD in economics from Yale University. Honors include the John D. Thompson Prize for Young Investigators awarded by the Association of University Programs in Health Administration and the Kenneth J. Arrow Award given by the International Health Economics Association.

ARINDRAJIT DUBE is Associate Professor of Economics at the University of Massachusetts–Amherst. He received his PhD in economics from the University of Chicago and has written extensively on the topic of minimum wage policies in the United States. His other work focuses on fiscal policy, income inequality, health reform, and the economics of conflict.

PETER V. HALL is Associate Professor of Urban Studies and Geography at Simon Fraser University in Vancouver, Canada. Trained as a city and regional planner, his research examines the connections between shipping and logistics chains, transport sector employment, and the development of cities. He is coeditor of *Integrating Seaports and Trade Corridors* (Ashgate, 2011) and *Cities, Regions and Flow* (Routledge, 2013).

CANDACE HOWES is Barbara Hogate Ferrin '43 Professor of Economics at Connecticut College. Her current work focuses on the problems of the long-term care workforce and low-wage workers, including the effect of job quality on the quality of care provided in institutional and home-based long-term care settings. She received a PhD in economics from the University of California, Berkeley, and a BA in Middle East languages and literature from Barnard College.

DONNA LEVITT was hired to lead the Office of Labor Standards Enforcement in 2002, having over twenty years of experience in the construction industry. She worked in the trade for over ten years as a carpenter, superintendent, and estimator. Levitt was also a widely respected union representative, the only woman to head a major construction local in the United Brotherhood of Carpenters & Joiners of America. She has served on the California Building Standards Commission, the San Francisco Landmarks Preservation Advisory Commission, and the executive board of the San Francisco Labor Council.

ELLEN LOVE joined the Office of Labor Standards Enforcement as an analyst in 2012. Her experience includes policy implementation and analysis for environmental policy and labor rights organizations. Ellen holds a master's degree in public policy from UC Berkeley and a bachelor's degree from Brown University.

VICKY LOVELL is former Acting Director of Research for the Institute for Women's Policy Research in Washington DC. Her research has focused on women's employment and economic security. She has provided extensive technical assistance on the development of paid family and medical leave and paid sick leave policies.

CHRISTY MALLORY joined the Williams Institute at the UCLA School of Law in 2008 as a law and policy fellow. Her research primarily focuses on sexual orientation and gender identity discrimination against state and local government employees. Her work on employment discrimination has been published in several journals and cited in a number of media outlets.

SURESH NAIDU is Assistant Professor of Economics and Public Affairs at Columbia University. He has an MA from the University of Massachusetts–Amherst and a PhD from UC Berkeley, both in economics. He was a Harvard Academy Junior Scholar from 2008 to 2010 and is currently a CIFAR junior fellow in the Institutions, Organizations, and Growth group.

BRAD SEARS is the Roberta A. Conroy Scholar of Law and Policy and Executive Director of the Williams Institute at the UCLA School of Law. He is also an assistant dean and adjunct professor at the UCLA School of Law, where he teaches courses on sexual orientation law, disability law, and U.S. legal and judicial systems. Sears has published a number of research studies and articles, primarily on discrimination against LGBT people in the workplace and HIV discrimination in health care. In 2012, he was the Shikes Fellow in Civil Rights and Civil Liberties at Harvard Law School.

MIRIAM J. WELLS is Professor of Anthropology Emerita in the Department of Human and Community Development at the University of California, Davis. She is the author of *Strawberry Fields: Politics, Class, and Work in California Agriculture* (Cornell, 1996), as well as numerous articles on U.S. farm labor and hotel industry unionization, immigration and immigration policy, economic restructuring in agriculture, and labor processes, class relations, and the law.

Index

Dallas-Fort Worth International Airport
(DFW), 89
Dana Corp decision (2007), 280
Dane County (Wisconsin), 168, 171, 194n
DeBartolo, Edward, 293
DeLeon, Richard Edward, 292
Democratic Party, 21–22, 24, 270, 271n
Denver, 24n, 205, 221, 288
discounts, employee, 6
Displaced Worker Protection Act (1998), 8
domestic partners, equal benefits for. See
equal benefit ordinances
Domestic Workers Alliance, 311–12
Domestic Workers Bill of Rights, 310–12
dot-com bust (2000), 16
Dow, William, 37, 125–55, 309, 316–17
Dube, Arindrajit, 25–26, 36, 37, 47–96, 309,
317
Dunn, Gibson, 220n
dynamic monopsony model, 50, 63

Earned Income Tax Credit (EITC), 11
East Bay Alliance for a Sustainable Economy,
310
East Palo Alto (California), 303
Eaton, Adrienne, 274n
economic development, urban. See urban
redevelopment
Emeryville (California), 310
employee discounts, 6
Employee Free Choice Act, 261
Employee Retirement Income Security Act
(ERISA), xiv, 6, 34, 128, 178, 185–88,
192–93
Employee Signature Authorization Ordi-
nance (ESAO), 38, 257–58, 270–82
Enforcement of labor standards, 38, 229–30.
See also Office of Labor Standards
Enforcement
England, 256
equal benefits ordinances (EBOs), 5–7, 31, 47,
156–96, 312; arguments against, 182–90;
compliance with, 170–82; costs of, 183–85;
implications for federal policy on, 191–
95; overview of, 161–70
Europe, labor market policies in, 1
Executive Order 11246, 191–93

Fair Labor Standards Act (1938), 34, 97, 111
Fairris, David, 73, 93
family leave, paid, 6, 14, 163, 310–11
fast-food restaurants, minimum wage workers in, 57, 59, 312
Federal Express, 6

Federal Service Contract Act (1965), 31
Figueroa Corridor Coalition for Economic
Justice, 288
Filipino Community Center, 244
Fortune 500 companies, 6, 195n
France, 256
full-time equivalent employment, 56–61
full-time work, effect of minimum wage on,
64–65

Garmon pre-emption, 265–67
Germany, 197, 257n
Glaeser, Edward, 17n
Gleeson, Shannon, 246–47
globalization, 2, 258, 281; labor rights
impacted by, 38, 256
Golden Gate Restaurant Association
(GGRA), 128, 136, 198, 219, 245, 272,
274n, 277, 279, 280
Gottlieb, Joshua, 17n
Government Accountability Office, 94
Great Recession, 16, 28, 312
Gross, Julian, 289

Hall, Peter V., 36, 70–96, 317
Hartman, Chester, 290
Hawaii, 34, 127, 221
Hayward, 51
health benefits, 6. See also specific ordinances and programs; minimum wage
and, 65
Health Care Accountability Ordinance
(HCAO), 9–10, 72; enforcement of, 232
health care reform, 37, 312. See also specific
legislation
Health Care Security Ordinance (HCSO),
12–13, 27, 31, 34, 110, 126–30, 133–53;
Annual Reporting Form, 141; changes in
health benefits after implementation of,
139–42; clarification and revision of, 245;
education and outreach on, 243; effects
on consumer prices of, 150; effects on
employment and wages of, 146–49;
enforcement of, 231, 236, 238, 247; offering and spending gaps relative to,
138–39
Health Reimbursement Accounts (HRAs),
27n, 126, 128, 129, 132, 139, 141, 142, 144,
151, 153, 245–46
Health Savings Accounts (HSAs), 126, 128,
129
Healthy San Francisco, 12, 13, 16n, 98, 109,
110, 125–26, 129–33, 135, 141–42, 144,
151–53